HCI is a multidisciplinary field focused on human aspects of the development of computer technology. As computer-based technology becomes increasingly pervasive – not just in developed countries, but worldwide – the need to take a human-centered approach in the design and development of this technology becomes ever more important. For roughly 30 years now, researchers and practitioners in computational and behavioral sciences have worked to identify theory and practice that influences the direction of these technologies, and this diverse work makes up the field of human-computer interaction. Broadly speaking it includes the study of what technology might be able to do for people and how people might interact with the technology. The HCI series publishes books that advance the science and technology of developing systems which are both effective and satisfying for people in a wide variety of contexts. Titles focus on theoretical perspectives (such as formal approaches drawn from a variety of behavioral sciences), practical approaches (such as the techniques for effectively integrating user needs in system development), and social issues (such as the determinants of utility, usability and acceptability).

Titles published within the Human-Computer Interaction Series are included in Thomson Reuters' Book Citation Index, The DBLP Computer Science Bibliography and The HCI Bibliography.

More information about this series at http://www.springer.com/series/6033

Graham Button • Andy Crabtree
Mark Rouncefield • Peter Tolmie

Deconstructing Ethnography

Towards a Social Methodology
for Ubiquitous Computing
and Interactive Systems Design

 Springer

Graham Button
Le Muy, France

Mark Rouncefield
Lancaster University
School of Computing and Communications
Lancaster, UK

Andy Crabtree
University of Nottingham
School of Computer Science
Nottingham, UK

Peter Tolmie
University of Nottingham
School of Computer Science
Nottingham, UK

ISSN 1571-5035
Human-Computer Interaction Series
ISBN 978-3-319-37365-2   ISBN 978-3-319-21954-7 (eBook)
DOI 10.1007/978-3-319-21954-7

Printed on acid-free paper

Springer International Publishing AG Switzerland is part of Springer Science+Business Media (www.springer.com)

Ask for this great Deliverer now, and find him
Eyeless in Gaza, at the mill with slaves,
Himself in bonds under Philistian yoke.

Samson Agonistes
John Milton, 1671

Acknowledgements

As we submitted the manuscript of this book to the publishers, the sad news reached us that our friend and colleague, John Hughes, had died. John was a noted sociologist, publishing critically acclaimed texts on sociological research and the foundations of the discipline. His work on ethnomethodology, with Bob Anderson and Wes Sharrock, was of a handful cited by Harold Garfinkel, ethnomethodology's founder, as exemplary. He was also one of the early pioneers of ethnography for systems design. Mark, Peter and Andy were all students of John and completed their PhD theses under his supervision. John was for each us, and will remain, a very special person. He will be greatly missed, and we would like to take this opportunity on our own behalf, and on behalf of the broader community, to acknowledge his contribution and support. Thank you John.

The writing of this book was partially supported by the Tembuso College, National University of Singapore, and the Engineering and Physical Sciences Research Council grant EP/M001636/1.

Contents

About the Authors

Graham Button has worked in the fields of ethnomethodology and conversation analysis since 1973. Following 17 years of working in the University sector in the UK, involving periods at the University of California Los Angeles and Boston University, he founded the Studies of Technology, Organisation and Work group in 1992 at Xerox's European Palo Alto Research Centre (EuroPARC) in Cambridge, UK, and was the group's principal scientist and the area manager. He subsequently became laboratory director of the Cambridge lab of Xerox's Research Centre Europe (XRCE) and then the laboratory director of XRCE's Grenoble Lab in France. He re-entered the University sector in 2005 as pro-vice-chancellor for the Faculty of Arts, Computing, Engineering and Science at Sheffield Hallam University in the UK. He has published extensively in the areas of ethnomethodology and conversation analysis and on how they may be used in the design of interactive systems. He has now retired from working within formal organisations and works on projects of interest.

Andy Crabtree is associate professor and reader in the School of Computer Science at the University of Nottingham. He has published widely on ethnography and systems design, including the books *Designing Collaborative Systems: A Practical Guide to Ethnography* and *Doing Design Ethnography*. He has conducted ethnographic work in a variety of social contexts, including workplaces, domestic environments, mixed reality and rural settings. His research has made substantive contributions to computer-supported cooperative work, human-computer interaction and ubiquitous computing, and he has contributed to methodological debates concerning the nature and role of ethnography in systems design and IT research.

Mark Rouncefield is a senior lecturer in the School of Computing and Communications at Lancaster University. He was awarded a Microsoft European Research Fellowship in 2006 studying social interaction and mundane technologies and how these might afford 'social translucence', which involves making socially significant information visible, providing an awareness of others and their actions, rights and obligations and providing a mechanism for accountability. More broadly his research interests are in the field of computer-supported cooperative work (CSCW) and involve the empirical study of the organisation of human interaction and how this impacts interactive systems design. He has published widely in CSCW conferences and journals and is a recognised champion of ethnography in systems design.

Peter Tolmie is a senior research fellow in the Mixed Reality Laboratory (MRL) at the University of Nottingham, where he conducts a wide range of ethnographic studies to inform systems design. He was originally a member of the Centre for CSCW at Lancaster University. In 2000 he was recruited by Xerox Research Centre Europe and worked at XRCE's Cambridge laboratory until 2002, when he moved to XRCE's sister laboratory at Grenoble in France and became area manager of XRCE's Work Practice Technology group in 2005. He joined the MRL in 2006. He has conducted a variety of ethnographic studies spanning workplaces small and large, domestic environments, museums, television and music production and pervasive gaming. He has published widely in the domains of computer-supported cooperative work, ubiquitous computing and human-computer interaction and is the author of a book on intimacy in domestic life, joint author of a book on ethnographic work in design and joint editor of two recently published volumes of ethnomethodological studies of work and of play.

Chapter 1
Introduction

Abstract The arguments made in this book were first articulated in sketch form in a conference paper in 2009 called *Ethnography Considered Harmful.* The paper tackled contemporary propositions that there was a need for 'new' approaches to ethnography to contend with a changing and broadening milieu for design, and presented a number of reasons for handling such calls with care. We explain here how that paper was received and the range of misunderstandings it gave rise to. We also outline how we were effectively left with the sensation of a job only half-done and how this current volume sets out to properly articulate for systems design what it might be engaging with really when it turns to ethnography for an understanding of the social. As a frame for this latter point we go on to present in outline the concern this volume has with the relationship social science in general and ethnomethodology in particular have with members' methods for the accomplishment of orderly action and interaction in the world. We do this in order to begin to elaborate *a systematic method* for building the social into systems design, and give some initial indications as to how design might choose to engage with such a method. We explain how, in order to accomplish this, it will be necessary to closely inspect and deconstruct how ethnography has evolved in social science and what this might amount to in systems design. We outline how the various chapters of this book contribute to this job of deconstruction: how they take the reader, step-by-step, to an understanding of what kinds of choices confront systems design when it seeks to engage with the social, and what kinds of consequences may ride upon the choices it makes.

1.1 Ethnography Considered Harmful

In 2009 the authors of this book presented a research paper called *Ethnography Considered Harmful* (Crabtree et al. 2009) at the annual ACM CHI conference on Human Factors in Computing Systems, the premier conference in the field of Human Computer Interaction (HCI). The paper was co-authored by Button, Crabtree and Tolmie, all experienced 'ethnographers', and computer scientist Tom Rodden, who has pioneered ethnographic studies in systems design. The paper reflected on

© Springer International Publishing Switzerland 2015
G. Button et al., *Deconstructing Ethnography*, Human-Computer
Interaction Series, DOI 10.1007/978-3-319-21954-7_1

new approaches to ethnography in systems design that were being proposed by a number of different people. The presentation was done as a special panel session open to the conference at large and was followed by responses from four panellists, including the fourth author of this book Mark Rouncefield.[1] This book has its origins in *Ethnography Considered Harmful* and the subsequent misunderstandings and misinterpretations given of it by three panellists and other parties to the event. It is not our intention in writing this book to take the panellists and other researchers to task, however, but rather to open up for broader and more detailed consideration than was possible in a CHI paper, even one given a longer presentation time than normal, why it is that we think ethnography *could* be harmful to systems design.

We appreciate that this is a serious claim to make. It is not one we make or take lightly. The central issue we want to address is how building the social into systems design can be made a *methodical* matter rather than a piecemeal or pliable activity. Simply put, we want to address the core question, what could be a social methodology for systems design? To date the standard way in which systems design engages with the social is through 'ethnography'. However, in the development of 'new' approaches to ethnography we are concerned that design could, unwittingly, buy into what can be shown to be problematic ways in which the social sciences at large go about the business of investigating the social. This could in turn anchor design in the disciplinary worlds of social science rather than the natural attitude of the everyday, commonly understood world into which systems are placed and must operate.

We are all sociologists working in the particular field of ethnomethodology.[2] Our work for the most part has not been conducted within the institutional and organisational structures of sociology, but within computer science departments at the universities of Lancaster and Nottingham or the research arm of a company famous for inventing many of the components of modern computing – the Xerox Corporation. In this respect we have conducted a broad range of empirical studies that address actual social situations and the locally ordered character of human action and inter-action for the purposes of supporting system design, both in terms of developing general sensitivities to the social and shaping particular design endeavours around it. We have been content, for the sake of convenience, to call these studies and to have them called *ethnographies* insofar as they make use of materials gathered through fieldwork.

---

[1] The other panellists included Bill Gaver (Goldsmith College London), Tracey Lovejoy (Microsoft Redmond), and Wendy Kellogg (IBM Yorktown Heights). William Newman (University College London) chaired the session.

[2] Ethnomethodology was developed by Harold Garfinkel, and his book *Studies in Ethnomethodology* (Garfinkel 1967) outlines many of ethnomethodology's basic issues. Very simply, Garfinkel eschewed the traditional social science preoccupation with generating theoretical accounts of society and the social character of action and interaction in favour of *studies* of action and interaction located within actual social situations. This current book is not an introduction to ethnomethodology, though we do elaborate Garfinkel's rejection of traditional social science, including 'new' developments in social science which have, ironically, in part been developed through misunderstandings of his work. Although not itself an introduction to ethnomethodology Mike Lynch's *Art and Artifact in Laboratory Science* (Lynch 1985) expands upon many ethnomethodological themes in an erudite and accessible way.

However, in doing this, our studies have come to be parcelled up with other sorts of social studies that are also called ethnography, which we entertain disciplinary misgivings about. In writing *Ethnography Considered Harmful* we were attempting to address three key misgivings. First, we were attempting to address calls that were being made for 'new' approaches to ethnography to be developed to address the challenges of ubiquitous computing. Second, and related to this, we were attempting to address misunderstandings about ethnomethodologically-informed ethnographies, which have it that they are all about work and the workplace and that new approaches are therefore required to support the diversification of computing in everyday life. Third, we were attempting to show that the 'new' approaches on offer were not new at all, but well-established in mainstream social science and that they traded on problematic understandings of the social that are pervasive in the social sciences, as ethnomethodology has attempted to make visible.

Our paper upset people from a number of different groups. First, some of the designers and computer scientists with whom we have worked over the years could not understand why we appeared to be so confrontational. Second, though rather less surprisingly, were those whose work we were either criticising or distancing ourselves from. Third, were members of the panel itself. Despite the fact that two of us had worked as senior researchers in industry for a combined total of 25 years, working very closely with the business groups of our company, we, as a collection of authors, were chided by the panellist from Microsoft for not understanding how products are produced and placed. The panellist from IBM played music to us, seeming to suggest that we suspend our intellectual concerns in order to be happy and get on well with other people, and the panellist from academia spoke in defence of those we had criticised, and attempted to show how our criticisms were based upon ill-informed, partial and distorted readings of their work. A fourth group was made up by a number of people in the audience whose questions seemed to be aimed more at us than they were at the arguments we were making.

With the exception of those whose work we criticised, we were puzzled by the paper's reception. Critique is not new for CHI. Lucy Suchman's critique of cognitive approaches to systems design (Suchman 1987) is now a seminal text in HCI, for example. Within our home discipline of sociology critique is the norm, for there is much dispute about how the study of the social is possible and how it can be conducted, and disputes are often worked through in terms of criticism of one another's work. Critique figures as an important tool in systems design and sociology then. In critiquing 'new' approaches to ethnography in systems design, we were addressing other bodies of *sociological* work. Sociological in the sense that even if they were not done by sociologists they were nevertheless examinations of *social life* done for professional purposes. We were trying to make visible what we considered to be their shortcomings and the consequences this could have for systems design if designers were to try and build systems on their basis.

In this latter respect, we were not just engaged in sociological argument for its own sake. Rather, we were concerned that the problems of sociological description, which have plagued sociology and other social science disciplines such as anthropology, were now being played out in and for systems design. We wanted to make sure that designers did *not* view all ethnographies as apiece, but had the resources to differentiate between different kinds of ethnography. That there are ethnographies such as our own, which are concerned with the methodical ways in which people assemble and order their situated actions and interactions; ethnographies that provide interpretations of and commentaries on society and culture through a theoretical apparatus; and ethnographies that describe what anyone can see but no more than that and thus leave the socially organised nature of action and interaction untouched (empirically or theoretically). Irrespective of their differences, these studies were and still are lumped together under the term 'ethnography' in HCI and we argued that if they were not disentangled then confusions over how to build the social into design could proliferate to the detriment of design. In making these distinctions we wanted to underscore the fact that there are crucial differences in how the social can be approached that are masked by the blanket term 'ethnography', and that these differences might lead design to construe the social in demonstrably problematic ways as it attempts to build social matters into its considerations.

The social now occupies a significant place in systems design thinking, just as 'the user' once did. Understandings of the user were underpinned by consensus as to how the user was to be addressed – cognitively – and cognitive theory thus became the vehicle through which the user was delivered into design. With respect to the social, however, there is as yet *no* consensus as to how it is to be driven into design. On the face of it ethnography would seem to be that vehicle. However, on the arguments we presented in *Ethnography Considered Harmful*, the term 'ethnography' is turned and used in different ways by different social science perspectives or viewpoints on the social, which do not agree as to how it is to be addressed. Design is not so much rubbing up against different types of ethnography then, which it might be invited to view as fit for different design purposes, as *different understandings* of the social and how it can be addressed. We wanted to make this clear in order to show that if it were thought that ethnography per se could be a vehicle for driving the social into systems design then that might well be a mistake.

Building the social into the design mix is a non-trivial matter, and perhaps the CHI conference was not the best place to 'out' our worries and concerns. Our arguments are rooted in old arguments and confusions in social science, and the word limit on CHI submissions only allowed us to gesture at these. Furthermore, many involved in systems design have only a utilitarian interest in ethnography, in the material insights it can deliver for design, and these interests are strongly represented at CHI. Our arguments were and are more principled than utilitarian in nature: we were not offering studies of the social, but querying the very grounds upon which design can effectively understand the social. We have thus produced this volume in order to try to do justice to our arguments and to elaborate what is a complex and far from trivial matter for systems design: *how to methodically build the social into systems design practice.*

Our premise is that the design of interactive systems, applications and services in any context, be it in support of workplace activities, domestic activities, leisure activities, whatever, requires a systematic understanding of the social. If the reader does not share this premise, then this book should not be read as an attempt to convince them otherwise. Rather, it is directed at those in the systems design community who are already convinced that designing computer systems to support or automate human action and interaction requires some understanding of how action and interaction is done and organised by those who do it. On the basis of that premise our major argument is that the social is currently understood in systems design in a piecemeal fashion, and requires next-step attempts to build it into the design of systems. What is needed is the development of a systematic method for building the social into design practice. Ethnography is *not* that method because it is not, in itself, a method at all. It is rather a gloss on a host of competing perspectives on the social that conceal conflicting understandings as to how the social can be apprehended and tracked into systems design. This may be a surprise to those in systems design who turn to ethnography as a solution. However, a key thrust of this volume is to make the divisions visible and to reflect on what this can mean for systems design. Doing so requires that we highlight important arguments and differences in the social sciences, and show how these are being played out in and for systems design.

We are aware that some within systems design might argue that they do not need to know about, and are not interested in, the twists and turns of social science thinking. We accept that this may well be true for many designers. Design is a very broad church. Only some of its members have an interest in the social and of these many might consider that they only need to have light traction on it. Some designers might simply be interested in a particular cultural matter, or some interactional issue, or some aspect of the professions that touch upon the social. For them, society, how people do the things they do, how they act and interact, the particular undertakings involved, etc., may be little more than a resource for stimulating their design interest. From our point of view we note, as the field of Computer Supported Cooperative Work (CSCW) compellingly illustrated when it emerged out of HCI, that the lack of serious and sustained attention to the *organisation* of human activity *in* action and interaction undermined the effectiveness of computing technologies for the social settings that introduced them and the people who had to use them. Seriously addressing the interactionally organised character of human activity provided not only a resource but also a *focus* for rethinking how to approach the design of collaborative systems. From our experiences in CSCW it seems to us that the social should be far more than just a resource for stimulating the imagination of designers, it should be a resource in the actual design of systems. However, we do not want to legislate as to what designers' interests should be and we appreciate that many designers may believe they only require a light touch on social matters and that they may, consequently, find this volume only of passing interest.

For those in the design community who are interested in drawing the social into the design mix in a *systematic* manner, we would maintain that calls for 'new' approaches to ethnography covertly draw them into the murky waters of social science thinking. These new approaches inevitably implicate the design community in the twists and turns of social science theory and method, though this may not be a particularly visible feature of such calls. It is ironic too that these calls badge themselves as 'new' ways of approaching the social. They might be new in HCI but they drive systems design towards traditional ways of understanding the social in the social sciences, which produce abstract and general descriptions that *hover above* social life as it is ordinarily encountered by the very people engaged in society's day-to-day business. Calls for new approaches to ethnography as a means of apprehending the social introduce systems design to old confusions in the social sciences, which provide little traction on social reality as this is understood as an everyday matter. In arguing against these calls we are obliged to lay out the grounds we have for rejecting foundational ways of describing the social in the social sciences. In challenging the 'new' it is necessary to open up old problems involved in describing the social for systems design, for without some appreciation of these issues design may well wander up the same blind alley that the social sciences in general have ended up in. Does design, as it grapples with building social matters into the mix, want to be saddled with the theoretical, methodological and philosophical confusions that beset the social sciences? Probably not, but in the short term it may have to as it gets to grips with the problems of sociological description. In writing this book it is our hope that it will go some way towards helping those designers who have a foundational interest in the social make their way through the social science maze.

1.2   Deconstructing Ethnography

In the spirit of hope this volume sets out to deconstruct ethnography for the systems design community in an attempt to elaborate a systematic method for building the social into systems design. The term 'method' in the social sciences usually implicates a body of practices built up within a discipline through which it addresses and develops knowledge of its subject matter. The social sciences have developed, and otherwise borrowed from other disciplines, a range of methodological practices through which they purportedly generate knowledge about social matters. By and large these practices are aimed at answering the foundational question posed by Thomas Hobbes (1651), "how is social order possible?" The social sciences have set about attempting to answer this question by constructing a diverse methodological apparatus, for example: systematic observation, experiments, statistical analyses, typologies and taxonomies, ideal types and a broad range of theoretical frameworks. Thus methods in the social sciences are disciplinary 'things', artefacts of the disciplines making up and articulating the social sciences as sciences.

The ethnomethodological tradition in which we work respecifies the ways in which social science works (see Garfinkel 1991). This respecification has various dimensions to it that we will elaborate in due course, suffice to say here that they underpin ethnomethodology's break with traditional sociology, anthropology, and other social science disciplines. One aspect of this break is a fundamental respecification of methods. As we will expand upon later, ethnomethodology recognises that people already have knowledge about how the social world works, which they use in methodical ways to bring off their actions and interactions as orderly endeavours, and actually make the social world work. This knowledge is displayed in knowing how to do, see and describe social activity, and is held in common by the members of society. To take a very simple example, just reflect on all the things we display we know in 'going to the pictures'. Setting aside how we get there, once there we display our knowledge of how to queue *in* actually queuing, of how to take turns at talk *in* asking for a ticket for a particular show, of economic institutions and transactions *in* offering our credit card, of interpersonal relationships *in* offering to buy the drinks and popcorn, of appropriate ways of being hygienic *in* using the urinals, and so on and so forth. The simple point to appreciate is that our actions are possessed of and display methodically ordered knowledge, and if that is in doubt just try to go to the head of the queue, walk in without paying, or use the corridor as a urinal and the full force of the everyday knowledge of how to do these things will be brought to bear on you by the other people around you.

This knowledge of how to do and recognise social action is also relied upon and used, in unacknowledged ways, across the social sciences. Thus, and for example, an explanation of the exploitative power of marketing that accounts for us purchasing a cinema ticket takes for granted and relies upon common-sense knowledge of how to purchase a ticket, relies upon what it is that we actually *do*, on what constitutes the act of purchasing. We will elaborate upon this argument subsequently, but note here that the upshot of this argument is that any and all scientific disciplines engaged in the study of the social tacitly rely upon common-sense knowledge, common-sense understandings and common-sense reasoning, which is drawn upon to *re-describe* what anyone knows about society and the ordering or organisation of social life. A social scientist might describe the actions of a software engineer working for a global corporation as contributing to world hegemony, for example. This description not only re-describes the ordinary work of software engineering, it relies on recognising that there are persons in the world engaged in software engineering in the first place. Just what the work of software engineering consists of as an orderly enterprise is, however, left untouched by sociological re-descriptions of the common-sense world.[3]

---

[3] One of the authors of this book was involved in a series of studies with the sociologist Wes Sharrock of software and hardware engineers involved in a number of projects to do with photocopiers, printers and multi-functional devices. At the time of the studies we were intrigued by the way in which social science colleagues, mainly in the area of Science and Technology Studies (STS), construed of scientists and technologists almost as though they were 'the enemy', involved in the technocratic subjugation of the world (see, for example, Law 1991). Whereas we were confronted with ordinary people not so much involved in working out the best mechanism of subjugation but in figuring out mundane practical solutions to technical issues and, more taxing for them, organising the running of the projects they were involved in within various and often conflicting constraints mainly to do with time and budget. Although we never included the hegemony example in the papers we published, it figured in our notes and helped us work our way through a number of issues. It will be used on various occasions in the present volume to illustrate particular analytic points. As on so many other occasions we thank Wes Sharrock for sharing his thoughts and contributions in this regard.

The methods of the social sciences are, then, at one and the same time ensnared by, and in competition with, methods of common-sense reasoning (Pollner 1987). They seek to replace common-sense knowledge of society with what they consider to be more rigorous, more objective, more systematic knowledge of the social world. Yet the descriptions they provide are *rooted* in the common-sense perspective. This produces an ironic situation in which social science descriptions treat the ordered properties of the common-sense world as *resources* for scientific elaboration, rather than as *topics* for investigation in their own right, and in doing so recast common-sense knowledge and understandings of the social. This results in descriptions of social life that are *at odds* with the very world they claim to be describing, and render a familiar world strange. Harvey Sacks, who developed what Harold Garfinkel described as the jewel in the crown of ethnomethodology, Conversation Analysis, describes the typical way in which social science proceeds:

> A curious fact becomes apparent if you look at ... revolutionary scientific treatises back to the pre-Socratics and extending up to at least Freud. You find that they all begin by saying something like this, "About the thing I'm going to talk about, people think they know, but they don't." (Hill and Crittenden 1968)

From a social science stance it is an appalling thing to argue that, contrary to their insistence, the social sciences actually build-in common-sense knowledge of the social world; that their methods of accounting for the things they address are based upon common-sense methods; and that this results in descriptions that are parasitic upon what 'anyone' knows about society. What is appalling about this situation for the social scientist is the *reliance* of social science *on* common-sense, which inevitably throws the foundations of social science into disarray. The conflation of topic and resource and the inseparable entwining of social science description with common-sense knowledge, common-sense understanding and common-sense reasoning drives ethnomethodology's respecification of method (Zimmerman and Pollner 1970). Thus, rather than see and treat methods as disciplinarily owned things, ethnomethodology orients us to methods as common-sense things ordinarily used by society's members in their everyday lives, be they engaged in work or leisure or play, etc., to order their endeavours. Methods, for ethnomethodology, belong *to the members of society* and the activities they engage in. This may be a surprise to system designers. However, if design wants to move beyond a piecemeal engagement with the social and develop a methodical engagement with it, and we understand that this is a big *if*, then this argument takes on an importance for design. Design can pick up on methods as disciplinarily owned things, pick up on the methods of the social sciences, *or* it can turn to the methods ordinarily used by society's members to bring about the ordered courses of action and interaction in which systems will actually be embedded.

Ethnomethodology's respecification of method is, we think, key to the attempt to systematically build the social into systems design. On this view, human activities are seen to be possessed of their own methods – *members' methods* – for assembling and ordering the distinctive courses of action and interaction that make up the recognisable features of society. The methodical ordering of social life – the real world, real time social organisation of human action – is an investigable matter and the sustained *topic* of ethnomethodological inquiry. *Studying* members' methodologies is what the term 'ethnomethodology' refers to: the study of folk knowledge and its procedural use in ordering the familiar scenes of everyday life. It means that when we point to a methodology for engaging with the social world we are not describing some disciplinarily owned apparatus and arguing that systems design pick it up. Rather we are arguing, or making the argument again to be more precise, that in attempting to build the social into the design mix in systematic ways designers should turn to members' methods as a means of getting a fix on the social. Such an argument may seem strange to systems designers. It may be of some small comfort to hear that it is perhaps even harder for those in the social sciences to grasp. For it is being argued that we turn away from established social science methodologies, turn away from disciplinarily generated knowledge of the social, and turn instead to methods whose existence is tacitly traded on but not acknowledged by the social sciences: methods that ordinary people use to do the ordinary things they do; methods that reflect an order of knowledge the social sciences are in direct competition with and seek to systematically replace.

We note here then, and address in detail later in this volume, two issues with respect to this concern with members' methods. The first is that the term does not refer to some armoury of *instructions* for the doing of human action that human beings possess and which they come by either innately or through socialisation. Computer science is familiar with the idea that sets of instructions are integral to the organisation of human action. The idea of a *plan* in Artificial Intelligence, for example, seeks to provide for action in terms of sequences of instructions for doing things. This cognitive conception of the methodical character of action was disputed by Suchman (1987), whose studies showed that such plans are always accountable *in action* to the situated, occasioned and contingent circumstances of realising them. Although not overtly marked in her book, Suchman's arguments resonate with Garfinkel's examination of 'instructed action', at least with respect to the way in which plans and instructions are organised in practice (Garfinkel 2002), and Wittgenstein's philosophical reflections on rule-following. Wittgenstein (1958) has described how rules do not determine their own application, that there are situated judgements involved in the use of a rule that are not themselves covered by the rule (Baker and Hacker 2009). Do you follow the signpost in the direction of its pointed end or its blunt end, for instance? Garfinkel describes how people do instructed action, such as following a set of instructions for reaching a destination: "Take the first left past the third set of traffic lights." Does that include the lights at this pedestrian crossing, or does it just refer to the lights governing road intersections, and does that alley count or should I turn at the first road? Much has been written in the social sciences relating to normative action and the idea that it is rule-governed. We do not intend to launch ourselves into this body of work, but simply point out here that members' methods cannot be reduced to this kind of account.

What members' methods refer to is simply that there is a methodical character to social undertakings, not that there are a bunch of rules for doing them. Take, for example, the very simple act of answering a phone. There are a number of methodical matters involved here. (1) Simply picking up the phone is to acknowledge the action of being 'summoned'. (2) The answerer, in immediately speaking rather than just holding the phone, recognises that the summons is providing for them to do a next action. (3) That next action usually consists of doing a greeting and in using a greeting term such as "hi" the answerer is displaying that not anything can be an appropriate next action but that some particular action, a greeting, is an appropriate response to the summons. (4) In using a greeting term the answerer is providing for another appropriate next action to be done, a reciprocal greeting by the caller. Now of course it is possible to try and codify these things into a set of rules for answering phone calls. But in so doing little is gained because it is not the case that people are following them to do the things they account for. Rather in noticing these features of phone call openings we are describing the sort of thing that everyone knows about them, and knows by being competent members of a culture brought up and schooled in society's ways (Sacks 1984). These 'ways' constitute the methods through which we accomplish the doing of social action and they are broadly recognisable, seen, known and understood by other members who share the same forms of social life.

This takes us onto the second concern we have with members' methods: that they provide for common-sense knowledge of society. Common-sense knowledge does not refer to people's opinions or beliefs about social life. Rather it refers to the knowledge society's members possess and display when, for example, they pick up the phone when it rings, rather than being puzzled as to what to do about it. Ethnomethodology recognises that common-sense knowledge, common-sense understandings and common-sense reasoning is wrapped up in the methods that people use to order social activities. It is these common-sense methods – *ethno methods* – that we refer to when we speak about building the social into systems design in a systematic and methodical way. We are arguing, then, that insofar as systems design is concerned to draw the social into the design mix it should orient itself to members' methods, and undertake empirical analyses that make these methods visible and available to design practice. Thus a social method for design is not a method of *our* construction. It is rather to provide design with access to members' methods for doing and organising human activities and social life, and for design to thereby be instructed in social matters *by those involved in their doing*, rather than through the disciplinary methods of social science. Ethnomethodology is all about making members' methods inspectable, and making visible the consequences of this inspection for studies of the social world. It is our objective that the first of these issues is made to matter for design. To do so we are obliged to forage into aspects of the second.

1.3   Volume Structure and Content

In Chap. 2, *Building the Social into Systems Design,* we lay down the contours of our argument and the intellectual territory we are working across throughout this book. We take up the central claim that ethnography is not all of apiece, examining its contested character in the social sciences. We review the origins of and motivations for ethnography in systems design, addressing the uptake and use of a marginal social science approach at Xerox PARC in the 1970s and its subsequent development in the 1980s in CSCW amongst broader efforts to develop workplace systems. We argue that over the course of its adoption in systems design ethnography has come to stand as a proxy for the social, which legitimates a diversity of perspectives and glosses over its origins in a design context in ethnomethodological studies. Calls for 'new' approaches to ethnography reflect mainstream social science concerns with the problem of social order, substituting ethnomethodological concerns with situated action and the local production of order with top-down theoretical views that emphasise the formative role of social and cultural structures on the orderliness of situated action and interaction. We argue that 'new' approaches to ethnography trade on mistaken assumptions about the ethnomethodological approach and mask the very insights into the social that have been of value to design to date. In elaborating these issues, we are not arguing whose version of ethnography is more appropriate to systems design. We are arguing that *ethnography is not the issue*. Understanding the social and building it into design is what matters. The rest is a divergence.

In Chap. 3, *Ethnography as Cultural Theory,* we begin our deconstruction of ethnography, examining how 'new' approaches trade on and in old assumptions about how the social should be described. We turn to the origins of ethnography in anthropology, elaborating Bronislaw Malinowski's immersive approach to the study of culture and society and how it becomes problematic (Malinowski 1922). Of particular issue is the grounding of observations of what people do in social or cultural theories to explain observed events. This substitutes descriptions of *how* action is done for competing accounts of *why* it is done, and what its doing *means*. It results in the production of interpretations of and commentaries on action and its organisation, which foreground the cultural meanings of action and its perceived structural character. Situated action therefore becomes a site to witness generic social and cultural institutions at work, rather than something to be understood in its own terms. The substitution produces descriptions or accounts of social order that stand at odds with common-sense understandings. The incarnate orderliness of action as known, seen and recognised by society's members is left untouched and is never unpacked. Thus the naturally occurring orderliness of action is *surplus* to the analytic requirements of ethnography. How society's members organise action *in action* remains to be described.

In Chap. 4, *'New' Ethnography and Ubiquitous Computing,* we address so-called 'new' approaches to ethnography, which track the old problems of sociological description elaborated in Chap. 3 into systems design. We explore the notion of 'messiness' and 'infrastructure' in ubiquitous computing and 'multi-site ethnography' as an analytic lens on society and culture (Dourish and Bell 2011). We attempt to show that there is nothing new in these arguments; that they simply represent a call to build the traditional role and apparatus of ethnography in anthropology into systems design. We critically examine the occasioned use of everyday concepts as a means of rendering general sociological descriptions. We argue that this central analytic practice trades on common-sense methods of interpretation, which reify generalised sociological accounts and make abstract theoretical concepts real-worldly. The result is that the descriptions generated through the analytic apparatus of contemporary ethnography provide generalised accounts of social life that are of an order, despite the disciplinary rhetoric, that anyone can provide: the man in the street, the tourist, the journalist, *anyone whomsoever*. This begs the question as to why systems design has need of ethnography at all?

In Chap. 5, *Interpretation, Reflexivity and Objectivity,* we examine contemporary anthropological concerns with the relationship between the observational act, which is at the heart of ethnography, and that which is observed, along with the impact of participation as an observer. These concerns have developed in part as a reaction to problems with the more traditional understanding of ethnography in anthropology that we have previously examined, and are being introduced as matters that design should attend to. Thus we address the assertion that all observation is theory-laden and inherently interpretive, showing that this argument again trades on and abuses ordinary language concepts that are used in unproblematic ways in the everyday world. The alleged necessity of theory to observation is supplanted by the 'praxio-logical' character of perception, i.e., the ordinary ability of society's members to see and recognise action. It is not an intellectual ability rooted in 'reflexive' practices of academic theorising, which focus on the ethnographer's observational and literary practices, but one rooted in the practical organisation of action and the reflexivity of members' descriptive practices, which enable them to account for the world around them. We consider the rebuttal to this, which is that we are advocating an outmoded 'realist' agenda, which we counter through an examination of the problem of objectivity in social science research. In tackling the issues of reflexivity and objectivity we attempt to relocate them in members' methods and *restore them to the everyday world* from which social science has appropriated them, thereby confusing itself with respect to its remit.

In Chap. 6, *The Missing What of Ethnographic Studies,* we focus upon the use of ethnography in sociology. We examine Anslem Strauss's call for studies of the work that people actually do, in contrast to studies of the imputed structural conditions under which work is assumed to be done. This involves us in examining old and new misunderstandings of what the notion of 'work' means in ethnographic studies and systems design. We also look at the studies of interaction that came out of the Chicago School of Sociology, which represent a serious and sustained attempt to get to grips with how the social world is organised within the things that people actually do. Despite their claims, however, we argue that these interactionist studies never-theless miss the interactional work involved in the doing of human activity. In its place are put 'scenic' descriptions: descriptions of social features of action that frame the interactional work involved in doing it; descriptions of the interactions that surround work; descriptions that again return us to what anyone can see but this time in terms of mere observations rather than general theoretical interpretations. We say 'mere observations' because these descriptions lack analytic focus and coherence. They replace theoretical descriptions with empirical ones for sure, but fail to get to grips with *the interactional 'what' of human action* and the orderly ways in which social phenomena are thereby brought about and pulled off in the course of their very doing. We then turn to some of the 'new' ethnographies offered to design and argue that they similarly embody scenic descriptions and let the interactional what of members' actions slip by in favour of heuristic devices that settle by fiat what is going on in social settings and what is relevant about it to systems design.

In Chap. 7, *Ethnography, Ethnomethodology and Design*, we explicitly turn to the ethnomethodological respecification of the study of social order as a locally produced interactionally achievement. We draw an explicit contrast between ethnographic studies and ethnomethodological studies that make use of ethnographically-gathered materials. In doing so we elaborate how the social sciences come to routinely and systematically ignore the interactional order in treating the orderliness of action as a taken for granted resource for investigating social life, rather than as a foundational problem for sociological investigation. The distinction highlights key differences in the descriptive practices of ethnography and ethnomethodology. The difference contrasts the abstract descriptive practices of mainstream social science with concrete descriptions of "work's things" (Garfinkel 1986), which relocate what anyone knows about the orderliness of everyday life in the methodical undertakings that recognisably constitute particular social endeavours. Ethnomethodological studies replace the artful, political, intriguing, and sometimes exotic descriptions of social life produced by mainstream social science with descriptions of mundane order. This is not to advocate that common-sense be accorded some special status and privilege; we are not trying to rival science with what anyone knows about society. Rather, we are saying that relocating what anyone knows in members' methods for mundanely producing the social order roots design in the lived work of interaction and that this, in turn, provides *a systematic means of anchoring systems design in the social world*.

Having built an understanding of ethnomethodology we turn in Chap. 8, *Members' Not Ethnographers' Methods*, to demonstrate that the study of members' methods can provide a resource for building the social into design. We do this by examining particular studies that have been previously undertaken. We make visible how they are descriptions of members' methods and how these methods have been built into design. The studies we treat range across ethnomethodology's historical engagement with design, and across work and leisure settings. In the course of doing this we disabuse design of the idea that ethnomethodological studies of work are only applicable for studying jobs, occupations or workplaces. We also draw together the considerations of the previous chapters by summarising what can be learnt through the deconstruction of the term 'ethnography' for undertaking empirical studies of human action and interaction, and lay out how this provides a method for design to build-in the social. We emphasise that we are not attempting to be prescriptive: design can look to whatever quarters it cares for inspiration, for context, for legitimisation, for whatever. We are, however, providing for those designers who want as a methodical matter, as opposed to a piecemeal matter, or an occasional matter, to build the social into design practice, just such an analytic method, and the grounds for proposing this method, as opposed to an interpretive or a scenic ethnography.

The need to write this book is immensely frustrating for us. Garfinkel's *Studies in Ethnomethodology* created a fork in the road for social science. Social science has largely ignored ethnomethodology's arguments and continued on in the same direction, ending up in the blind alley which the academic concern with reflexivity so aptly demonstrates. It could take a new direction, studying the methods through which society's members achieve, display and make use of the social order in their mundane actions and interactions. Although ethnomethodology in part exists in a dialogue with social science, in which the exhibits of its studies are used to sign-post the fork in the road, it also exists in making those exhibits visible in their own right as the direction of travel. It is in this latter direction that we have worked within systems design, undertaking studies of members' methods and making the exhibits of our studies tell for design purposes. The frustration then resides in having to back track to the fork and emphasise it less systems design should wander up the same blind alley and lose sight of the *incarnate orderliness* of everyday life that systems must gear into if they are to live and thrive in practice.

References

Baker, G. P., & Hacker, P. M. S. (2009). *Wittgenstein: Rules, grammar and necessity*. Oxford: Wiley-Blackwell.

Crabtree, A., Rodden, T., Tolmie, P., & Button, G. (2009). Ethnography considered harmful. In *Proceedings of the SIGCHI conference on human factors in computing systems* (pp. 879–888). Boston: ACM.

Dourish, P., & Bell, G. (2011). *Divining a digital future: Mess and mythology in ubiquitous computing*. Cambridge, MA: MIT Press.

Garfinkel, H. (1967). *Studies in ethnomethodology*. Englewood Cliffs: Prentice-Hall.

Garfinkel, H. (Ed.). (1986). *Ethnomethodological studies of work*. London: Routledge and Kegan Paul.

Garfinkel, H. (1991). Respecification: Evidence for locally produced, naturally accountable phenomena of order. In G. Button (Ed.), *Ethnomethodology and the human sciences* (pp. 10–19). Cambridge: Cambridge University Press.

Garfinkel, H. (2002). *Instructions and instructed actions* (Ethnomethodology's Program: Working Out Durkheim's Aphorism, pp. 176–181). Lanham: Rowman and Littlefield.

Hill, R., & Crittenden, K. (1968). *Proceedings of the purdue symposium on ethnomethodology, west Lafayette*. Purdue Research Foundation. http://aiemcanet.files.wordpress.com/2010/07/purdue.pdf

Hobbes, T. (1651). *Leviathan*. St Paul's Churchyard: Green Dragon.

Law, J. (Ed.). (1991). *A sociology of monsters: Essays on power, technology and domination*. London: Routledge.

Lynch, M. (1985). *Art and artifact in laboratory science: A study of shop work and shop talk in a research laboratory*. Boston: Routledge and Kegan Paul.

Malinowski, B. (1922). *Argonauts of the western Pacific: An account of native enterprise and adventure in the archipelagoes of Melanesian New Guinea*. London: Routledge.

Pollner, M. (1987). *Mundane reason: Reality in everyday and sociological discourse*. Cambridge: Cambridge University Press.

Sacks, H. (1984). Notes on methodology. In J. M. Maxwell & J. Heritage (Eds.), *Structures of social action: Studies in conversation analysis* (pp. 21–27). Cambridge: Cambridge University Press.

Suchman, L. (1987). *Plans and situated actions: The problem of human-machine communication.* Cambridge: Cambridge University Press.

Wittgenstein, L. (1958). *Philosophical investigations.* Oxford: Basil Blackwell.

Zimmerman, D., & Pollner, M. (1970). The everyday world as a phenomenon. In J. Douglas (Ed.), *Understanding everyday life* (pp. 80–103). Chicago: Aldine Publishing Company.

Chapter 2
Building the Social into Systems Design

Abstract This chapter lays out some necessary context for the book by examining how the problem it addresses first came about as systems design encountered the need to engage more concretely with the social. We start by looking at the interdisciplinary character of work in systems design and how Human Computer Interaction (HCI) arose as an area of interest within it. A point of particular focus here is how systems design has mistakenly presumed social science to be a relatively univocal affair whereas, in fact, it contains a concatenation of different voices. A naïve conflation of ethnography and social science therefore overlooks the contested character of ethnography within social science itself. Thus, when called upon to consider 'new' approaches to ethnography design is therefore confronted with a choice between a number of *divergent* perspectives upon the social. Much of design's engagement with the social to date has been through collaboration with ethnomethodologists, who locate expertise in the social milieu. This contrasts with 'new' approaches, which locate expertise in the long-standing traditions of social science. This being the case we seek to highlight the real nature of the choice designers are being asked to consider. In the ethnomethodological approaches that characterise much of design's early engagement with the social, the expertise design is being asked to engage with is the expertise of the members of society themselves who populate the settings that are investigated for design purposes. By contrast 'new' approaches, built upon traditional understandings of ethnography within social science, invite design to engage with the *social scientist as expert*, where the goal is to replace members' expertise with the theoretical and conceptual machinery of social science.

2.1 Systems Design and Social Science

Systems design is one of those few academic areas in which interdisciplinary work is routinely conducted. Collaboration between disciplines is encouraged by research councils and funding agencies, who stress the advantages of working together, though much of what passes as interdisciplinary work involves cognate disciplines within engineering, or involves disciplines that have a relatively established relationship, such as programming, operating systems, networks and distributed

© Springer International Publishing Switzerland 2015
G. Button et al., *Deconstructing Ethnography*, Human-Computer
Interaction Series, DOI 10.1007/978-3-319-21954-7_2

systems, and other areas of expertise that 'naturally' go together. However, systems design has also occasioned the coming together of very different disciplines, which are not necessarily cognate or 'naturally' associated, and it has often been creative in its development of different disciplinary design mixes. Today the development of computer systems is shaped not only by computer scientists, mathematicians, and engineers of different hues, but also by social scientists, psychologists, artists, graphic designers and others who have been drawn in different proportions and at different times into the design mix. This holds true across the different contexts within which systems design takes place, be it in large corporations, small and medium-sized enterprises, universities, or even peoples' homes.

As computing has developed over the decades, the disciplines involved in systems design have grown. The advent of the programmable computer occasioned collaboration between those who built hardware and those who built software, and this gave birth to particular, closely allied, disciplines and areas of expertise. However, as interest in computers developed beyond those who created them, and outside of the rarefied circles in which they were initially used, attention shifted towards understanding those who might want to make use of computer programs. This was driven by commercial and research interests, commercial in the sense that an understanding of what a customer might require from a commercially available program might support sales of that program if it could build in their requirements, and research in the sense that researchers became interested in how to build some appreciation of the non-expert users of systems into their design.

The field of Human Computer Interaction (HCI) institutionalised 'the user' in the design of computer technology. In its early years, HCI was strongly associated with ergonomics, itself an interdisciplinary collaboration drawing off disparate disciplines which emphasised the design of hardware around the anatomical features of the human body. HCI sought to design software not just around the physical characteristics of humans but also their imputed cognitive features, on the premise that human-computer interaction is essentially a matter of communication between man and machine (Grudin 1990a). Incorporating the user therefore centred on the design of the 'interface' between the user and the computer. The enterprise was founded on cognitive theory and interfaces began to be designed with an understanding of what was generally referred to as human 'mental models' and 'information processing' and the engineering challenges involved in creating the 'software control dialogue' to support these and facilitate effective communication between man and machine. Through the design of the computer interface HCI introduced *human factors* into thinking about the development of computing systems. In so doing the human sciences started to be incorporated into the design mix.

Jonathan Grudin (1990b) describes the history of the interface in five stages, each characterised by different users and different disciplines being drawn into the mix. He describes stage one as being where hardware constituted the interface and interaction centred on the ergonomics of switches, dials and panels. Stage two was the development of software programming interfaces. Stage three introduced the idea of the 'end user' and saw the terminal as the interface, drawing off the disciplines of human factors, psychology and graphic design. The 'end user' is preserved in the fourth stage – the 'interface as dialogue' stage – which draws heavily off cognitive psychology and cognitive science. The fifth stage of the interface is the interface as work setting. This involves groups of end users and inevitably draws the *social and organisational sciences* into the design mix. We neither want to endorse nor dispute Grudin's history of the interface but note two matters of significance in it for our present undertaking. First, that taking account of the work setting in design introduces the idea that disciplines to do with *the social*, and not just humans or human factors themselves, should be incorporated into the design mix. Second, that this 'turn to the social' in design does not address *how* the social should be factored into design. It is assumed to be a non-problematic matter to introduce the idea of designing with the social in view. However, in practice this is not turning out to be the case.

One of the reasons for this is that the disciplines investigating social matters are drawn from the social sciences, such as anthropology, sociology, management and organisational sciences, etc., and their ways of proceeding are unlike the ways in which the disciplines involved in systems design had proceeded before they entered the mix. Within the engineering disciplines, for example, there is a more or less agreed upon *consensus* as to how to proceed. A disciplinary paradigm holds sway over the disciplines' investigatory theories and methods. This is also generally true when the disciplines described by Grudin as involved in his third and fourth stages become involved. Although there is more flex involved in the theory and methods involved in human factors and cognitive science when compared to engineering, and even disagreement as to the best ways in which to do design, there is still broad agreement as to the principles of investigation and theory within cognitive science, human factors and psychology. All three areas would aspire to a unification of theory and method that, at least in received wisdom, typifies the disciplines of engineering and science. However, the social sciences are far from unified over matters of theory and method; indeed they often seem to revel in the differences between perspectives.

In stark contrast to the broad consensus within other disciplines involved in systems design, social science often seems to be driven by dissent, and its theories and methods are often sites of bitter contest. It sometimes appears that social science largely proceeds on the basis of argument about how the social world should be investigated, or what it is that drives and organises that world, rather than actually investigating social matters and social occurrences themselves. This is an ordinary and unremarkable fact of life for social scientists, and its taken for granted character may well have masked it from view in design's initial engagement with social science. Consequently, in elaborating the fifth stage of the interface's evolution and approaches towards its development Grudin refers to ethnography as if it were a unified approach. It might have appeared that way as well to the computer scientists at Xerox's Palo Alto Research Centre (PARC), where ethnography was first drawn into the design mix (Syzmanski and Whalen 2011). It might well have been the case that the PARC scientists, and those outside of PARC who followed this initial engagement with the social, viewed ethnography as what investigating the social amounted to, and as something that provided an uncontroversial approach to uncovering it. This is not the case.

Ethnography is as contested as any other matter within social science. There are arguments that it is not a method, for example, just a loose assembly of data collection techniques. There are arguments with respect to how the data gathered is used in descriptions of social life and its organisation, and arguments as to the quality of those descriptions and the quality of the data gathered. As systems design's engagement with the social has gathered steam, and as ethnography has become more entrenched in design activities, these sorts of divisions within the social sciences have started to surface and the issues that are raised within the social sciences are now being raised within design (e.g., Crabtree et al. 2009; Irani et al. 2010; Taylor 2011). This may well baffle designers, especially those who appreciate the merit of what may initially be seen as a way of bringing in matters to do with the social in descriptions of the activities they want to design systems to either automate or support. Nevertheless, the question of how disciplines involved in systems design are to react to this division in social science over what they might have reasonably supposed was a unified method is a timely and an important one as design's engagement with the social begins to mature.

There are of course a number of possible reactions to the fissures within ethnography. First off, one could ignore them. Designers share some traits of the magpie, which on seeing a glittering object takes it back to its nest: it does not matter if the object is made of glass or is a jewel, it suits its purposes. Thus, a description of some aspect of the social world produced by a social scientist may spark the designer's imagination, and that spark is all they need. It does not matter for their purposes if the description is, from the point of view of another social science perspective, methodologically flawed. Secondly, designers know what they like and what they trust. Here, the relationship that is built up between particular people, or the continued use of descriptions and accounts derived from a particular social science methodology may be the important matter, and if it has worked before then it will more than likely work again. With respect to these two reactions, it may well be that designers do not need to follow very carefully methodological arguments within the social sciences; their work can proceed without becoming sucked into the mire of social science dispute and debate.

A third reaction could be to try and understand the strength of an account of the social that might appear to be relevant for design matters, and there is a major lesson to be learnt from not having done that in the past. The idea of Artificial Intelligence (AI), for example, has taken many engineers, computer scientists and designers up a blind alley. AI is based upon cognitive theory and although we will not elaborate the many problems it is afflicted with here, a proper appreciation of its arguments and an understanding of the arguments of its opponents (see, for example, Button et al. 1995) may have given some who merely accepted its premises and proceeded from there pause for thought. A fourth reaction could be to reflect upon the multidisciplinary character of systems design. Rather than it being seen as an arena within which a number of disciplines contribute, it could be viewed instead as an emerging discipline in its own right, a *hybridised* discipline. In this respect a social methodology might become an important ingredient in systems development methodology, transforming the social from something turned to and treated in a piecemeal fashion into something turned to and treated in a methodical way. Understanding social science methodologies in themselves might then become an important step in developing a social methodology within and for the purposes of systems design.

Both the third and fourth reactions would require systems designers to understand at least some of the methodological issues within social science and the grounds of the various arguments which propel them. This book is aimed at people who fall into these categories, though it is hoped that other categories of reader might also reflect upon the fact that ethnography is not all of apiece and consider what might be an appropriate reaction to this. There is of course a fifth reaction, which is to just give up on social science, because there is just too much baggage to deal with. However, the option for that reaction has really gone by; the genie is out of the bottle, and the social *is* part of systems design thinking. The fact that designers and users are in social relationships with one another is a difficult matter to turn a back to and ignore, and the social is broadly recognised to now infuse systems design.

As the relationship between systems design and the social sciences matures an interesting aspect in the relationship has emerged. Once the social sciences might have hesitantly hovered around the design table but as the relationship has developed the social sciences have gained more confidence in what they might contribute to the design mix. In this respect another set of interests is now actively involved in understanding systems design in addition to those of system designers and developers: the interests of social scientist themselves. At every major design conference there will be found numerous papers situated in or derived from some study of the social. Major journals publish studies of social matters developed for design purposes, or descriptions of systems rooted in studies of the social, or speculations about systems that derive from studies of the social.

With developed confidence in what they can contribute, the social sciences may be able to reflect in a mature and critical way on how they can make their contributions to systems design without the fear that they will be banished from the table, even if it makes waves. Whilst design has turned to the social and the social has begun to be incorporated into design oriented conferences and journals, the reaction of some social contributors to other social contributions might well be different to what they would be if aired in social science conferences or journals. While it might have appeared initially to design that ethnography was a unified and unproblematic social science methodology, in the social sciences themselves not all studies of social matters rooted in ethnographic observation would be given equal weight: social scientists might contest the veracity of the observations made, for example, or the methodological and theoretical validity of the particular approach taken. Questions with respect to the strength of the relationship between the things a study might observe and the things it says about them are important matters within the social sciences. As the incorporation of the social into the design mix develops it becomes more important that *how* the social is incorporated is overtly considered if that mix is to result in a firm design platform. It might have served design for the social scientist sitting in a design-oriented conference to suppress the kinds of professional concerns they would raise if they were sitting in a social science conference for the purposes of just getting the social into design in some way. But now that it is firmly part of the design mix does it still serve design for social scientists to continue to be mute and not offer critical reflection upon descriptions of the social? Would one programmer suppress criticism of another programmer's code for being clumsy or inelegant? Would one designer accept the output of another designer just because they were a designer?

Suppressing critique by social scientists of social science descriptions developed for design purposes would be to negate a significant resource for system design. Critique has been used widely within design circles in general as a method to assess systems or proposals for systems. It is used within systems design to propel the enterprise forwards. The emergence of the field of Computer Supported Cooperative Work, and associated calls for a turn to the social, was based upon critiques of systems that were problematic in their support of group work and collaborative activities in the workplace. In this respect, early ethnographic studies of systems in use provided critiques of systems. Case studies found that people had to work around particular systems to get the job done, or that particular systems interfered with work practices and organisational structures. Many of the initial studies that heralded the relationship between systems design and social science sensitised design to the problems for social interaction and organisational process that particular systems created when they were introduced into the workplace. Critique has, then, an important role to play in the interdisciplinary mix.

This book provides a critique of ethnography in design for the purpose of making its contribution stronger. It provides an examination of ethnography in the social sciences and different orientations to the social that characterise different ethnographic approaches and considers their ramifications for systems design. The point and purpose of the exercise is not to make social scientists out of designers, but to show that an understanding of these differences can actually support design practice and enable the social to be built into design in more methodical ways. The methodological focus of the book makes it relevant to a particular audience and it is aimed, as we have mentioned, at those design practitioners and researchers who fall into the third and fourth categories outlined above. Thus it is intended to be a resource for those in systems design who want systems design to be a methodologically grounded matter. Building the social into design can be no less methodical than any other aspect of system development. Achieving that requires the development of an appropriate social methodology for systems design, and the development of an understanding of what could be appropriate requires some understanding of methodology in the social sciences.

2.2   The Turn to Ethnography

Within the social sciences there are a range of ways in which the social is studied. Ethnography emphasises observational, participatory techniques, but questionnaires, structured interviews, social modelling, ideal type construction, typologies, taxonomies and statistical surveys also figure strongly. Across anthropology and sociology the development of theories of society and culture have been stressed and, in recent social science history, feminist social theory, postmodernism and the lingering influences of Marxism have all propelled thinking around social matters. So given Grudin's developmental stages in interface design, we could ask the question: why is it that the method that is associated with the social in systems design is ethnography and not some other, more prominent method for investigating social matters such as a statistically driven method? Part of the answer to that question perhaps has more to do with the historical development of the personal computer and the introduction of computing technologies into the workplace, than it has to do with developments and trends in the social sciences. We are fully aware, given the nature of histories, that alternative historical accounts can be given, indeed await being given, and that engaging in them is a treacherous business. However, from our position within its history it seems possible to point to a number of key interrelated factors involved in the forging of a relationship between systems design and ethnography. These include research emanating from Xerox's Palo Alto Research Centre (PARC), the emergence of the field of Computer Supported Cooperative Work (CSCW), the Scandinavian School of Design, high profile system failures, and critiques of cognitive theory.

Research conducted at PARC made a decisive move in the introduction of the social into the design mix. As noted by Symanski and Whalen (2011),

> … in the late 1970s …John Seely Brown (JSB) brought a sensibility for social scientific research to the Palo Alto Research Centre … Before coming to PARC, JSB deepened his conviction that social scientific inquiry is powerful while working at BBN Technologies, where he realised that the challenge is not the building of technologies, but the *creation of technologies that fit into the workplace*. (our emphasis)

Part of PARC's research agenda became the need to understand the social context in which computing systems were to be placed, for while PARC had developed the personal computer and the work station there was still the realisation that these systems were not just being used by individuals but that they had to fit into the real time character of work and organisations. Although there was no lack of physiological and cognitive theory 'input' to the design of the interface for workplace systems, there was also the recognition that PARC designers knew little about the social character of the work that their systems were to fit into. Not only might they not know about it but the simple question that might provide for a useful answer – what do you want this system to do? – turned out not to be as simple as it seemed and PARC, for contingent, local reasons, therefore turned to anthropology and ethnography to start to understand how to answer it.

It is worth noting at this point that Bell and Dourish (2011) consign ethnographic interests in the workplace, and with it much of what ethnography has been for design to date, to that of the development of requirements, and propose 'new' horizons for ethnography in design instead. We take issue with this simplistic apportioning later. However, 'requirements capture' does well illustrate not only the need to understand social settings in designing for them but also the complexities involved for design in attempting to grapple with social matters. Within the area of requirements engineering, for example, the apparently simple and straightforward matter of asking (as above) the question "what do you want the system to do?" turns out to be a very complex one. In real world contexts, it is a question that has seen many large-scale developments flounder. Who are you to turn to answer the question? The people running the organisation would seem to be an obvious choice, but people in leadership positions do not always know what is going on in their organisations or how the work of the organisation actually gets done. 'Information seals' are rife in large complex organisations. Such information may not find its way up the organisational hierarchy and, consequently, asking about the nature of work in an organisation may not be as simple as posing enquiries to those occupying senior management positions.

Consulting organisational processes, workflow charts, job descriptions and other formal instruments may not result in clear-cut answers to questions about the way an organisation operates either. This is because, as anyone knows, formal specifications do not capture the ways in which they operate within actual contexts. Within organisations, there is what is supposed to happen and what actually happens, and while people might strive to align the two there are many examples in the literature which show that alignment is, at best, only approximate (see, for example, Rouncefield and Tolmie 2011). One might, then, turn to the purchasers of systems to elicit an understanding of the work the system will automate or support. However, purchasers are not the end-users, they do not understand the details of the work, the work-arounds that have developed, and actually how, in practice, the work is done. Purchasers might, at best, have previously done the work themselves before being promoted but again, as found in many studies, purchasers are all too often divorced from a detailed understanding of how the work is done now and the swarm of contingencies that currently play upon it.

Requirements engineers might instead turn to and ask the end-users. Again, this might appear to be a simple enough matter, but how is this to be done? Will a questionnaire do the job? The problem with this approach is that a questionnaire designed to make visible the work requirements for a system cannot be constructed without first knowing about that work. A pilot questionnaire might be put together in order to address the problem, to make visible what needs to be asked about in the proper questionnaire. However, now the requirements engineer is beginning to step into the murky waters of questionnaire methodology and the more they wade into those waters, the more the ground on which they stand might not seem as firm as it did at the outset as probabilities take hold. The end-users might be interviewed. However, interviews are a course of social interaction involving different parties with different interests. Some people are more skilled than others and those being interviewed may use the interview for their own purposes. Like the use of questionnaires, interviewing end-users to gain an understanding of the requirements for a system might not present the simple solution it at first appears to offer.

Furthermore, requirements engineers themselves work within an organisational structure and occupy a particular status position within it. Fujitsu, one of the largest interaction software houses, commissioned a study from PARC under the leadership of Jack Whalen to understand why 60 % of its developments failed. The study, amongst many other matters, found that the problem resided in its requirements capture and analysis and was directly related to the relative status of the requirements engineers and customers. The requirements engineers were often of a lower organisational status than those in the customer organisation they were talking to. Within Japanese business dealings relative status can be important within an interaction, and the study found that these status disparities could account for the developed software failing to satisfy customer need. In short, the requirements engineers were not able to elicit requirements, but had to merely listen to requirements. They were not in a position to challenge, to search, to probe, but were merely there to record.

On top of this, as any large development house will confirm, one of the key problems encountered in software development is often the customers themselves. Customers change their minds as to what they want, even though they may have been confident as to their requirements at the beginning of the development. Trying to pin down what the customer wants through tightly worded contracts and sign offs does not always work because the meaning of the words and phrases can change depending upon the person articulating them. Thus, just by taking one example – requirements engineering – in the whole complex of designing, developing and building a system for complex organisations, it is possible to see that attempting to bring in social considerations is not in practice a simple matter for those doing the development. Defining user requirements is itself a socially organised matter and is, as such, often a much more complicated job than defining systems specifications. The required capacity of a particular wire can be specified through a mathematical calculation of resistance, for example, but there are no corresponding mathematical formulations that will yield the organisational or work requirements that a system must satisfy. Some form of social enquiry and analysis *has* to be undertaken.

PARC's initial engagement with social enquiry and analysis was through Eleanor Wynn, one of six anthropology graduates from UC Berkeley hired as summer interns in 1976, who stayed on at PARC to do her PhD thesis. It would not be inappropriate to characterise her work as 'ethnography' (Wynn 1991). Ethnography had come to epitomise the way in which anthropologists engaged in their research by collecting materials 'from within social life' – being present as social life unfolds and witnessing it directly. Wynn, and the other early ethnographic pioneers in design, demonstrated that an ethnographic approach could provide a way through for those who needed to know more about actual social settings, particularly office settings at that time, and could help them grasp what was actually occurring within those settings. In this respect ethnography helped designers understand, in part at least, the general workplace requirements a system might need to satisfy.

Running concurrently with developments at PARC, some within HCI were arguing that the real world, real time character of work was not reflected in prevailing design models. As Schmidt (1994) observed, for example,

> In the design of conventional computer-based systems for work settings the core issues have been to develop effective computational models of pertinent structures and processes in the field of work (data flows, conceptual schemes, knowledge representations) and adequate modes of presenting and accessing these structures and processes as represented in computer systems (user interface, functionality) … the issue of how multiple users work

together and coordinate and mesh their individual activities – 'through' the system or 'around' it – was not addressed directly and systematically, as a design issue in its own right. So far as the underlying model of the structures and processes in the field of work was 'valid', it was assumed that the articulation of the distributed activities was of no import or that it was managed somehow by whoever it might concern. It was certainly not a problem for the designer or the analyst.

The development of Computer Supported Cooperative Work emphasised that the issue of how multiple users work together and coordinate their individual activities needed to be a major focus in the design and development of workplace systems. What was known as the Scandinavian School of Design was a major driver of CSCW, and a particular concern was to develop workplace systems in a way that empowered 'the worker'. This meant bringing in people who were engaged in the actual work that systems were being designed to support, and *their* understanding of the organisation of the workplace. It also meant that designers needed to enter into their world of work.

This turning to the social was driven by very public and embarrassing system failures. For example, the "comedy of errors" that beset the London Ambulance Service (LAS) was often cited (Finkelstein and Dowell 1996). LAS introduced a Computer Aided Despatch (CAD) system in October 1992. The CAD system exploited an automatic vehicle location system (AVLS) and mobile data terminals (MDTs) to automate ambulance despatch.

> Immediately following the system being made operational the call traffic load increased (but not it should be noted to exceptional levels). The AVLS could not keep track of the location and status of units … multiple units were being assigned to some calls. As a consequence of this there were a large number of exception messages … exception messages generated repeated messages and the lists scrolled off the top of the screens so that … messages were lost from view. Ambulance crews were frustrated and, under pressure … could not (or would not) use their MDTs … The public were repeating their calls because of the delay in response … The entire system descended into chaos (one ambulance arrived to find the patient dead and taken away by undertakers, another ambulance answered a 'stroke' call after 11 hours–5 hours after the patient had made their own way to hospital). The CAD system was partly removed and aspects of its function (notably despatch decisions) were performed manually. This part-manual system seized up completely 8 days later … … …
> … there is a very strong message in the report about the attempt to change working practices through the specification, design and implementation of a computer system. (ibid.)

The prescient need to shape systems to the social contexts in which they would be deployed and used consequently resulted in a broad turn to the social sciences. But social science is a vast territory. What sections of it might best support design objectives of fitting systems into the workplace? One might think, for example, that management science would be a primary candidate to support the design of workplace systems. Nonetheless, systems designers gave it short shrift.

> … the field of management science and its offspring organisational theory are like the emperor with no clothes … Organisational theory acts like the magic cloth that keeps us from looking at the essential issues within the workplace … [it] throws us off that course, as it defines organisations and their behaviour as rational entities acting through managerial practices. (Knudsen et al. 1993)

Knusden is making visible a divide here between theoretical orientations to work and organisation and empirical goings on in the workplace. Recognition of this divide was importantly made for design in Lucy Suchman's (1987) deconstruction of theoretical models of cognition and the empirically based examination of photo-copier use she provided. Descriptions of what people *actually do* were juxtaposed against theoretically generated models that provided for what they do.

These various factors occasioned the development of what was understood to be ethnographic explorations of work and the workplace to support design thinking with respect to workplace systems. However, as ethnographic work began to build momentum within Xerox's systems research, and within CSCW in general, we would argue that a sleight of hand occurred with respect to an understanding of what ethnography was. Really, and hopefully this will be come more clear as we examine ethnography and its various guises in depth, all that ethnography means is that we should orient ourselves to the study of society *'from within its midst'*. The idea of studying society from within is a radical departure from standard sociological alter-natives, such as studying society through statistical representations, or theoretical constructs, and to say 'all that it means' is not to ignore the important move that ethnography takes in stepping inside of the social to witness everyday life at first hand. But that is all that the term ethnography describes. It says nothing about *what* it is that such a study would apprehend. Nor *how* it would apprehend it. Certainly ethnographic work done at PARC, and elsewhere, brought the social into design, but *what* it saw and *how* it saw it was not derived from the theories and conceptual frameworks to be found in the ethnographic accounts of anthropology, be those derived from classical or contemporary studies. In the next chapter we will explore the origins of ethnography and part of its development within anthropology. It will be seen that ethnographic observations were used to fuel particular theoretical accounts of society and culture, and were part of a theoretical and definitional approach to social matters. We will also explore in Chap. 4 how some calls for new approaches to ethnography are actually not new at all but calls to return to this old social science practice.

However, ethnography as it was developed at PARC, and to some extent in CSCW and HCI, could not be more removed from this classic way of apprehending social matters through the generation of cultural theories and the production of defi-nitions and interpretations for and of social actions and interaction. Ethnography in design as it developed at PARC and as it made its early appearance in CSCW articu-lated *ethnomethodological* studies of work (Symanski and Whalen 2011). Ethnomethodology was a radical departure from traditional social science concerns and understandings. Harold Garfinkel, its founder, had provided a respecification of sociology in his book *Studies in Ethnomethodology* (Garfinkel 1967). We will be examining this respecification in detail in Chap. 7, but as a precursor we note here that in distinction to traditional social science, and included in this are undertakings that draw off ethnographically collected materials to generate theoretical and defi-nitional accounts of social order, ethnomethodology instead does the job through describing the practices of those involved in its achievement. Social order is, in ethnomethodology's view, a members' matter, not a matter of sociology and anthropology. In a way Garfinkel was putting sociology and anthropology out of business, because he was providing for an alternate social science. Unsurprisingly ethnomethodology has been marginalised by mainstream social science and is certainly organisationally dwarfed by the mainstream social science institution.

Ethnomethodological studies of work are key to Garfinkel's program (Garfinkel 1986; Rouncefield and Tolmie 2011). The idea of 'work' here, as we will explain later, does not just relate to what people do for a living, to 'jobs of work', but is more extensive and focuses on the work involved in doing action and interaction. This may involve studies of people's jobs but may also apply to the other non-paid activities that people engage in (see, for example, Tolmie and Rouncefield 2013). There certainly have been many ethnomethodological studies of 'jobs of work', and initial studies done for design purposes focused on the workplace. Lucy Suchman and her group put the study of work into high gear at PARC, which overflowed into HCI and CSCW. This research agenda was underpinned by Harold Garfinkel's ethnomethodological interest in how people order their activities in the course of doing them. This ethnomethodological influence is not only visible in PARC's lab studies (Suchman 1987), but also in studies of office procedures, airline operations, document retrieval, and broader reflections on 'studies of work' and their relevance to systems design more generally (Suchman 1983, 1995; Suchman and Trigg 1991; Blomberg et al. 1994). This body of work, as much as what happened within the labs at PARC, gave rise to the idea of 'situated action' and 'work practice' and came to epitomize PARC's interest in the social, an interest wholly grounded in ethnomethodology.

This initial ethnomethodological impetus in what were often just described as 'ethnographies' was strengthened by two further developments: the opening of a European PARC Lab in Cambridge in the UK (EuroPARC), and the development of a CSCW centre at the University of Lancaster, involving a collaboration between members of the sociology and computer science departments. EuroPARC recruited sociologists who were rooted in, and explicitly articulated, an ethnomethodological approach,[1] and although not all of the sociologists in the Lancaster CSCW Centre would own to ethnomethodology, one of the driving forces, John Hughes, and the graduate students around him, pursued ethnomethodological interests. Lancaster played a key role in a major European Union funded project called COMIC, which brought together a range of social scientists, computer scientists and systems designers, many from within the Scandinavian School of Design, who were concerned by the limitations of computing to support cooperative activities in the workplace. The COMIC project reinforced the usefulness of ethnography in closing the gap between systems design and the workplace (see the COMIC deliverables, particularly 2.1, 2.2, 2.3, 2.4 and 5.4). Again, however, the particular ethnographers involved employed an 'ethnomethodologically-informed' approach. Thus, the sleight of hand involved in the introduction of ethnography into systems design was to be content to have ethnomethodological studies labelled and called

---

[1] These included Bob Anderson, Wes Sharrock, Christian Heath, Richard Harper, Graham Button, Jon O'Brien and Peter Tolmie.

'ethnographies', rather than making clear that they owed little to ethnography as conducted in anthropology and elsewhere in sociology, but had all to do with ethnomethodology.

Within our potted history of the beginnings of ethnographic research in design, and again we acknowledge the fragility and vulnerability of such histories to alternative accounts, it may not have mattered that the 'ethnography' systems designers encountered was ethnomethodologically driven. Indeed many might have supposed, if they actually thought about it, that when they heard the term ethnomethodology that it was just another word for ethnography, that the two were one and the same. What mattered was not the name but the practical utility for their undertakings of the observations that ethnomethodologists cum ethnographers cum anthropologists and sociologists generated.[2] It also probably meant little to the social scientists involved as well that they did not make it explicit that they would *not* present themselves as ethnographers in their home discipline, though they used materials that were collected ethnographically, that is, through fieldwork, through observing society from within its midst.

However, developments within systems design, and really the occasioning circumstance of this book, are proving that while it might not initially have mattered that it was ethnomethodology rather than ethnography itself that drove many of the early social science engagements with systems design, *it now does*. This is because as the computer has moved out of the workplace – a setting which shaped previous design thinking with regard to the social – there have been calls to re-think ways of incorporating the social into design, driven in particular by the various writings of Genevieve Bell and Paul Dourish over recent years (see Crabtree et al. 2009). However, these calls are rooted in confusions about what was being leveraged into design at the outset. These are not necessarily confusions on the part of systems designers however, but confusions on the part of those calling for 'new' ethnographies to incorporate the social into design as the computer reaches out into novel contexts.

These calls have accompanied the interest that systems design is showing in non-work activities. With the development of 'ubiquitous computing' (Weiser 1991) the computer started to move away from the workplace and the focus of design shifted to society at large and a myriad more playful and leisurely domains. This has occasioned, for some, a need for design praxis to reinvent itself and move beyond prevailing models of workplace design towards new and poorly understood settings and situations. As design moves out from the workplace so-called 'new' ethnographic perspectives have emerged in a bid to accompany it, supplanting the focus on understanding users and their practices with "alternative viewpoints on assumptions in the design process", which are intended to "help us rethink the opportunities" as the computer reaches into new development sites (Bell et al. 2005). In short,

---

[2] The title of an early paper in the development of the relationship between design and ethnography says it all "Sociologists can be surprisingly useful in interactive systems design" (Sommerville et al. 1992). However, the cited sociological ideas and work are those of ethnomethodology, not sociology at large.

the reinvention of design praxis has opened the door to what social scientists generally refer to as *reflexivity* in ethnographic praxis. Gilbert Brown and Doblin (2004) sum up the idea in saying that,

> ... ethnography is discovering new sites for praxis, occupying new theoretical topoi, developing new signifying practices, articulating a new ethnographic subject, redefining its goals, reinventing its methodologies, and revising its assumptions in what constitutes a radical ontological and epistemological transformation.

This reflexive turn has been widespread, cutting across the social sciences and into systems design too as it turns towards novel sites and rubs up against new sociotechnical themes and new kinds of users, seemingly requiring new approaches, new conceptual frameworks, and new knowledge to make systems fit new social contexts of use.

On the face of it this might make sense to those in system design who do attempt to build the social into design. Ethnography as it has developed in systems design has largely concerned itself with work related activities and workplace contexts. In this respect it might seem a reasonable proposition that as systems designers have to adapt their development concepts and heuristics to handle design in novel settings and situations, then so too the methods of ethnography need to adapt in order to apprehend the social character of the new contexts that designers are reaching into. However, this line of reasoning begins with the wrong assumption that the ethnography 'traditionally' associated with design was itself designed for studying the sociality of work-related activities and the workplace. *Nothing could be further from the truth*. The original development of ethnography by Bronislaw Malinowski was done in studying the Trobriand islanders in the Western Pacific (Malinowski 1922), whose way of life was as far removed from the industrial conception of work and the workplace as is possible. Similarly, the ethnomethodological approach that has driven studies of work and the workplace originated in studies of what many social scientists, including those who studied work and occupations, considered trivial matters; matters such as walking, crossing the road, queuing, having a conversation and other mundane actions and interactions far removed from the work setting.

It is not ethnography per se that is the issue – i.e., observing social life from within its midst – but *bringing an appropriate understanding of how to describe the social into design*. It is in this respect that ethnography becomes problematic as it can be used by a whole range of different perspectives in the social sciences with very different results. Take, for example, the ground-breaking investigations of scientists' laboratory work by Lynch (1985) and by Latour and Woolgar (1979). Both studies exploited ethnography, witnessing first hand the matters they describe. However, both studies provide us with strongly contrasting understandings of how the actions and interactions of lab members are ordered and organised. Lynch's ethnomethodological examination elaborates the embodied practices through which scientists establish the situated intelligibility of their work as science. Latour and Woolgar, on the other hand, elaborate the idea that scientific work is a matter of inscription and can be inspected through literary practices. Both studies examined the same type of work, laboratory-based scientific investigation, both were ethnographic in character in that they entailed the sociologists being party to the setting, witnessing the work first hand and collecting materials that detailed that work, but there the resemblance ends.

If we look across the social sciences we can observe that ethnographically collected material has been used to construe the social in different ways. Within anthropology, Malinowski, 'the father of ethnography', produced a functionalist description of Trobriand society, while for example, Levi-Straus (1963) produced an important 'structuralist' analysis. Generally, anthropology has been concerned with understanding society through a *cultural lens*, with ethnography only being a way of collecting material to do that. As the influential American anthropologist Clifford Geertz (1973) makes clear, it is not the setting that is of concern to anthropology:

> The locus of study is not the object of study. Anthropologists don't study villages (tribes, towns, neighbourhoods ...) they study *in* villages.

What anthropologists study *in* a setting of any kind is not so much how that setting is organised in the actions and interactions of the people who inhabit it, as per the early ethnographies found in systems design with respect to the work setting, but the *broader culture* which is said to shape action and interaction in the setting. In this respect the setting, and the actions and interactions that animate it, are mechanisms through which the anthropologist can grasp the broader culture at work. This cultural lens, however, is not all of apiece but made up of (and fractured by) many different and competing social theories such as, as noted above, functionalism and structuralism and, more commonly today, post-modernism and feminism.

Although ethnography is strongly associated with anthropology, the sorts of 'studies of work' that have been done for systems design purposes, which designers familiar with early PARC and CSCW studies will recognise, are far removed from anthropology's diverse interests in 'culture'. For design studies it matters that the locus of study *is* the object of study. It also matters that *local* features of work, especially the particular activities and interactions through which the work is done, can be examined. However, from the point of view of anthropology, and for that matter sociology, the setting is a platform from which to view the operation of general cultural matters, such as class, or religion, or race, or gender, etc., rather than the setting-specific activities and their internal organisation in action. The reflexive turn in the social sciences masks different ways of apprehending the social. Within design, the reflexive turn masks just what is being introduced into the design mix – not 'new' forms of ethnography, but different ways of viewing the social to that which has been predominantly viewed in design to date. So while the term 'ethnography' might, on the face of it, seem to be a relatively straightforward matter, it is really an umbrella term sheltering a complex array of different views on, and different ways of viewing, the social.

In deconstructing ethnography, and producing our abbreviated history of its emergence in design, we must, however, be careful not to give the impression that all of the ethnographic engagements with design around work and the workplace

have been fuelled by ethnomethodological interest. Sheltering under the ethnographic umbrella in the past, as we will examine in more detail in Chap. 6, it is also
possible to find ethnography driven by and serving different views on the social. For
us this fact reinforces the point that the issue that is consequential for systems design
as it grapples with the social is not ethnography per se but *how the social is apprehended and understood*. As design moves out into other areas of everyday life the
call for the new is all too seductive. The seduction lies in taking and treating ethnography as if it were all of apiece, such that whatever description of the social is
offered it is assumed to be appropriate because it has been derived from 'ethnography'. The term ethnography has become a way of legitimising a broad range of
social scientific investigations. Thus, and although we have been strongly associated with the idea of ethnography in design, we now want to open that term up and
make it available for critical scrutiny by those in systems design who are interested,
as we are, in developing a social methodology for it. We want to open up 'ethnography' because it has become the default methodology for building in the social but
it cannot be a methodology in that sense: the competing and conflicting viewpoints
it harbours undermine the possibility of any such unified coherent method.

2.3 Why Should Systems Designers Care?

It was the recognition of the fact that systems are used within organised settings by
people interacting with one another, and that understanding the social character of
the design context is not an easy matter, that motivated PARC scientists to turn to
the social sciences in the first place. In effect PARC recognised that social matters
are important for the design of systems, but that the designers of systems may not
necessarily be the best equipped people to develop understandings of them. 'Experts'
in the investigation of the social were required and, in an attempt to build the social
into systems design, PARC turned to the academy and the social science faculty
staffed by people who spend their careers immersed in the study of social affairs and
arrangements, and to anthropologists in particular. There was good precedent for
turning to experts in other fields. The developments with respect to interface design
were supported (as noted by Grudin) by 'experts' in the field of psychology and
graphic design. Anyone who started to use word processors in the late 1970s and
early 1980s will remember how command instructions had to be inserted into the
text they were writing in order to introduce new paragraphs, italics and the like. The
move to graphical interfaces, and the concept of 'What You See Is What You Get'
(WYSIWYG) was a step change in design.

   The development of the graphical interface design was, in part, driven by the
concept of the user – an understanding rooted in cognitive theory and articulated
particularly within psychology. While the position of psychology within the human
and natural sciences has often been debated, some arguing that it belongs within the
realm of the natural sciences, others maintaining that its scientific bed-fellows are to
be found among the human sciences, psychology does share at least one thing in

common with the natural sciences that it does not share with other human sciences, which is that it is dominated by one particular paradigmatic theory: cognitive theory. Thus in having successfully turned to the experts with respect to interface design, underpinned by a unifying theory, it might have appeared that the same potential existed within the social sciences with respect to building the social into systems design.

However, as we have been arguing, unlike psychology, the social sciences do not have a ruling paradigm. Within the human and social sciences there are competing ways of grounding an understanding of the social. If there is any commonality amongst the social sciences then it lies not in a shared paradigm but in their interest, as noted in Chap. 1, in the Hobbesian problem of social order (Hobbes 1651); that is, in the question of how social order can be *accounted* for. The social sciences are predicated on the plainly observable fact that social life is organised or ordered. People are not just individuals, but individuals operating within an organised ensemble, a collectivity, a 'society', and in their dealings with one another display an orientation to that *fact*. As mentioned in the introduction, the way that anyone in the UK can go into a cinema that they have never been to before, in a part of the country they have never been to before, and ask a person they have never met before to purchase a ticket for a film displays and exemplifies not only that our mundane activities are orderly affairs but also, and to boot, that the social order is an unremarkable feature of everyday life for its members. Furthermore, the social order cuts across national boundaries. Thus, and for example, wherever the social institution of the cinema exists an orderliness of action and interaction will be involved in coming to watch a film. Of course there can be local variations in, for example, how people queue for a ticket, or pay for it, or find a seat, but there will, nevertheless, be some social 'system' at work.

There is then, a *universal phenomenon* for the social sciences – social order – and a universal recognition that social order involves a relationship between society and the individual. In place of a ruling paradigm, the social sciences have traditionally positioned themselves as falling into one of two camps with respect to the primordial question of how social order comes about and thus be accounted for. This is often framed in terms of a relationship between *social structure* and *social action*, or 'structure and agency' to avoid relativising the issue to a particular society and individual. At its most simple the divide has been construed of in *top down/bottom up* terms, sometimes as 'macro' vs. 'micro'. That is to say that, on the one hand, social structure is said to constrain and provide for social action thereby providing for a top down view on social order; on the other hand is the idea that structure is a product of agency, thereby providing for a bottom up view on social order. In these terms, social order is the product of constraining social structures that exist outside individuals and shape their actions, posed against the idea that social order is constituted through individuals and their actions. Within the social sciences the structure camp is exampled by Karl Marx, Emile Durkheim and Talcott Parsons, and articulated through theories of functionalism, consensus, and conflict, whereas the agency camp is exemplified through methodological individualism, interactionism and phenomenology. Ethnomethodology would be characterised within the social sciences as falling into the agency and micro side of the proposed divide. It would certainly be true to say that the prevailing wind in the social sciences has always been the top-down view, with theories of patriarchy and globalisation being examples of current social science top-down thinking.

Why should the fact of this broad dichotomy matter to design? The answer is that until recently it has not mattered a jot, and really we would prefer that it continued not to matter. However, it is now being made to matter for design by the calls that are being made to develop 'new' forms of ethnography, ones that for example argue that cultural theories are needed to move design beyond a 'requirements' engagement with the social (Bell and Dourish 2011). Without probably realising it, design is now being confronted with the old divide in the social sciences with regard to structure and agency, and is being invited to see that the 'macro' concerns of structure can replace the 'micro' concerns of agency. Since ethnomethodology would normally be associated with the micro, agency side of this supposed divide, it follows that it too can be transcended by the traditional emphasis on structure and the macro.

So did the PARC scientists wrong-foot systems design when they turned to ethnomethodologically-informed ethnography as epitomising the practice of expertise in the social? Should they have looked elsewhere? Should they have turned to the predominant top-down theories and methodologies in social science for the expertise they sought? Certainly they should have asked the question, "What are we buying into?" If they had, the answer might have surprised them. They would have discovered that the expertise they were appropriating was not and is not at all typical in the social sciences. Further still, they would have found out that *that* expertise is not even typical in anthropology, for despite the fact that the discipline utilises ethnography in collecting its materials, the predominant focus of anthropological studies was and still is on social structure. Thus, in turning indiscriminately to anthropology and ethnography for expertise, and rather by chance picking up on ethnomethodology, PARC unwittingly created an interesting issue for systems design, for design's initial foray into the social was through what was and is considered by mainstream social science a marginalised, 'micro' interest in agency not typical of anthropology or sociology at all.

This irony was not particularly apparent in the early ethnographic work. While occasionally discussed by ethnographers working in a design context (e.g., Jirotka et al. 1992) there was little interest or engagement from the broader social science community with design. Mainstream social science, as epitomised by fields examining the social 'shaping' and 'construction' of technology (MacKenzie and Wajcman 1985; Bijker et al. 1987) instead preferred to treat technology as an object of critical scrutiny rather than something that it would actually want to help develop. Within systems design research a growing band of social scientists interested in CSCW and ethnomethodologically-informed ethnography had the job to themselves to some large extent. Nonetheless, the turn to ethnography as an expert means of understanding the social has over time attracted broad interest in systems design, and the demand for expertise has brought more traditional or mainstream kinds of ethnographers to the table. With them, however, comes the top-down view of the social that predominates in anthropology and sociology, as it does elsewhere in the social sciences.

What is also brought into play here is an interesting issue around the very idea of 'expertise' in social affairs. We will elaborate key issues raised by ethnomethodology with respect to the description of human action in Chap. 7, but one thing we note here is that ethnomethodology in its respecification of sociology took the idea of expertise in understanding and describing social matters out of the hands of social scientists as social scientists and placed it back in the hands of those who actually *do* social life. This is because, as we have touched upon in the introduction and will expand on later, social science accounts of social matters inevitably rely upon and build in everyday accounts, which makes them re-descriptions of what everyone knows. Ethnomethodology rather directs attention to what it is that everyone knows, making explicit the ordered features of common-sense knowledge and the ways in which people use that knowledge methodically to achieve their actions and interactions. Thus, although PARC scientists and others in CSCW and HCI might have turned to the supposed experts in social matters – anthropologists and sociologists – in as much as initial engagement with the social was heavily influenced through encounters with ethnomethodological studies, the expertise designers encountered was the expertise *of those studied* not the expertise of social science. It was what those who were working within particular settings knew about organising that setting and organising their work activities and interactions, not what the social scientist knew, that was being brought into design. Ethnomethodological studies of work brought *members' expertise* into the design mix, not social science expertise.

Calls for 'new' approaches to ethnography are placing the social scientist in the driving seat rather than those involved in actual settings, whatever and wherever they might be, by introducing a top-down view with respect to the social structuring of action and interaction. In doing so they track old confusions about the relationship between structure and agency into systems design. Although this dichotomy is one that has been consistently held to in the social sciences since their inception, and despite many attempts to synthesise them, we understand it to be one that rests in large measure on misunderstandings of those in the structure camp of the arguments being made in the agency camp (Sharrock and Button 1991). Rather than treating the dichotomy as an either/or proposition to be continually debated it needs to be recognised that agency arguments are not about the inappropriateness of understanding structural matters for how the social is ordered, but are ones that *relocate* the site for the production of structure. They are not about dismantling the idea of structure but respecifying it as something that is *internal* to the sites of its production (Garfinkel and Sacks 1970) to the effect that structure and agency are seen and understood to be *mutually elaborative*. As Sharrock and Watson (1988) put it,

> … we cannot conceive of an individual action except as an-action-in-a-structure, any more than we can conceive of a single word as other than a-word-in-a-language … The relationship between 'action' and 'social structure' is not to be conceived … as one between cause and consequence (whichever way the causal connection is supposed to run …). It is, instead, to be conceived as that of pattern and particular, where the articulation of the two provides

for their mutual visibility: the particular is recognisable for what it is as part of the pattern but the pattern itself is made out of and manifested in the particulars (as the elements of a mosaic and the mosaic-as-a-whole comprise one another). The pattern and the particular are mutually constitutive ...

Thus action (the particular) elaborates structure (the pattern) and vice versa. Nevertheless, despite such arguments, the dichotomy between action and structure remains as a fulcrum around which many contradictory debates in the social sciences revolve and, in calls to move design beyond the micro, beyond agency and into matters of social structure and culture, design is being lured into accepting an old confusion. The confusion results in designers being told that the understandings of social order they have encountered in studies of the workplace are not relevant to the sorts of social and cultural understandings that that they are being now presented with, and that approaches to studying work and the workplace are only good enough for design as generative of requirements and not grappling with grander social matters. But this is not so, for ethnomethodological studies of work are just as much concerned with the idea of social structure as any top-down perspective. It is just that they have respecified structure as a matter of *local production* and that, in these terms, understanding structural matters requires an understanding of the situated methods – members' methods – for *bringing them about*. This interactional interest in structure holds whatever the setting, be it at work, at home or at play.

The whole reason for turning to the social in the first place in systems design was the recognition that designers did not know much about what it was that people actually *do*. In turning to ethnomethodologically-informed ethnography, design was encountering first order understandings of social structures *in action* rather than the second order reinterpretations of the social sciences. Design really has an option: contend with what people do, their actions and interactions, be they in the workplace or elsewhere, and engage with social settings as they are organised, structured and understood by those who are party to them, or have understandings of the social mediated by social science through the descriptive apparatus of theory and interpretation. Of course social science will try to ascribe to ethnomethodology that it inevitably uses this apparatus itself. It will be argued, for example, that it is just as theory-laden as any other perspective, but as we hope to make clear when we turn to these matters in depth, this misunderstands the idea of ethnomethodological study and what it is that is studied.

It might seem, as we have gestured towards before, that design could consider itself to be above these concerns; that it can pick and choose what it cares for and whatever suits its purposes. However, if the point is not perspicuous by now, then let us be forthright. From our point of view, having worked with designers since 1990, we understand that the reason that ethnographic expertise has come to be valued by them lies in its ability to make visible how the orderliness of a setting is achieved *by those who are party to it*. We appreciate that designers themselves might not put it in these terms, but however it is worded it is a demonstrable fact borne out of long interdisciplinary experience. It is not the expertise of the social scientist that has been of value to systems design, but the conspicuous expertise of members in accomplishing their social affairs that has been made available to design reasoning through 'ethnography'. This has involved focusing upon members' methods for achieving order in action and interaction and thus placing emphasis upon surfacing how those involved bring the social order about. However, the unwitting turn to the traditional and predominant concerns of the social sciences brought about by the call for 'new' approaches to ethnography brings in the theoretical and conceptual machinery of social science, which is used to *replace* members' methods. The replacement is being done surreptitiously, masked by the term 'ethnography' and the unquestioned acceptance of ethnographic expertise.

The issue then is this: will traditional, disciplinary sanctioned, top-down views on the social do the job that designers want and expect them to do? Will designers be able to build the social into their systems if the local orderliness of action and interaction is no longer made visible and available to design reasoning? In surfacing these issues we seek to encourage those designers who are concerned to build a social methodology into the construction of computational machines to consider whether or not the 'new' breed of ethnographic expertise is sound and fit for purpose. In deconstructing ethnography we want to reveal how the term masks concealed understandings of the social. In doing so we want to create a space for reflection on the practical adequacy of mainstream, traditional, top-down, structural views on the social for systems design. In the following chapter we take a critical look at the classical roots of ethnography in anthropology and how the local orderliness of social action becomes a *surplus* phenomenon – something to be dispensed with – before moving on to elaborate how this plays out in calls for 'new' approaches to ethnography in contemporary systems design.

References

Bell, G., & Dourish, P. (2011). *Divining a digital future: Mess and mythology in ubiquitous computing*. Cambridge, MA: MIT Press.

Bell, G., Blythe, M., & Sengers, P. (2005). Making by making strange: Defamilarisation and the design of domestic technologies. *ACM ToCHI, 12*(2), 149–173.

Bijker, W., Hughes, T., & Pinch, T. (Eds.). (1987). *The social construction of technological systems*. Cambridge, MA: MIT Press.

Blomberg, J., Suchman, L., & Trigg, R. (1994). Reflections on a work-oriented design project. In: *Proceedings of the 1994 participatory design conference* (pp. 99–109). Chapel Hill: Computer Professionals for Social Responsibility.

Button, G., Coulter, J., Lee, J. R. E., & Sharrock, W. W. (1995). *Computers, minds and conduct*. Oxford: Polity Press.

COMIC Deliverables. www.comp.lancs.ac.uk/computing/research/cseg/comic/

Crabtree, A., Rodden, T., Tolmie, P., & Button, G. (2009). Ethnography considered harmful. In: *Proceedings of the SIGCHI conference on human factors in computing systems* (pp. 879–888). Boston: ACM.

Finkelstein, A., & Dowell, J. (1996). A comedy of errors: The London Ambulance Service case study. In: *Proceedings of the 8th international workshop on software specification and design* (pp. 2–5). Washington, DC: IEEE.

Garfinkel, H. (1967). *Studies in ethnomethodology*. Englewood Cliffs: Prentice-Hall.

Garfinkel, H. (Ed.). (1986). *Ethnomethodological studies of work*. London: Routledge.

Garfinkel, H., & Sacks, H. (1970). On formal structures of practical action. In J. C. McKinney & E. Tiryakian (Eds.), *Theoretical sociology: Perspectives and developments* (pp. 160–193). New York: Apple-Century-Crofts.

Geertz, C. (1973). *The interpretation of cultures: Selected essays* (pp. 3–30). New York: Basic Books.

Gilbert Brown, S., & Dobrin, S. (2004). New writers of the cultural sage. In: *Ethnography unbound: From theory shock to critical praxis* (pp. 1–10). Albany: State University of New York Press.

Grudin, J. (1990a). Interface. In: *Proceedings of the ACM conference on computer supported cooperative work* (pp. 269–278). Los Angeles: ACM.

Grudin, J. (1990b). The computer reaches out: the historical continuity of interface design. In: *Proceedings of the SIGCHI conference on human factors in computing systems* (pp. 261–268). Seattle: ACM.

Hobbes, T. (1651). *Leviathan*. St Paul's Churchyard: Green Dragon.

Irani, L., Vertesi, J., Dourish, P., Philip, K., & Grinter, R. (2010). Postcolonial computing: A lens on design and development. In: *Proceedings of the SIGCHI conference on human factors in computing systems* (pp. 1311–1320). Atlanta: ACM.

Jirotka, M., Gilbert, N., & Luff, P. (1992). On the social organization of organizations. *Computer Supported Cooperative Work: The Journal of Collaborative Computing, 1*(1), 69–94.

Knudsen, T., Bansler, J., Bjørn-Andersen, N., Greenbaum, J., Nurminen, M., & Thoresen, K. (1993). The Scandinavian approaches: Theories in use, of use and organisation of interdisciplinarity. In: *Proceedings of IRIS 16* (pp. 29–38). University of Copenhagen, Association for Information Systems.

Latour, B., & Woolgar, S. (1979). *Laboratory life: The construction of scientific facts*. London: Sage.

Lynch, M. (1985). *Art and artefact in laboratory science: A study of shop work and shop talk in a research laboratory*. London: Routledge and Kegan Paul.

MacKenzie, D., & Wajcman, J. (Eds.). (1985). *The social shaping of technology*. Buckingham: Open University Press.

Malinowski, B. (1922). *Argonauts of the western pacific: An account of native enterprise and adventure in the archipelagoes of Melanesian New Guinea*. London: Routledge and Kegan Paul.

Rouncefield, M., & Tolmie, P. (Eds.). (2011). *Ethnomethodology at work*. Farnham: Ashgate.

Schmidt, K. (1994). The organisation of cooperative work: Beyond the 'Leviathan' conception of the organisation of cooperative work. In: *Proceedings of the conference on computer supported cooperative work* (pp. 101–112). Chapel Hill: ACM.

Sharrock, W. W., & Button, G. (1991). The social actor: Social action in real time. In G. Button (Ed.), *Ethnomethodology and the human sciences* (pp. 137–175). Cambridge: Cambridge University Press.

Sharrock, W., & Watson, R. (1988). Autonomy among social theories; the incarnation of social structures. In N. Fielding (Ed.), *Actions and structure: Research methods and social theory* (pp. 56–77). London: Sage.

Sommerville, I., Rodden, T., Sawyer, P., Bentley, R. (1992). Sociologists can be surprisingly useful in interactive systems design. In: *Proceedings of the 7th conference of the British computer society human computer interaction specialist group* (pp. 341–341) York: BCS.

Strauss, L. (1963). *Anthropologie structurale*. Paris: Plon.

Suchman, L. (1983). Office procedures as practical action: Models of work and system design. *ACM Transactions on Office Information Systems, 1*(4), 320–328.

Suchman, L. (1987). *Plans and situated actions: The problem of human-machine communication*. Cambridge: Cambridge University Press.

Suchman, L. (1995). Making work visible. *Communications of the ACM, 38*(9), 56–64.

Suchman, L., & Trigg, R. (1991). Understanding practice: Video as a medium for reflection and design. In J. Greenbaum & M. Kyng (Eds.), *Design at work: Cooperative design of computer systems* (pp. 65–89). Hillsdale: Lawrence Erlbaum Associates.

Syzmanski, M., & Whalen, J. (2011). Introduction: Work practice analysis at Xerox. In M. Szymanski & J. Whalen (Eds.), *Making work visible: Ethnographically grounded case studies of work practice* (pp. 1–17). Cambridge: Cambridge University Press.

Taylor, A. (2011). Out there. In: *Proceedings of the SIGCHI conference on human factors in computing systems* (pp. 685–694). Vancouver: ACM.

Tolmie, P., & Rouncefield, M. (Eds.). (2013). *Ethnomethodology at play*. Farnham: Ashgate.

Weiser, M. (1991). The computer for the 21st century. *Scientific American, 265*(3), 94–104.

Wynn, E. (1991). Taking practice seriously. In J. Greenbaum & M. Kyng (Eds.), *Design at work: Cooperative design of computer systems* (pp. 45–64). Hillsdale: Lawrence Erlbaum Associates.

Chapter 3
Ethnography as Cultural Theory

Abstract In this chapter we take a closer look at the workings of ethnography in social science, in particular in anthropology, to understand better the work it has traditionally done as pointed to in Chap. 2. As an introduction to this matter we explore how the rise of ubiquitous computing in systems design has generated calls for 'new' ways of handling the social milieu. However, upon examination, it becomes apparent that these calls actually return ethnographers to an old and traditional role: that of acting as *interpreters of* and *commentators on* the organisation of society and culture at large. To understand what is being offered here it is necessary to understand the role ethnography has traditionally played in anthropology. We begin with ethnography's 'founding father', Bronislaw Malinowski, and show that despite an apparent resonance between the early ethnographies done for systems design the only real overlap lies in an interest in fieldwork. At the heart of Malinowski's approach, and 'new' forms of ethnography alike, is the grounding of what is observed through fieldwork in a theory of culture and society. This produces a visible *disjuncture* between society and culture as it is understood by its members, and society and culture as understood by anthropologists and other social scientists making use of fieldwork. The net result is that the everyday life of people studied through ethnography becomes a *surplus* phenomenon and disappears from view in social science accounts, a point we demonstrate in reviewing two ethnographic studies of the same social setting: Tepoztlán in Mexico.

3.1 New Calls, Old Ways

In Chap. 2 we described how interest in building the social into systems design originated in various initiatives: the realisation by scientists at Xerox PARC that they did not have a sufficient appreciation of the social character of work in the office, which was the focus of design in the 1980s; the development of Computer Supported Cooperative Work (CSCW) and the recognition that work involved the interaction of individuals-within-groups, not just individual users; the Scandinavian school of design's interest in building 'the worker' into the actual design process; highly visible systems failures; and the undermining of cognitive theory as a means of addressing social matters. We also described how, in attempting to build the social into the design mix, PARC turned to 'the experts' – that is, those with a disciplinary interest in social matters – and how, for a variety of reasons, the discipline they first drew upon was anthropology, and in so doing encountered what passes as 'ethnography' in systems design.

Although ethnography as a 'method', to use the term in a loose fashion to begin with, was first developed in anthropology, it might not have been anthropology per se that attracted the interest of designers. While anthropology was interested in culture, society, and social structures, in retrospect, it might rather have been the *investigatory practices* of anthropology that came to hold researchers' interests. The study of the social through *fieldwork* was of particular note. PARC was striving at the time to reinvent the office, yet there was little information about how office work was conducted other than that derived from anecdotal or personal experience. Ethnographic investigations of the office provided insights into the actual nature of work in the office, including group work and the relationship of machines to the collaborative conduct of office work. While other social science disciplines had a longstanding interest in work – there was, for example, a sub-discipline of sociology called 'the sociology of work and occupations' – they more often than not seemed to be concerned with the social conditions of work, rather than with *the actual work itself*. The interest in work and the workplace within social science at large was not focused on the conduct of work and its enacted organisation but, for example, in studies of the statistical spread of genders in the office, the hierarchy of office life, the politics of it, and such 'structural' matters, which in turn shaped general theoretical understandings of the position of the office worker in society. These concerns dominated social science interest in work, the office being but one platform from which to view them operating, rather than an understanding of what it was that office workers actually *did*.

Although researchers and designers at PARC and elsewhere did not articulate it in these terms, it was, perhaps, an interest in 'getting closer to the work' that new computing systems would automate or support which sparked and drove the turn to the social sciences and to ethnography in particular. It appeared that in situating the researcher *in the midst of work* that anthropology actually studied what people did through fieldwork, rather than holding them at arms length through statistical procedures of investigation and theoretical representations of work. However, although anthropology might emphasise ethnography and fieldwork as data gathering activities, as a discipline it has a predominant *structural* interest in social and cultural affairs, whether in regard to work or any other kind of social enterprise and endeavour. This disciplinary concern with social and cultural structure was not pursued by the designers who had begun to forge links with anthropology however, and PARC became known, not so much for its anthropological interests per se, but for its interest in building in an understanding of the *situated work practices* of those whose work it was developing systems to automate or support. The structural disciplinary concerns of anthropology were rarely touched upon in design as ethnographic investigation of work practice spread outside of PARC and gathered pace in CSCW, and to an extent in HCI. As interest in ethnography burgeoned the focus largely remained centred on the design inspiration that ethnographic studies could foster and how they could play into the practicalities of particular design efforts, rather than on anthropology's disciplinary interest in the structure of culture and society at large.

This initial lack of interest in anthropology's disciplinary concerns is now becoming a source of some 'confusion' as to how to build the social into the design mix (Dourish 2014). This is because, as we have noted, while interest in the workplace and work-related activities remains potent, computing in the twenty-first century is marked by the movement of the computer away from the desktop into the fabric of everyday life: into streets, buildings, machines, mobile devices, clothes, and even the body. The spread of the computer beyond the workplace and rise of 'ubiquitous computing' (Weiser 1991) has been accompanied by calls for 'new' approaches to ethnography and understandings of the social. These 'new' approaches seem to stand in contrast to the ethnographic approaches that typified PARC's interest in work practice. Thus, in distinction to the previous genre of ethnographic studies that focused upon 'the situation' – i.e., on the unfolding action and interaction of participants in real time and the practices through which they methodically organise their undertakings as they do them – 'new' approaches are, as we have argued in the last chapter, returning ethnography back to its original remit in anthropology and the production of generalised accounts of social and cultural structure.

Paul Dourish and Genevieve Bell are notable champions of 'new' approaches to ethnography in systems design. Their efforts have been driven in substantial part by the perceived paucity of a standard 'ubicomp' vision that continuously regurgitates Weiser's view, developed at PARC, of a future world in which human action and relationships are mediated by an invisible technological infrastructure (Bell and Dourish 2007). Bell and Dourish set about remedying this by turning to anthropology's interest in social and cultural structures, an interest largely neglected in systems designs' engagement with ethnography around work and the workplace. It concerns us that Bell and Dourish's emphasis upon imputed structural forces shaping contemporary culture and society returns ethnographers to their old and traditional role, which is that of acting as *interpreters of* and *commentators on* the organisation of societies and cultures at large.

This stands in contrast to the role that emerged from out of PARC, which was subsequently developed in CSCW, where the ethnographer was an *analyst* responsible for making it visible how people do the things they do as a resource for design. In recasting ethnography anew, Bell and Dourish miss the fact that the *practical role* that has developed for social science in systems design is just as relevant for systems to be used outside of the workplace as it is for systems used within, and just as relevant for non-work activities as it is for work activities. In returning ethnography to its traditional role in the social sciences the original focus on situated action and interaction, which drove ethnography in design, is being replaced by a focus on a generalised social milieu needing interpretation by a social scientist as a *context for design*, as opposed to the social being a *source of data* either for design inspiration or for the practical development of particular systems. Simply put, some old confusions about the role of the social scientist, and mistakes about how to describe the social, are (unfortunately) being tracked into design with the turn to the 'new'. Thus the potential arises for old confusions in the social sciences around structure and agency, and top down/bottom up understandings of the social, to muddy the waters for those in design interested in building the social into the design mix.

One of the strengths of ethnography in design is that it has developed as an *analytic*, *investigatory* matter rather than involving itself in disputes about how to approach the social. However in doing that, and as outlined in Chap. 2, design has unwittingly aligned itself, or at least drawn from, the agency side of the so-called 'structure/agency' divide and inadvertently taken this way of approaching social matters as the consensus in the social sciences. Ethnography, as mainly encountered in design, does not represent the consensus view on the social in the social sciences. Rather, the consensus is represented by a theoretical interest in culture and society at large and the interpretation of situated action and interaction in terms of an overarching theoretical apparatus. In calling for the 'new' Bell and Dourish are actually returning to the old consensus view of social science. This may seem like a good idea. After all, if theorising generic social and cultural structures is good enough for the social sciences, it may well follow that it is good enough for systems design. However, it should be appreciated that the role of the ethnographer in systems design and social science is very different: one provides empirical data and analyses for the practical purposes of shaping and building computing systems, the other provides theoretical interpretations and commentaries on the social that might be used to define contexts for design.

The turn to 'new' approaches to ethnography is problematic then for those designers who are interested in developing a systematic approach to building the social into design. The turn to the 'new' is built on some very old assumptions about the social and how it should be described, which are rooted in anthropology. These assumptions, and their consequences for design, are masked by the ubiquitous use of the term 'ethnography' to convey what are really very different understandings of how to investigate and describe the social. We begin our attempt to unpack the assumptions that the call for the 'new' turns upon by making these differences visible, first by attempting to show that, as a discipline, anthropology's development of ethnography has been to drive a top-down, structural understanding of social and cultural matters. We pick up and elaborate the key issues raised here in the next chapter to show how a disciplinary concern with general theoretical description of social and cultural structures is leaking into systems design with the turn to 'new' approaches to ethnography.

3.2   The Beginnings of Ethnography in Anthropology

If we are to understand the 'new' we need first to appreciate how ethnography *began* its examination of 'the social'. Ethnography is in many respects, as recorded in many histories and introductions, an accident of the First World War. The term was coined by the Polish anthropologist Bronislaw Malinowski. A student at the London School of Economics, he was working in Australia studying the exchange practices of Australian aboriginals when war broke out in 1914. He was prevented from travelling back to England because he was a subject of the Austro-Hungarian empire, and was thus deemed to be a 'hostile alien'. In place of internment he took up an offer from the Australian government to undertake research in Melanesia, and worked extensively in the Trobriand Islands where he continued his interest in 'exchange patterns' by studying the *Kula ring*, which involved a network of social actors in the exchange of valuable necklaces and bracelets throughout the islands of the Massim archipelago.

Anthropology had traditionally conducted its research through archival documentary material, interviews with travellers and *fieldwork*. One way the latter was typically undertaken was through the offices of a 'native informant'. A member of the society or tribe under investigation would be enlisted to guide the anthropologist through the intricacies of their culture, and explain the various activities, institutions, rituals and other social practices they encountered. Another mechanism was to learn about culture and society through colonial government officials. However, effectively stranded for an unknown duration, Malinowski was living *within* the culture he was studying, and experiencing it for himself, not just through the tongue of a native informant or the eyes of a colonial official. He was not just observing and having his observations explained, he was also *participating* in the culture as a matter of his daily round.

Anyone who has conducted fieldwork in, for example, a workplace which is unfamiliar to them and within which there are activities going on that are not readily comprehensible will appreciate the orienting explanations that a 'guide' might provide. Often this guide is a manager or someone whom the manager has appointed. The fieldworker will also appreciate that, after a time, as they become more familiar with the setting and have talked with and worked alongside others therein, they will begin to notice that there is often a disjuncture between what has initially been explained to them and the actualities of the social milieu they find themself in the midst of. This is because within organisations of all types there are, inevitably, information seals – managers might think they know what occurs on, for example, the shop floor, but it is not always in the best interest of shop floor workers for them to actually know, in detail, what really goes on. Also, managerial versions given to outside fieldworkers tend to be 'handbook' versions, formal versions of workplace activities, whereas actual practice may significantly differ from these. Furthermore, prejudices and personal opinions in one way or another can enter into descriptions – a manager's dislike of union activities, or a shop stewards distrust of management, for example. Inevitable disjunctures between the guided version and the experiences of actually participating in the setting arise, and otherwise unobtainable glimpses into the organisation of the social setting can be developed by going beyond 'received wisdom'.

Without knowing when he could return to England, Malinowski was living within and participating in the culture he was studying. This afforded him the opportunity to gain glimpses into that culture in a way that was not traditional for anthropologists before him. Rather than viewing a culture from afar 'on the veranda', mediated through others or documents of various kinds, Malinowski was immersed, as a daily matter, in the day-to-day culture of the Trobriand Islanders. He subsequently saw that this kind of experience needed to be a foundation for studying society and culture.

> It would be easy to quote works of high repute, and with a scientific hall-mark on them, in which wholesale generalisations are laid down before us, and we are not informed at all by what actual experiences the writers have reached their conclusion. No special chapter or paragraph is devoted to describing to us the conditions under which observations were made and information collected. I consider that only such ethnographic sources are of unquestionable scientific value, in which we can clearly draw the line between, on the one hand, the results of direct observation and of native statements and interpretations, and on the other, the inferences of the author, based on his common sense and psychological insight. (Malinowski 1922)

Although beginning a 'participatory' tradition of fieldwork in the social sciences, very few discussions of ethnography refer to the observations produced by Malinowski and why he came to emphasise experiencing "the native's point of view". Yet the problems he encountered of gaining traction on his subject matter ring as true today as they did for him then, and they are well documented in the first section of his book *Argonauts of the Western Pacific*. Those in systems design who have encountered the early ethnography emanating from PARC, the University of Lancaster, COMIC, and EuroPARC (as mentioned in Chap. 2), done for the purposes of design, will find Malinowski's observational principles very familiar.

Thus, early ethnographic studies done to support systems design deal with the *actions* and *interactions* of actual people, and not with statistical trends, for example. This dovetails with a first concern raised by Malinowski with the difficulties of using conventional social science tools:

> I took a village census, wrote down genealogies, drew up plans and collected the terms of kinship. But all this remained dead material, which led no further into the understanding of real native mentality or behaviour, since I could neither procure a good native interpretation of any of these items, nor get what could be called the hang of tribal life.

A second point of intersection between early design ethnography and Malinowski was the focus on *direct* observation of action and interaction, as a means of developing an understanding of how social life was organised, rather than mediating that organisation through a third party translator. Indeed, Malinowski was sceptical about the role of the traditional anthropological mediator:

> As to obtaining their ideas about religion, and magic, their beliefs in sorcery and spirits, nothing was forthcoming except a few superficial items of folk-lore, mangled by being forced into pidgin English. Information which I received from some white residents in the district, valuable as it was in itself, was more discouraging than anything else with regard to my own work. Here were men who had lived for years in the place with constant opportunities of observing the natives and communicating with them, and who yet hardly knew one thing about them really well.

Another important feature of Malinowski's ethnography and the early work practice studies was the examination of a setting's activities as they unfolded in *real-time*. This was key to the way in which Malinowski built up his experiences and understanding of Trobriand Island life. He describes how in living amongst the people he was studying, experiencing the intimacies of their unfolding day as it happened for them, becoming familiar to those around him, and more and more invisible as a stranger allowed him to understand how those he studied organised their social environment:

> ... there is a series of phenomena of great importance which cannot possibly be recorded by questioning or comparing documents, but have to be observed in their full actuality. Let us call them *the inponderabilia of actual life*.

Investigation driven by the nature of life on the ground – by the inponderabilia of actual life – contrasts with observation and the collection of materials seen through the lens of, and driven through, particular analytic interests:

> An ethnographer who sets out to study only religion, or only technology, or only social organisation cuts out an artificial field for inquiry, and he will be seriously handicapped in his work.

This again reflects the orientation of early work practice studies, which were not directed by preconceived interests arising from *outside* of the setting being studied – by something to be looked for and found in the setting as it were – but rather were directed from *within* the setting, by the focus of interest being defined by participants' actions and interactions.

Attendant to this, a significant feature of the early ethnographies in design was the interplay between formally specified rules, processes, and principles for how activities 'should' be carried out and the 'work arounds' or ad hoc implementation of formal procedures found in situ, which are often done so as to achieve the outcomes formal procedures are meant to result in but otherwise would not. Thus emphasis was placed on the observation of *actual human conduct* as opposed to the codification of conduct in terms of formal procedures, which are often taken to account for the organised character of social action. This interest provides a fifth resonance with Malinowski's ethnography:

> There is no written or explicitly expressed code of laws, and their whole tribal tradition, the whole structure of their society, [is] embodied in the most elusive of all materials; the human being.

A sixth connection is that seeing things from the native's point of view is not to take what any one person might say as 'the truth' or 'the whole matter' and for the ethnographer to merely become a mechanism for transmitting particular prejudices; to become a 'scribe' as it were operating under the auspices of what contemporary anthropologists call 'naïve realism'. Rather than simply reporting what anyone can see and hear, the "superficial registration of details" as Malinowski puts it, the focus on the native's point of view is a stipulation that data gathering and analysis should be *driven* by the inponderabilia of actual life:

> So far, it has been done only by amateurs, and therefore done, on the whole, indifferently ... ... There is no doubt, from all points of sociological, or psychological analysis, and in any question of theory, the manner and type of behaviour observed in the performance of an act is of the highest importance.

As we have said before, not all ethnography is of apiece, and in Chap. 5 we will take a closer look at the difference between 'scenic ethnography', which involves the superficial registration of details, and 'analytic ethnography' which is about elaborating the socially organised ways in which action is brought about and recognisably accomplished in its performance. The latter is characteristic of the early ethnographies of work and while those studies might not articulate matters in the scientific and professional language employed by Malinowski, there is certainly some resonance with Malinowski's attempts to lift the lid on observation and to employ it to drive analyses of the organisation of society and culture *in action*.

3.3 Social Structure and Culture

It is, however, at this juncture that those in systems design who are familiar with the ethnographies done in the tradition of early work practice studies will find a break with Malinowski's interests. The same interests run through anthropology as a whole and are now being resurrected – on our arguments problematically so – through the overtly anthropological kind of ethnography now being done for the purposes of systems design. The key interest for Malinowski and contemporary anthropological ethnography alike is one of *grounding* what is observed in a *theory* of society and culture:

> ... the ethnographer has to be inspired by the knowledge of the most modern results of scientific study ... the more problems he brings with him into the field, the more he is in the habit of moulding his theories according to facts, and of seeing facts in their bearing upon theory ... The field worker relies entirely upon inspiration from theory.

Thus, what lifting the lid off observation amounts to in these terms is not a description of how action and interaction is organised as the thing that it recognisably is for those who do it, as per the early workplace ethnographies in design. Rather, the situated recognisability and intelligibility of action is taken for granted and anthropology instead attempts to provide a theoretical *interpretation* of what has been observed.

> ... the ethnographer has to construct the picture of the big institution, very much as the physicist constructs his theory from the experimental data, which always have been within the reach of everybody, but which need a consistent interpretation.

This interpretation is provided through the construction of an abstract, generalised theoretical description of social life. In other words Malinowski's ethnography, and the principles he develops for the production of ethnographic accounts in anthropology, is used to service a *general theory of society and culture*.

Malinowski's description of the Kula ring is instructive in this respect. His work with the Trobriand Islanders became focused on the exchange of Kula *vaygu'a* or valuables: *mwali* (armbands) and *soulava* (necklaces) made out of seashells and passed on constantly between people and groups within a ring or network of relationships – a 'Kula ring'. The exchange of Kula valuables was done through ceremonial practices described by Malinowski. However, throughout his description Malinowski puts great emphasis upon asking a particular kind of question with respect to these practices: why are they done? Asking this question is a turning point for how ethnography has developed within anthropology. All disciplines, at least all human and social science disciplines, have their turning points; points at which they could have developed in one way or another. Gilbert Ryle noted how psychology turned on a particular question, for example. Thus, instead of enquiring into what something has to look like in order for it to be recognised as the thing that it is – e.g., what something has to look like for it to be described as 'thinking' (Ryle 1968) – psychology instead took 'mental' attributes as a given in posing questions of how to measure them. Understanding what mental attributes look like and *how*, therefore, they are *ordinarily recognised and understood* by a society's members is consequently passed by and left untouched. Ryle thus describes a fork in the development of psychology, one prong leading to phenomenology, the other to experimental psychology.

A similar point can be made about ethnography as it was fashioned in the hands of Malinowski. Instead of seeking to elaborate what the Kula has to look like in order for it to be recognised as the Kula – i.e., how the exchange of seashells is performed and pulled off *as* the Kula – Malinowski sought to explain why the Kula is done.

> … even though usable and sometimes used, this is not the main function of these articles …
> why, then, are these objects valued?

The former concern would lead to the description of the situated practices through which the Kula is recognised and understood as the act it is by the Trobriand Islanders themselves as opposed, for instance, to acts of mere economic trading. Thus, where an outsider may observe trade or barter in the exchange of armbands and necklaces, an insider recognises the practices of the Kula ring. The question in this respect, then, is what are the social practices through which the Kula is done so that it *is* recognisable *as* a constituent feature *of* the Kula ring on any occasion in which such an exchange is taking place? Without knowing about those practices it would not be possible to perform the Kula, any more than it would be possible for an outsider to understand that they were witnessing a particular set of ceremonial actions and interactions, as opposed to, for example, an occasion of trading or barter.

The latter concern, which enquires into the *why* of an activity, leads to a very different understanding. It led Malinowski to propose, for example, that the Kula ring serves an integrative *function* in Massim society, binding people together in reciprocal relationships; people or groups, who are geographically separated from one another, are nevertheless connected through the exchange of Kula valuables. Understood in these terms it is what Kula exchanges *mean* that is of importance, not so much how they are recognisably performed and ordered in action.

> Science … has to analyse and classify facts in order … to incorporate them in one of the
> systems in which it tries to group the various aspects of reality … It is therefore the chroni-
> cler's task to finish his account by a comprehensive, synthetic *coup d'oeil* upon the

institution described ... ... Each piece of *vaygu'a* of the Kula type ... has one main
function and serves one main purpose – to circulate round the Kula ring ... Thus, one of the
most important and unusual features of the Kula is the existence of the Kula *vaygu'a*, the
incessantly circulating and ever exchangeable valuables, owing their value to this very cir-
culation and its character.

Thus, the organisation of action and interaction is made subservient to the *cultural
meaning* that the *ethnographer attaches to it*. Malinowski is, then, providing an
interpretation of what the Kula exchange means and his interpretation is that the
Kula has social rather than economic significance enabling Massim society to
cohere and maintain itself as a society over time. Although Malinowski is at pains
to describe how Massim society emanates from the clan or the tribe, from the daily
round that he experienced, his interest is in what that daily round means in terms of
a theoretical understanding of social organisation or social order which, as discussed in Chap. 1, propels much of social science.

It is notable that Malinowski's interpretation of the Kula has various meanings
attached to it, some of which have an *analytically critical* edge to them insofar as
they seek to *respecify* other disciplinary understandings of the organisation of society. In the specific case of the Kula ring the critique is applied to economic theory:

In one or two places in the previous chapters, a somewhat detailed digression was made in
order to criticise the view about the economic nature of primitive man ... the conception of
a rational being who wants nothing but to satisfy his simplest needs and does it according
to the economic principle of least effort. This economic man always knows exactly where
his material interests lie, and makes for them in a straight line. At the bottom of the so-
called materialistic conception of history lies a somewhat analogous idea of a human being,
who, in everything he devises and pursues, has nothing but his material advantage of a
purely utilitarian type at heart ... the meaning of the Kula will consist in being instrumental
to dispel such crude, rationalistic conceptions of primitive mankind, and to induce both the
speculator and the observer to deepen the analysis of economic facts. Indeed, the Kula
shows us that the whole conception of primitive value, the very incorrect habit of calling all
objects of value 'money' or 'currency'; the current ideas of primitive trade and primitive
ownership – all these have to be revised in the light of our institution.

It is interesting too that such a critique *does not* turn upon theories of society, but
rather on observation and explication of the ordinary ways in which a society's
members conduct and organise their day-to-day affairs (the Kula, in this case). In
this sense, the virtue of ethnography might well be understood to provide for the
elaboration of 'epistopics' (Lynch 1993) – i.e., empirical understandings of the
ways in which a society's members conduct and organise particular phenomena
described in scientific theories and methodologies (such as the foundational notion
of 'value' in economic theory). However, the epistopical character of ethnography
is *not* one that takes precedence in Malinowski's interpretation of the meaning of
the Kula.

Rather, the why question predominates and the continual re-enactment of the
Kula is therefore taken to epitomise what Durkheim, before Malinowski, had
described as a 'mechanical' form of 'solidarity' or social order. Malinowski's ethnography thus seeks to make a contribution to the development of a *functionalist*
theory *explaining* social order. Functionalist explanations place particular emphasis

on the cultural 'institutions' that structure social life (e.g., the Kula ring), and how these work or function over time to create a socially cohesive system, a stable society. In this respect, Malinowski stands in an historical line which has many influential social scientists associated with it, such as Comte and Durkheim before him, and Mauss, Radcliffe-Brown, Spencer, Parsons, Davis, Moore, and Merton, following him. While systems designers might not be interested in the history of structural functionalism as a social theory, even this brief excursion makes it visible that the interest pursued by Malinowski falls squarely on the *structuralist* side of the agency/structure divide. This might be immensely surprising, since the initial ethnographies done for the purposes of systems design were not geared towards developing explanatory theories, but towards explicating through direct observation what it is that people *do*.

The surprise might be all the greater in light of our review of Malinowski's ethnographic principles and their resonance with early ethnographic interest in design. However, we can now perhaps see that the only common feature between early ethnographies in system design and Malinowski's ethnography is *fieldwork*. There is some resonance with the arguments that Malinowski made concerning the native's point of view and participant observation, and if it were these which defined ethnography as it developed in anthropology then there would be a coherence between the ethnography of early systems design and ethnography as it is done in anthropology. However, having conducted fieldwork and witnessed the daily round from within, how fieldwork findings are then *used* gives rise to immense differences. Malinowski used his observations to fuel a top-down, explanatory theory of society. Consequently, it is sociological phenomena such as societal intuitions, social solidarity, social cohesion, and the like that are the concern, not the organisation of situated social action and its own inherent intelligibility.

How can we reconcile what would appear to be Malinowski's interest in 'the situation' – his emphasis on observing things from within and on experiencing the daily round from the natives point of view – with the reification of these matters through sociological theorising? The quotation by anthropologist Clifford Geertz in the second chapter concerning the locus of study illuminates this seeming dilemma, for as Geertz makes crystal clear it is not the situated acts witnessed, the daily round, and the natives point of view that are in themselves of interest, but how *within them* it is possible to see social and cultural institutions at work. Thus 'the locus', the situation, is merely an observation point, a place from which to view the workings of society at large. This interest has driven the development of anthropology, which although seemingly grounded in the situation has, as a discipline, actually pursued an interest in developing generic theoretical descriptions of large-scale social and cultural forces. It is not our intention to provide a history of anthropology post Malinowski, detailing the deconstruction of structural functionalism and the development of other top-down social theories. It might be useful, however, to briefly examine one of these developments to highlight a particularly *problem* occasioned by this sort of top-down approach – a problem that systems designers will inevitably encounter as they come up against anthropological ethnographies done for design, and one that may cause chronic indigestion unless properly chewed over.

The development of the *British School of Anthropology*, and the *Manchester School* in particular, will suffice to make the problem visible. The ideas of functionalism provide an integrative 'consensus' view of society at large. In strong distinction to this, the Manchester School developed an influential 'conflict' view of society. Max Gluckman, the first Professor of Social Anthropology at Manchester and the founder of the Manchester School, had attended some of Malinowski's lectures at the London School of Economics and like Malinowski he emphasized the importance of studies in the field, indeed he developed the idea of the 'case study' in anthropology. However, in contrast to Malinowski, rather than viewing society as driven by forces of cohesion and integration, Gluckman understood the driver to be *conflict* between different groups in society, as defined by their relative positions to the means of production. Thus, in the case of Malinowski, his functionalism could be traced to one of the founding fathers of sociology, Emile Durkheim, but Gluckman's emphasis upon on conflict could be traced back to a different founding father, Karl Marx.

So, while Malinowski viewed, for example, the Rand Mines of Africa and the African tribe that supplied the labourers who worked there "as part of the same social field", Gluckman opposed Malinowski's integrative schema and condemned it as "stultifying" (Gluckman 1949). He subsequently outlined his ideas on conflict in a series of BBC broadcasts, gathered together in *Custom and Conflict in Africa* (Gluckman 1955). His thesis, and one that was developed by other prominent UK anthropologists and sociologists such as Frankenberg, Clausen, Kapferer, Worsley, and Mitchell (who along with Barnes and Bott developed the idea of social network theory) was that it was not the forces of cohesion that drove society, but the forces of class conflict:

> I have touched here on a series of conflicts which it seems to me must exist in every political system. There are conflicts between the interests of different individuals within a group, and between the interests of smaller groups within a larger society. There is also conflict between society with its law and the individuals and groups within a larger society. (Gluckman 1949)

Setting aside the question of how you choose between them for a moment, there is an important consequence here for how the social sciences proceed with respect to fieldwork. If observations made in the field are fuelled by a theory of the social, and if there can be more than one theory, then what is observed by the field worker may be understood differently depending on the particular social theory the field worker has elected to use. Simply put, different theories of society can lead to *different* interpretations of the *same* situation and social milieu.

This problem is starkly exemplified by two separate studies of the same Mexican village, Tepoztlán, one done by Robert Redfield (1930), the other by Oscar Lewis (1951). Although making their observations in the same village, and witnessing the same daily round of the villagers, both interpret that daily round very differently and develop very different understandings of the process of social change and 'acculturation'. Redfield articulates a more functionalist perspective and developed the idea of 'folk society' and 'folk culture' in understanding the effects of social change on communities as they moved from a tribal to an urban life. Tepoztlán was a different type of society to that which anthropology had traditionally studied. It fell between an urban society and a primitive society, and Redfield argued that it required the development of new concepts to understand it. To this end he used the concept of 'ideal type' originally employed by Max Weber, another founding father of sociology. The ideal types of 'folk society' and 'folk culture' were situated at one end of a continuum with 'urban' at the other. He thus rendered social change in terms of an interaction between 'the little traditions' of folk culture and the 'great traditions' of urban society, and in so doing provided a functionalist view of 'acculturation' with its essentially integrative cast.

On the other hand, rather than seeing social change as being propelled by the forces of integration, Oscar Lewis, drawing off his own study of Tepoztlán, came to paint a very different picture where the poor become marginalised as society develops. Lewis suggested that a 'culture of poverty' is generated, which is characterised by a dislocation from the structures of society and the disintegration of the bonds that are said, within a functionalist view of society, to integrate people, such as the bonds of family. This dislocation is viewed as a culture because it becomes perpetuated through the generations as a society develops from (in Redfield's terms) a folk to an urban society. For Lewis, then, the poor are not integrated into society as society progresses, but become marginalised from it, living a dislocated life in slums and ghettos. Redfield's emphasis had led him to a particular view of humanity which was integrative, emphasising society as a whole, while Lewis saw people trapped in a culture of poverty – a fatalistic view in which people feel helpless and inferior. For Redfield as society moved to a cash economy, people grew and society grew. For Lewis, this movement led to low wages for the unskilled or unemployment and a feeling of inadequacy.

Both of these different theories of society involve ethnographic studies. Both have their beginnings in observations made from living in the same settlement. Both provide a different interpretation of social and cultural matters. A pertinent question for anyone who confronts these two different interpretations is: how do you choose between them? Which one is right and which is wrong? There is no empirical way of telling, as the evidential grounds for choosing – the day-to-day activities of the villagers themselves – are not visible and available to the reader. Thus, the grounds for deliberation do not reside *in* the ethnographic materials themselves, in the witnessed conduct of everyday life and its recognisable organisation. Rather, they reside in the power of the narrative, the argumentative ploys, the political persuasion and sympathies of writer and reader, and in other matters that stand *outside* of the actual social situation described. These matters exist over and above the inponderabilia of actual life and the particular actions and interactions it consists of. Such inponderabilia are appealed to but only, at best, hazily so, yet they provide the fertile grounds from which social theories spring in the first place. Their absence, and with it the observable orderliness of everyday life, is curious.

As we have already said, we do not want to produce a history of anthropology, and we could therefore be accused of just picking up bits, and old bits at that, to prove our point. Contemporary anthropology is well aware of the fact that there is a relationship between social theory and the production of a particular account or description of that which is observed through 'the lens' of the theory. As we will see in Chap. 5, this leads anthropologists to consider the 'reflexive' relationship between theory and the ethnographer in the constitution of what they observe. For the moment, however, we are attempting to demonstrate that although ethnography may well have developed in anthropology, the predominant way in which the discipline has used fieldwork emphasizes very different considerations to those emphasized by a bedrock of ethnographic studies conducted within systems design to date. Within anthropology, ethnography has traditionally been used to fuel theories of culture and society, to provide *abstract interpretations* of everyday life ordered by overarching theoretical structures. It has pursued, in the traditional manner of the social sciences, a top-down approach to social action and interaction which has little to say in actuality about how action and interaction is done and understood by those who do it. It is highly unlikely that the Trobriand Islanders would have described the Kula ring in terms of it functioning as an integration mechanism, for example, any more than the villagers in Lewis' study would have described the man who abandoned his family and took up with another woman as perpetuating a culture of poverty. The curiosity of anthropological ethnography consists, then, of a visible *disjuncture* between society and culture as it is accountably understood by its members, and society and culture as accountably understood by anthropologists and other social scientists making use of fieldwork.

3.4 Consequences

If theoretical interpretations provide accounts of the orderliness of everyday life that specify the broader structural and cultural meaning of observable events what, then, is the attitude of this sort of theorising to action and interaction as it is done and naturally understood by those who do it? The 'natural' accountability of action and interaction does not disappear just because a disciplinary account has produced a different understanding. The sense that something has for those who do it remains despite different theoretical interpretations provided by social science 'experts'. In this respect, everyday accounts and understandings are *surplus* to sociological and anthropological theories, left over and disregarded. On the rare occasions when they are not ignored they are usually treated as 'mere' common-sense understandings – partial, truncated, ill-informed, naïve, pub and bar-talk understandings. Sometimes a bolt-on to the theory is added to account for the fact people hold to different understandings of what they do to those understandings produced by the theory. Marx's concept of *false class consciousness* exemplifies this: the proletariat do not understand their objective conditions as rendered in Marx's materialist theory of society because, for various reasons accounted for by the theory, they are unable to see those conditions. They remain in a deluded state, which is maintained by various social mechanisms such as religion.

There are, however, a number of problems with the stance that the social sciences take towards the everyday understandings of those who are doing the things their theories interpret. Those providing anthropological or sociological interpretations are in effect saying, as we noted in Chap. 1, and to borrow again from Harvey Sacks, that people think they know what they are talking about, but they don't; they are walking in a dreamworld (Hill and Crittenden 1968). This attitude of social science to the everyday world results in two orders of account (the natural and the scientific) that treat the same topics but not in the same ways. The traditional social science view has is that the kind of accounts it produces have *primacy* because their production is organised, if not according to the principles of the natural sciences, at least according to principles that have been developed within a system of supposedly rigorous thinking. However, such a view is misplaced because social science accounts are *parasitic* on everyday accounts. The reason for this is that the interpretations offered by the social sciences are inevitably built on everyday accounts; one comes first and that is the everyday account, the natural sense that something has for those who are doing it. As Geertz (1973) puts it,

> In short, anthropological writings are themselves interpretations; and second and third order ones to boot. (By definition, only a 'native' makes first order ones: it's his culture.)

Recall, by way of example, the dichotomy between software engineers understanding of their activities and social science understandings that we cited in the introduction. In conducting a number of studies of software engineering activities Button and Sharrock (1996) found themselves straying into a territory well examined by social studies of science and technology. These studies are also largely based upon ethnographic fieldwork, and in the ways we have outlined above. One theoretical viewpoint that was particularly powerful at the time of Button and Sharrock's studies held that technologists such as the software engineers they were studying were, through their work, contributing to a new global 'hegemony' (see Law 1991 for example). It was very noticeable, however, that the engineers did not describe what they were doing in these terms. Rather, and for example, an engineer working on a faults module was seen to draw a diagram and was asked what he was doing. He did not say, "I'm contributing to world hegemony", but rather that "I am having difficulties in understanding how to relate various components in this guy's module to my faults module and am trying to represent it all diagrammatically to see if that helps."

The *natural accountability* of engineers' work, like any human activity, is often not the same as its social science accountability. Rather, the social science account re-describes what is already a well-understood world for members and this has very particular consequences. Of particular note is the plainly observable fact that such re-descriptions contain things that (a) are not well understood by social scientists and (b) are nevertheless taken-for-granted (Sacks 1963). For instance, the natural accountability of engineering work is not well understood by social scientists, yet the intelligibility of engineering work is nevertheless taken for granted in saying that engineers are contributing to world hegemony. The re-description trades upon the reader knowing what kind of things engineers do for its sense, but the brute reality is that unless the reader is a qualified engineer then they do not really know what kinds of things engineers do at all. One might wonder at the wisdom of an investigatory practice that routinely builds things that are not well understood into its 'scientific' apparatus. It might also be wondered at that when such taken for granted matters are investigated they turn out to be more interesting than second or third order accounts, something again pointed to by Sacks (1984).

The point we are making here about the natural accountability of human activity is not simply an argument with practices of generic description (i.e., theorising) in ethnography and the social sciences more broadly, but something of direct relevance to systems design too. It manifests itself in practical ways. The study of engineers was undertaken for the purposes of shaping the design of tools to support their work. The engineers were using CASE tools and the computer scientist involved in the research, Ian Sommerville, was interested in the practical work the engineers were engaged in and how they were using CASE tools in practice. It was mentioned that the engineers might be considered to be involved in practices of world hegemony, but Sommerville seemed more interested in the engineers' own understanding of the work they were doing.

There is a general point here then. If design is to use social science as a tool then it may serve design to understand its practices, at least to the extent of understanding how certain assumptions may leak into design and thus rest design on what might be considered problematic ways of understanding and accounting for the social world. The interpretive tendency of anthropology and conventional (theoretical) social science effectively *divorces* meaning from action. We mean by this that arguing that the social world requires disciplinary interpretation is to say that there is action that is undertaken on the one hand, which has then to be interpreted and given meaning on the other. Thus there is what someone does, their bodily movements for example, and the meaning that is then given to those movements. In these terms there are the things that are done when someone is involved in a Kula exchange or engineering work, and then the interpretation of that as a Kula act or engineering. However, this is a strange understanding of what people do, for they do not just engage in bodily movements, they engage in action, the sense of which is already incorporated into its doing. So there is not the bodily movement of the driver shaking his fist at another driver, for example, which then awaits interpretation. What the driver is doing is being angry *in* the shaking of his fist. The meaning is *part and parcel* of the doing, not something that stands outside of it and has to be bolted-on afterwards.

Garfinkel (1967) described the accountability of an action as *part of the action itself*; that action is done so that it is recognisable and thus available to account. If action were not done in this way it is difficult to see how social life would actually be possible, for people witnessing a social event would not understand what was going on and be able to respond appropriately. For instance, if a greeting were not done so that it was recognisably a greeting, then an interlocutor would not be able to respond appropriately by, for example, returning a greeting. The issue then is not so much one of the necessity of interpretation, as we will make clear in Chap. 5, but of understanding how action is recognisably done. However, the predominant tendency in social science to divorce the meaning that action has from its doing and to provide interpretive theories of society and culture prohibits treatment of the in-built accountability of action. This means that the everyday understanding that people have of action is lost from view, surplus to requirements. The surplus dispenses with the very phenomenon that has been historically important to systems design: what it is that people actually *do* and its in-built, naturally accountable *organisation.*

3.5 Social Science Is Not Privileged

The objection we, and ethnomethodologists in general, have to the traditional ways in which disciplines such as anthropology and sociology have approached their subject matter is thus twofold. First, they provide theoretical interpretations of the social that although couched in seemingly systematic and methodological terms are parasitic on naturally accountable or 'common-sense' understandings. The second is that common-sense understandings, and the practices for their construction, are taken for granted and left unexamined. In as much as many of the initial ethnographic studies done for the purposes of systems design were grounded in ethnomethodology, their concern with the social was with how people use their common-sense understandings, and how they construct them in practice, to practically accomplish the activities they are engaged in. Such studies elaborated, for example, the situated practices through which air traffic controllers work together 'here and now' to practically accomplish the smooth flow of aircraft across flight sectors and create a shared understanding of the order in the sky (Hughes et al. 1992); or the situated practices through which workflow is accomplished and understood on the shop-floor in real time (Button and Sharrock 1997); or the situated practices through which call centre operatives handle photocopier break downs and build up a reciprocal understanding of 'the problem' and potential 'solutions' with ordinary users of the machine (O'Neill et al. 2005); etc. These studies were not concerned to produce theoretical interpretations of air traffic control, workflow, photocopier fault handling, etc. It is perfectly possible to spin some anthropological and sociological interpretations out of them though, as examples of the way in which organisations function in the modern world. However, having done that, the work as done and understood by those who do it, still *remains* to be described.

Now it is perfectly possible that theoretical worldviews may provide designers with general heuristics. For example, the Scandinavian school of design was clearly interested in empowering workers in the workplace through the design of systems, as opposed to developing systems that extend the remit of managers. But on our arguments, drawing off anthropological or sociological accounts provides no special or privileged access to the social that stands over and above any other interpretation of the world and its organisation. Thus if designers are looking for general heuristics, or inspiration, then as far as the social is concerned, *anything* will do, anthropology and sociology can await selection along with literature, philosophy or art. We are not trying to legislate as to how design draws off the social then. However, if design wants to be serious about building the social into the design mix by developing this methodologically and making an understanding of the social part of design practice, then social science itself needs to be taken seriously along with the objections to traditional social science concerns such as the ones we have outlined above. It is perhaps a lack of understanding of these objections both within social science and within design that has led to calls for 'new' approaches to ethnography. As we have suggested, these calls are not providing new forms of ethnography at all, but are in fact returning ethnography to its old and traditional role in social science. Having in this chapter explicated that traditional role, and examined the problems of sociological and anthropological description it involves, we turn in the next chapter to a detailed consideration of the call for the 'new' and how it embodies the same problems once again.

References

Bell, G., & Dourish, P. (2007). Yesterday's tomorrows: Notes on ubiquitous computing's dominant vision. *Personal and Ubiquitous Computing, 11*(2), 122–143.

Button, G., & Sharrock, W. (1996). Project work: The organisation of collaborative design and development in software engineering. *Computer Supported Cooperative Work: The Journal of Collaborative Computing, 5*(4), 369–386.

Button, G., & Sharrock, W. (1997). The production of order and the order of production. In: *Proceedings of the European conference on computer supported cooperative work* (pp. 1–16). Lancaster: Kluwer Academic Press.

Dourish, P. (2014). Reading and interpreting ethnography. In J. Olson & W. Kellogg (Eds.), *Ways of knowing in HCI* (pp. 1–24). New York: Springer.

Garfinkel, H. (1967). What is ethnomethodology? In: *Studies in ethnomethodology* (pp. 1–34). Englewood Cliffs: Prentice-Hall.

Geertz, C. (1973). Thick description: Toward an interpretive theory of culture. In: *The interpretation of cultures: Selected essays* (pp. 3–30). New York: Basic Books.

Gluckman, M. (1949). *An analysis of the sociological theories of Bronislaw Malinowski*. London: Oxford University Press.

Gluckman, M. (1955). *Custom and conflict in Africa*. Glencoe: The Free Press.

Hill, R., & Crittenden, K. (1968). *Proceedings of the Purdue symposium on ethnomethodology*. West Lafayette: Purdue Research Foundation. http://aiemcanet.files.wordpress.com/2010/07/purdue.pdf

Hughes, J., Randall, D., Shapiro, D. (1992). Faltering from ethnography to design. In: *Proceedings of the conference on computer supported cooperative work* (pp. 115–122). Toronto: ACM.

Law, J. (Ed.). (1991). *A sociology of monsters: Essays on power, technology and domination*. London: Routledge.

Lewis, O. (1951). *Life in a Mexican village: Tepoztlán restudied*. Urbana: University of Illinois Press.

Lynch, M. (1993). From quiddity to haecceity: ethnomethodological studies of work. In: *Scientific practice and ordinary action: Ethnomethodology and social studies of science* (pp. 265–308). Cambridge: Cambridge University Press.

Malinowski, B. (1922). *Argonauts of the western pacific: An account of native enterprise and adventure in the archipelagoes of Melanesian New Guinea*. London: Routledge.

O'Neill, J., Castellani, S., Grasso, A., Roulland, F., Tolmie, P. (2005). Representations can be good enough. In: *Proceedings of the European conference on computer supported cooperative work* (pp. 267–286). Paris: Springer.

Redfield, R. (1930). *Tepoztlán, a Mexican village: A study of folk life*. Chicago: University of Chicago Press.

Ryle, G. (1968). The thinking of thoughts: What is 'Le Penseur' doing? *University Lectures No. 18*, University of Saskatchewan.

Sacks, H. (1963). Sociological description. *Berkeley Journal of Sociology, 8*, 1–16.

Sacks, H. (1984). Notes on methodology. In J. M. Maxwell & J. Heritage (Eds.), *Structures of social action: Studies in conversation analysis* (pp. 21–27). Cambridge: Cambridge University Press.

Weiser, M. (1991). The computer for the 21st century. *Scientific American, 265*(3), 94–104.

Chapter 4
'New' Ethnography and Ubiquitous Computing

Abstract In this chapter we inspect how the movement of the computer away from the desktop and the workplace has led to calls for 'new' approaches to ethnography within systems design, with the accompanying suggestion that ethnography should now be used to provide an understanding (rather than an explication) of culture and the meaning that technology has for people in their everyday lives. What we see in these calls are some old social science arguments about the 'macro' and the 'micro' being dusted off and played out anew in design. More than this, we see old social science practices of description at work, which rip familiar everyday concepts out of everyday contexts of use and distort them to provide *generalised analytic accounts* of culture and the social order that have arisen as a consequence of ubiquitous computing. Something we especially see unravel for the reader here is the way in which, for all of their claimed purchase upon the social character of computing in the twenty-first century, the generalised analytic accounts provided by 'new' approaches to ethnography fail to give design any kind of *privileged* insight into the contemporary social world. The accounts they offer are of much the same order that *any* competent member of society might give, in so much as they are demonstrably rendered through *common-sense* practices of description.

4.1 Ethnography as Cultural Tourism

As noted at the beginning of the last chapter, computing in the twenty-first century is marked by the movement of the computer away from the desktop into the fabric of everyday life; a shift that is often characterised as 'ubiquitous computing'. As also noted this shift has been accompanied by calls for 'new' approaches to ethnography within systems design, which differ from those that have been predominantly engaged with to date (Dourish and Bell 2011). The argument that underpins the call is that ethnography in design has until now had a utilitarian cast. As Plowman et al. (1995) had previously observed, ethnographies have often been undertaken and milked for 'implications for design', which are typically tagged on to a study in a section at the end to provide some relevance for design, either in terms of requirements for designing with 'this setting in mind' or to highlight particular issues of relevance for a specific kind of design solution. Consequently, ethnography in

© Springer International Publishing Switzerland 2015   61
G. Button et al., *Deconstructing Ethnography*, Human-Computer
Interaction Series, DOI 10.1007/978-3-319-21954-7_4

design to date is largely construed of in such accounts as an 'under-labourer' approach with respect to the development of *requirements* for systems design (see Dourish 2006).

In distinction to this it is argued that ethnography can be used to provide an understanding of culture and the meaning that technology has for people in their everyday lives, in order for designers to reflect upon the kinds of interventions they are proposing or making when designing computer systems (ibid.). This pits what is called 'analytic' ethnography – i.e., ethnography that provides interpretive understandings of culture – against (merely) 'factual' ethnography developed in order to derive implications for design and requirements for particular systems.[1] The sorts of ethnomethodological studies done for the purposes of design that we have been associated with are by implication, though not actually referred to as such, contrasted with ethnographic studies undertaken for the purposes of understanding general cultural drivers such as power, value, and emotion. Analytic ethnography providing an understanding of cultures and societies at large is, then, juxtaposed against what is reconfigured as factual ethnography that focuses on the practices of situated action and interaction in context.

We have some sympathy with some of the points made by Dourish and Bell. Early on in the engagement of ethnography with design there were often pressures from funding agencies and journals to develop sections in applications or papers on the relevance of a study for systems design. We have all had reviewers specifically call for the inclusion of an 'implications for design' section. This often results in a generalised, broad-brush connection between studies and design interests. However, these initial and sometimes blundering attempts to connect the social with design should really be thought of as *first steps* in working out how two very different sets of disciplines could engage with one another, rather than as a defining feature of the relationship. While crude or gross connections may have been made between an ethnographic study conducted in some setting for systems to be placed therein, or critiques of existing systems, the real benefit of these sorts of investigations was the contribution they made to the developing appreciation amongst designers that the social really did and does need to be built into design.

The issue at hand now, as we argue throughout this volume, is to mature this understanding so that the social can be built into the design process in a methodical way, as opposed to (merely) drawing implications for design from a study. That is, we are here exploring the opportunity for building the social into design so that ethnography is used *within* the enterprise in a methodical way, rather than it being something that is done *for* design and drawn upon in an ad hoc manner. Dourish and Bell may denigrate developing implications for design from out of ethnography, but we find it difficult to see how a generalised understanding of culture and society is

---

[1] Dourish's notion of 'analytic' ethnography, which emphasises the interpretive understanding of social matters by the social scientist, should not be confused with Button's use of the term (see Button 2000), where he was attempting to make a contrast between ethnography that produces descriptions of what anyone can see with ethnography that attempts to make visible *how* anyone can see what has been seen.

much different when push comes to shove or why building in the social should be disconnected from developing requirements for a system. In this respect, attempting to methodically address the social within design, although it may involve more than just pointing to social considerations, would (it seems to us at least) necessarily be part of building a system. If it is not, one might wonder what ethnography's role is *in* systems design?

A response to this kind of question, and the one offered by Dourish (2006), is that 'implications for design' are not the appropriate criteria by which ethnographic contributions should be judged.

> In thinking about ethnography (or indeed any social science contribution), it is important to distinguish two levels and two sorts of contributions – the analytic and the empirical ... The call for 'implications for design', I would argue, drawing upon the notion of requirements in traditional software engineering, is a request for empiricism. It is a request that the ethnography provide 'facts' – when people work, how they talk to each other, what they do when they sit down at the computer, and so forth – which can be translated into technological constraints and opportunities ... What has traditionally been more complicated has been to establish a deeper, more foundational connection between ethnography and design – to look for a connection at an analytic level rather than simply an empirical one.

A demonstration of the point was actually provided some 10 years previously by Dourish in collaboration with one of the present authors (Dourish and Button 1998), where it was shown that taking foundational matters that have driven ethnomethodological studies, such as the *fact* (as noted in the last chapter) that social action is done so that it is accountable, can be used to problematise design principles and re-construct new ones: surfacing the underlying operations of a computer system to make its actions accountable to users enables interactants to do appropriate next actions, for example. This recognises that systems are often designed to bury what they are doing beneath the mechanisms that provide for interaction; with it the resource for how to respond appropriately to some process being done by the system is lost. Dourish's description of problems in the copying of files from remote sites (ibid.) aptly illustrates what might be meant by establishing 'a deeper, more foundational connection' between ethnography and design – e.g., of building foundational matters that the social character of interaction turns upon *into* design to shape the development of general design principles.

So while we have some sympathy regarding the issues with just drawing implications for design from ethnographic studies, construing ethnography to date, and for us, construing ethnomethodological studies of situated action and interaction, as contrastable with socio-cultural accounts misses key points of difference between the two. The difference between previous ethnomethodological studies and the 'new' ethnography promoted by Dourish and Bell does not revolve around how ethnography is used, either for or within design. The difference, and it is a very real and marked difference, resides in understanding how social science can proceed in the first place. On the basis of our arguments in the last chapter, the call for a 'new' approach to ethnography is really a call to revert back to the social sciences' traditional manner of proceeding, which is to provide interpretations of culture and society through professionally generated, and often contradictory, social theories. It is then a call to repeat, all over again, the mistakes of anthropological and sociological theorising made in the social sciences in systems design. Thus our worry with the call for 'new' ethnographic approaches to support ubiquitous computing is that it is not really a call for new approaches at all. Rather it is bringing in very old and traditional, even 'classical', understandings of how to do social science into design; understandings which are problematic within the social sciences even if they represent the consensus view on how to do social science.[2] Indeed we see in Dourish and Bell's arguments the old problems that we have long had to contend with in social science now being played out in and for design.

In the process of advocating what is really a return to classical anthropological understandings of how to do social science, two further confusions are introduced. One is to provide a particular understanding of analysis. The other is to misunderstand what ethnography is in ethnomethodological studies of situated action, which have been lumped together with all sorts of ethnographies done for the purposes of developing design implications. Before moving onto ground what we are asserting it should be noted that we are *not* saying that designers should not look to traditional anthropological and sociological approaches, even 'new' approaches. Reading that people from one society may hide their emotions more than people from another (Dourish and Bell 2011), that some societies attach sacred meaning to certain kinds of site (Bell 2006), and that within some societies family living is more communal with less opportunity for privacy (Bell 2001), may well be of interest to designers. It may, for example, allow products to be more easily placed if they facilitate rather than cut across cultural concerns. It may provide for the broadening of 'the design space'. And it may flare the imagination.

In this respect it might seem that Dourish and Bell are proposing the ideal situation in their contrast between 'old' and 'new' ethnographic approaches in ubiquitous computing. On the one hand there are ethnographies that can support requirements capture because of their 'micro' concern with situated action and interaction, which are perhaps more suited to the constrained environs of workplace systems, and on the other there are ethnographies that can support the design of ubiquitous systems because of their 'macro' concern with culture and social structure, which transcend geographical and political boundaries. Such a distinction may well be welcome in design because it might appear that it can now draw from different ethnographic wells depending upon the particular undertaking: the development of situated workplace systems being supported by ethnomethodologically-driven studies of situated work practice, and ubiquitous computing by studies investigating cultural and societal structures.

---

[2] We will be told that anthropology and sociology have moved on from their classical foundations, which had a distinctly positivist caste, in addressing the idea of reflexivity, the body as a site of 'knowing', and the role of the ethnographer in the constitution of what they are observing. We take these issues up in the next chapter, where we will argue that although these are touted as new developments in social science they merely dress up old problems in new clothes and perpetuate classical problems involved in the description of social action.

While it would be absurd to try and legislate what designers may or may not find interesting it is, however, important to appreciate that traditional social science concerns, which put cultural interpretation at the heart of what are, as we say, ironically called 'new' approaches to ethnography, do not give design any kind of privileged insight into society and culture. Designers might find the journalist or tourist to be just as informative and fuel the imagination in equal measure. It may sound provocative to say this, and even unnecessarily confrontational, but we say it to underscore the fact that the account provided by the cultural interpreter is of the same *order* that a journalist or tourist and, indeed, just about any other member of society can give.

We are aware that this stark claim may sound strident, even absurd. How could the cultural observations of professional social science be categorised as being of the same *order* of description as that provided by the tourist? How could the interpretive descriptions of someone who has spent possibly years living in and observing another society be brought together with interpretive descriptions made by lay people? Standing behind this statement is the large and important question that the social sciences have contended with since their inception, which is the question of how social science can *warrant* its descriptions of social doings as standing over and above the descriptions that any competent member of society can give? This is a challenge that social science has attempted to address through its professional descriptive apparatus. One of sociology's founding fathers, Emile Durkheim, attempted to provide for the superiority of social science description in crafting sociology as a seemingly 'scientific' endeavour akin to the natural sciences (Durkheim 1897). More recently, appeals to the ways that literary theory conducts itself have been made. However, Garfinkel's concept of 'member', which has often be read as meaning 'member of …', points to a feature of social science justifications that makes them problematic. As Garfinkel and Sacks (1970) explain, member refers to *a mastery of natural language*. Members in that mastery display held in common knowledge of social and cultural matters, their competency in which is visible in the things they do and the accounts they provide of those doings.

In the everyday use of natural language we display *common-sense knowledge* of social arrangements; common-sense understanding of and common-sense reasoning about social structure if you like. Take the simple answer, "I got married last month, we went to the Seychelles", to the question "What have you been up to since I last saw you?" The intelligibility of this answer builds in a number of taken-for-granted, common-sensically known about features of social arrangements. Thus, amongst other things it requires knowledge of the institution of marriage; it invokes an understanding of legal arrangements in society; it trades on knowing about significant occasions in people's lives; and to someone overhearing it displays that the questioner actually may not know the answerer very well since, as a big occasion in someone's life it would be known about by friends and associates; it invokes an understanding of the fact that many people in the UK are having 'exotic' marriages abroad rather than run of the mill marriages at home; and other matters. Thus in intelligibly using natural language people in their descriptions inevitably *display* common-sense knowledge of social arrangements.

This is very far from saying that all descriptions are the same, that they are all equally correct. We have ways of contesting and verifying descriptions in law courts, for example, or through institutionalised procedures such as asking experts, or appealing to someone's status, or pointing to the eloquence of a description, etc. It is to say, however, and how could it be otherwise, that the use of natural language displays held-in-common knowledge of social structures, and that descriptions produced in natural language are therefore of the same essential *order* as each other. Here's the rub for social science: an obvious fact about social science description is that, inevitably, it has to use just the same tool that anyone has to use in describing social life, *natural language*. So it inevitably displays common-sense knowledge of social structure in its own descriptions. Take, for example, a social science description of marriage as, say, a subjugating institution in a patriarchally organised society. Here common-sense knowledge of the natural language expression 'marriage', held in common in society, is taken for granted, and traded on by the sociological description. Now 'marriage' can be interpreted in a multiplicity of ways. An alternative would be to view it not as a form of subjugation, but as a cohesive force in society and part of the glue that holds society together. Whatever the interpretation, it takes for granted that 'this' social arrangement is a 'marriage' and recognisable as such by any competent societal member.

This means, as Zimmerman and Pollner (1970) spell out, that social science descriptions and accounts of social matters, in as much as they use natural language, *build in* common-sense knowledge of social structure, and that common-sense knowledge is an unacknowledged *bedrock* and resource in social science description. Social science could contend that it takes, and indeed has to take, ordinary words as its resource but that it gives them special, rigorous meanings within the definitional framework of a social theory, and in that process cleanses them of common-sense knowledge, replacing them with disciplinarily sanctioned knowledge of social affairs. However, when the social science apparatus is then laid on top of the world it is all too plain to see that there is a *disjuncture* between the world commonly understood and accounted for by people in it, and the world as portrayed in the social science account, and inevitably, since there is no consensus in the social sciences, there are disjuncture's between social science accounts themselves. When used as a resource for sociological theorising common-sense terms such as 'emotion', 'sacred', 'privacy', etc. – categories which make perfect sense in ordinary accounts of the orderliness of action and events – are given generalised *explanatory* power across a whole range of situations where their familiar sense breaks down and the action and events to which they are being applied cannot be recovered from theoretical descriptions of them; this latter issue is a matter which begs serious questions as to their *veracity* as scientific descriptions (see Sacks 1963).

The assumption that because social science descriptions are discipline based, that because they are generated through the institutionalised methods and theories of recognised disciplines such as anthropology and sociology, they therefore stand over and above common-sense knowledge of social arrangements is something that we have to let go of. Social science description is a fraught matter, which revolves around the inevitable building of common-sense understandings into social science understandings in unacknowledged ways. Ethnomethodology provides an alternative path for social science to follow, which is to respecify social science's task as one of making visible the ordered properties of common-sense knowledge of social affairs and how those ordered properties are used by people methodically in the course of conducting their social lives. A prosaic way of describing this turn, one used by Zimmerman and Pollner, is to treat common-sense as a *topic of*, rather than a *resource for*, social science description.

Again we return to the question of why design should care about this sort of issue, of why should designers care about the topic-resource distinction. The reason why is that they are being told that ethnography can be so much more than what it has been so far in the relationship between design and the social sciences, it can be more than an empirical resource for their design. Design is now being told that, for example, it can be a tool through which the meaning technology has in people's lives can be explored and that this in turn will enable designers to build over-arching, complex cultural matters, even cross-cultural matters, into design, and not just empirical facts about restricted situated activities. Heady stuff one might think. However, such cultural interpretation inevitably has to draw on common-sense methods or practices of reasoning; inevitably because cultural interpretation is rooted in natural language and thus builds-in common-sense knowledge of the world even if it is disavowed. In this respect then, if ethnography is an interpretive enterprise, its interpretations of culture and society do not, and cannot, stand over and above interpretations provided by other societal members and institutions that provide descriptions and commentaries on social life. Journalists' descriptions and interpretations would be just as much a resource, as indeed might tourist guides. The social scientist, the journalist, and the tourist all produce accounts through natural language and therefore build into their accounts common-sense knowledge of the things they account for – it could not be otherwise. Thus, despite their obvious differences, they all provide the same *order* of account.

Below we attempt to demonstrate this more concretely with respect to the way in which Dourish and Bell's exemplary classical accounts of social and cultural order in the twenty-first century are put together and made to work. The demonstration is intended to make it visible that 'new' approaches to ethnography are shot through with common-sense-knowledge, common-sense understandings, and common-sense methods of reasoning. We are not doing this to denigrate these accounts; they are produced through the established ways in which the social sciences conduct themselves and are in these terms good examples of social science practice. What we are trying to do in unpacking how classical accounts are made to work is to make visible to design what is being bought into if these calls for 'new' ethnography are taken up. To start to unpack these issues we first turn towards the idea of there being old and new visions for ubiquitous computing.

4.2 Old and New Visions for Ubiquitous Computing

The idea of 'ubiquitous computing' or 'ubicomp' is one that invites us to consider the development of technology that 'disappears' into the fabric of everyday life (Weiser 1991). At the time of its publication, the idea was a radical one that represented a step change in computing: moving it away from the desktop and virtual interaction to embed it in the physical world and embodied interaction (Dourish 2004). Dourish and Bell (2011) suggest that the vision of ubiquitous computing provided a unifying vision for computer science, a shared paradigm as it were, which is still invoked today to justify and legitimate the construction of a 'proximate future'. The problem with this ongoing invocation of the ubicomp vision is that it has "already come to pass" (ibid.). Today's technological landscape is radically different than that of the late 1980s when Weiser was outlining the ubicomp vision, so much so that what was once a matter of imagination and envisionment is now a commonplace feature of everyday life. Ubicomp already exists and permeates our lives, being embedded in the devices in our homes, our cars, our streets, and a host of other settings too. Given this, Dourish and Bell suggest that it might be fruitful to put the vision on hold and instead draw on two cross-cultural studies to elaborate 'the computer of now'. They turn to Singapore and South Korea in particular, both of which have advanced technological infrastructures, and cite a range of statistics and anecdotes to help designers see the present day anew.

> ... by looking outside of the research laboratory, we are looking at ubiquitous computing as it is currently developing rather than it might be imagined to look in the future. In these settings, we ... see that the ubiquitous computing agenda is one that is fundamentally tied to other important but neglected issues such as multi-generational living, high density housing, public transit, religious observance, the practicalities of calling a cab, the politics of domesticity and the spatialities of information access – the messiness of everyday practice. (Dourish and Bell 2011)

Orienting us to the computer of now and how it is being shaped by the 'messiness' of everyday practice undermines the continued invocation of the ubicomp vision and recasts it as being just as misguided as 1950s science fiction speculations. Dourish and Bell's invocation of a 'messy' social world in which ubiquitous computing is already embedded suggests an alternative domain of ubicomp research – a ubicomp not of the future but of the present. This present view on ubiquitous computing sees a world in which computing technology is already embedded within social and cultural settings; that ubicomp already has a life beyond the research lab and is entwined with and inseparable from the social structures it is situated within and the cultural meanings that people already attach to it. Dourish and Bell would also have us recognise that society and culture are themselves entwined and inseparable; that to speak of the social is to speak about the cultural and vice versa such that any principled separation is meaningless. The upshot is a view on society/culture as something that is generative or productive of everyday experience – something that shapes the ways in which people encounter the world. This in turn leads to the view that ubiquitous computing (and technology more generally) is encountered in a very particular way; that we experience technology, as Dourish and Bell (2011) put it,

> … through cultural lenses, which bring it into focus in particular ways while also rendering it meaningful and accountable to us. These lenses frame what we see, and how we see and understand it.

Dourish and Bell's ubicomp of the present elaborates a view on technology that renders it inseparable from the socio-cultural lens through which it is encountered in everyday practice. The question is, *what does that lens look like*?

Rather than turn to everyday practice, Dourish and Bell turn to cultural studies by way of providing us with an opening answer. They turn in particular to studies underpinned by Critical Theory (Adorno and Hockheimer 1944) and contemporary ethnographies informed by Science and Technology Studies (STS) (Latour 1991). These studies locate technology in the cultural meanings created by consumers and the ways in which technology provides a means of enacting culture. In turn, the authors suggest that Critical Theory and STS provide alternative ways for us to think about the relationship between technology and culture and in so doing they prompt us to consider what a cultural account of technology might amount to. With this, the question of how technology is socially and culturally apprehended in everyday practice becomes a question of what a *socio-cultural analysis* of technology might look like and be about. In other words, it becomes a question of how the socio-cultural lens should be *configured*. This, for Dourish and Bell, is a methodological matter. A matter not only of method but of the epistemological foundations upon which the use of methods stands – foundations which would have us recognise that observation is 'always theory laden' and that ethnography is, therefore, 'inherently interpretive'. Configuring the socio-cultural lens is, then, a matter of adopting an *appropriate interpretive framework* for analysing culture.

> One of the more significant transformations of contemporary anthropological ethnography has been the concept of multi-sited ethnography, as developed particularly by George Marcus. Whereas traditional ethnographies since Malinowski have focused on a geographically bounded field site, Marcus observes that in the context of globalisation, culture can no longer be adequately circumscribed in such a manner. The Trobriand Islands can no longer (if they ever could) be approached as a 'realm apart', but must be understood within a broader web of relationships to other parts of the world and other forms of cultural practice … Contemporary ethnography must concern itself instead with transnational flows of people, capital, and culture. This is perhaps especially relevant when considering information technologies – technologies that are both means and embodiments of these globalised practices. (Dourish and Bell 2011)

The question of what constitutes an appropriate socio-cultural analysis is a radical one, at least in terms of what ethnography is currently understood to consist of and provide in a systems development context, and becomes a matter of *reframing* the analytic orientation that has largely driven ethnography in design to date from a focus on situated action and work practice to 'a broader web of relationships' and 'other forms of cultural practice'. The reframing is part of a broader move in anthropology that goes beyond standard concerns with observation and interpretation to the 'politics of knowledge'. As Marcus (1999) puts it,

Under the labels of postmodernism and then cultural studies, a bracing critical self-examination was initiated by many practicing scholars in the social sciences and humanities. This examination of their own habits of thought and work involved reconsiderations of the nature of representation, description, subjectivity, and objectivity, reconsiderations even of the notions of 'society' and 'culture' themselves …

Dourish and Bell's work stands testimony to the fact that the politics of knowledge are not confined to the social sciences and humanities. They are now playing out in systems development. Nurtured by Dourish and Bell, a new breed of design ethnographers cum social analysts are trying to position the critical sensibilities occasioned by anthropology's 'bracing' examination of itself within systems design. Much of this positioning is being done under the auspices of HCI4D and Postcolonial Computing (Irani et al. 2010), which focus on technology development in and for the so-called Global South. In this context, culture is particularly prominent in the visible differences between Africa or India, for example, and the Western way of life lived by a great many IT researchers and system developers. Culture thus becomes a special topic, something to sensitise developers to, and treating the exotic, the anthropological 'other', becomes a vehicle to open it up.

The multi-sited lens on culture seeks to map out what Marcus (1995) describes as brave new worlds in which the traditional macro-micro distinctions of social science collapse into one another. While invoked by design-oriented researchers in the context of HCI4D, the methodological precepts of multi-sited ethnography apply transnationally: to 'us' as much as 'them'. Multi-sited research reconfigures the ethnographic field site, transforming it from a particular bounded setting into an indefinitely connected array or network of local sites across which 'world systems' or social structures operate and are manifest. This reframes the ethnographer's task, making it a matter of following and tracking connections across local sites as a means of elaborating the relationship between the micro and macro. The multi-sited research lens thus seeks to make top down views on culture into an integral part of local situations rather than something monolithic and external to them. It might otherwise be said that multi-sited ethnography *contextualises* situated action (Falzon 2009), locating it 'within the larger framework of people's lives', integrating it 'with more inclusive social forms', and elaborating the various ways in which world systems are 'detectably' played out within it.

… the crucial issue concerns the detectable system-awareness in the everyday consciousness and actions of subjects' lives … getting at the 'white noise' in any setting … sorting out the relationships of the local to the global …

… this kind of ethnography maps a new object of study in which previous situating narratives … become qualified by expanding what is ethnographically 'in the picture' of research … (Marcus 1995)

So what is the 'white noise' (what should we be hearing) and what is 'in the picture' (what should we be seeing)? How should we configure the ethnographic lens and bring the social into view through 'new' kinds of cultural analysis?

A number of ethnographic studies have emerged in the HCI4D arena that provide us with the necessary instruction. Williams et al. (2008) undertook a multi-sited ethnographic study of a group of 'transnationals', people who travel between

Thailand and the US at regular intervals. Their findings report the results of 19 semi-structured interviews that elaborate a set of thematics, including what the authors describe as spatial, temporal and infrastructural 'anchorings' and how these are implicated in the production of domestic structures that span 'spatial locales'.

> I interview Nok and Kung at their home in Chantaburi province. Both were from that region originally, and their house, built in the last year and a half, was located on Kung's family's land. His brother lives close by, and there are plans for other siblings to build homes nearby in the future. They currently stay at this house for two to three months twice a year. Both have cell phones, on extended loan from a cousin, but the house currently lacks hot water, a land-line, and internet. When they settle there permanently ('someday') they will set those things up. For the time being, Nok checks email at her brother-in-law's house or at an internet café in town. Their orchard will soon produce an excess of bananas to share with relatives or sell at the local market. Over the course of a day, Kung's older brother visits to help in the garden, and we in turn use his house in town as our base of operations while visiting the afternoon market. His wife provides us with a spicy crab dip. We also run into Kung's younger brother at the morning market; later that afternoon he and his wife stop by with green mangoes and coconut. Kung's nephew comes and goes on his motorbike several times during the day, bringing materials for the garden. They normally spend most of their time in Thailand in Chantaburi, but on this trip Kung's sister is in the hospital in Bangkok and they are helping to take care of her. 'We take turns', says Nok. When we return to Bangkok at the end of the weekend, Kung's older brother will come with us.
>
> 'Ae' and 'Tui' live in Nonthaburi, just north of Bangkok, and maintain a home in Staten Island. They bought two halves of a duplex with their friends 'Ning' and 'Neung'. Ae and Tui's daughter 'Tina' looks after the house on occasion; their other daughter 'Helen' and her husband lived there for a while as well, in their absence. Ning also makes sure all was well, and maintains their shared backyard. Ae and Tui moved to their neighborhood in Nonthaburi largely to be near Ae's sister, who will look after that house when they are in the US. Tina had spent a year in Thailand recently, and they kept her old cell phone to lend out after she returned to the US. They will have to buy themselves another set of phones when they return to the US in April to do their taxes, for use there.

Stories such as this are cited to elaborate 'the production of domestic order' through the enactment of kinship practices, and how the home is spread across local, national and even transnational sites through mundane kinship-bonding practices. They are drawn on to identify a set of design implications to support social infrastructures and mobility across them in a global world.

Irani et al. (2010) report observations from a 7-week ethnographic study of mundane tool use in an Indian design firm and how these elaborate an 'intercultural infrastructure' that 'shapes' design work.

> At a brainstorm at the Bangalore office, Banita, Kurosh, Denis, and the field researcher gathered to generate e- classroom ideas. Lacking post-its, they began writing ideas on slips of white paper and sticking the slips to the wall with bits of blue adhesive tack. After some time, they decided that jury-rigging these sticky notes undesirably broke the flow of brainstorming. Banita, a senior member of the team, sent less senior Denis to Staples – the one place on that side of the city selling post-its – to purchase the notes before continuing the brainstorm. Brainstorms then resumed, now mediated by post-its. The post-its subtly changed the form of contributions from more graphical, narrative ideas to ideas expressible in short phrases. The group generated post-it contributions at a faster clip than with the previous slips and tack. In the above example, the materiality of available tools shaped the flow of interaction. Importantly, however, it also broke the flow of a kind of *broadly shared*,

symbolic *convention of practice*: brainstorming. To brainstorm with post-its is not only to functionally generate ideas at a fast clip. It is to talk and act like a designer, and to interact as a design team. In performing these recognisable innovation practices, designers leverage these practices' legitimacy. The post-its are an infrastructure *embedded* in other infrastructures. Selling 3Ms slips of papers in India relies on global distribution infrastructures, infrastructures of global finance, and in this case, a Staples chain store. Broadly, these are the infrastructures of 1990s Indian economic reforms inviting foreign companies into what had been a more planned, nationally-bounded economy.

Another tool, AutoCAD, was similarly central as an infrastructure of professional, collaborative practice. AutoCAD is a widely used software tool for 2-D and 3-D design. It is also a tool that costs approximately one third of a designer's annual salary at D-Design. Despite the cost, however, Rita, a junior designer, explained its importance in allowing the studio to engage in professional design-for-manufacture: "We should ideally use AutoCAD when we are, say, manufacturing the product 'cause it's much more accurate and standardised ... in the same way manufacturers and engineers use standardised industry processes ... Moreover, its just a way of simplified presentation and communication to different parties involved in the product development process." The materiality of the tools – the features and computational capabilities – enabled them to produce distinct kinds of design forms. Because these tools were de facto standards *built on an installed base*, designers were able to access knowledge and support from internet sites and from the professional partners and manufacturers with whom they worked. Even more explicitly than post-its, AutoCAD is a work tool that embodies a very expensive, transnational, professional standard.

These and other observations are drawn upon to elaborate a transnational intercultural infrastructure that links designers in specific locales to broader communities of professional practice, and how designers are 'forced to shape' their work around that infrastructure to make what they do professionally recognisable. In analysing the typically 'invisible' or taken for granted, material and symbolic character of intercultural infrastructures the authors suggest that they are not unique to design work or India but implicated in the social order more generally, 'producing broader forms of social life beyond work'.

Williams and Irani (2010) send us 'postcards from the field' to elaborate their ethnographic studies in Thailand and India.

Williams conducted a long-term ethnographic engagement with a charitable organisation in Bangkok, Thailand focusing largely on their use of digital imagery and media in configuring local and trans-national networks of financial support. Much of the field work took place on site over the course of several months: visiting the arts and crafts space, hanging out with the children who lived and attended school there, designing the organisation's website and annual report, and providing various computer support as needed. While the participants in this study would not have characterised themselves as professional designers, or even as particularly tech savvy, much of the everyday work at the field site consisted of various forms of design, creation, and critique. To leave Bangkok for North America, however, was not to leave the field site. The activities around which Williams designed the website continued in her absence, requiring her to intervene in and maintain the site. Feedback from supporters, breakdowns in webhosting, and donation processing problems all informed Williams' understanding of the field as a site for design. The time interacting with the organisation from across the world offered crucial insights into technology, social order, and meaning in the organisation.

> Irani spent several weeks as part of a team designing water filters for village households in Andhra Pradesh, India. Using ethnographic approaches, the team sought to understand the role of water in everyday family life to inform filter design. Researchers planned to screen participants, and to engage with the household through observations and one-on-one interviews. These plans were quickly revised, however, when the team arrived to see not a household but a loose union of homes and water infrastructure shared among extended families. Their first participant slept under his aunt's roof while he built a neighboring home for his mother and sister. As researchers began a planned one-on-one collage exercise meant to provoke discussion of health and lifestyle issues, more and more neighbors gathered round, drawn by the unusual encounter. Rather than attempt to single people out for individual exercises in which the participant might feel self-conscious, researchers decided to change the exercise into a cooperative group activity, reasoning that their underlying goal had been to understand shared (rather than individual) hopes, ideas, and meanings. The improvisation did, they reasoned, not undermine the research goals.

In place of a particular set of findings about transnational, intercultural practice and social order in Thailand or India, Williams and Irani instead offer a series of methodological reflections that 're-present' the user and 'relocate' fieldwork, culminating in the re-specification of 'criteria for ethnographic rigor'. These criteria seek to cement 'reflexive accounts generated by the body as an instrument of knowing' into the epistemological foundations of ethnographic research. In more prosaic terms, multi-sited ethnography would have us recognise that the user and field site are not natural facts but *discursive constructs* made by the ethnographer as he or she follows connections, selects topics of interest, and puts boundaries around fieldwork. This in turn, means that rigor (on this view) should be located in the ethnographer's account of how he or she constructs an understanding of 'the field', rather than in 'unbiased' or objective measures (e.g., duration of fieldwork, frequency of observations, sample size, etc.).

Dourish and Bell's critique of the dominant ubicomp vision is fostering 'new' ethnographic approaches in an effort to (re)configure the socio-cultural lens. In place of ethnomethodologically-informed ethnography and the focus on situated action and work practice, a multi-sited approach that seeks to elaborate a broader web of relationships and other forms of cultural practice is being imported into design from contemporary anthropology. The multi-sited research lens focuses on following connections between sites to bring into view the social, intercultural, and transnational infrastructures and practices that 'shape' (generate and produce) social order both locally and globally. Technology is embedded in those infrastructures and practices and multi-sited ethnography is therefore seen by Dourish and Bell, et al., to provide design with an appropriate lens for observing, interpreting and understanding technology in the twenty-first century – a century in which technological infrastructures are globally distributed. In short, the suggestion is that multi-sited ethnography reflects the connected world in which we live today, and the substitution of objective measures for reflexive accounts generated through the ethnographer's movement across connected sites ensures trustworthy insights into the orderliness of a massively networked, mobile, global world.

4.3   Messiness and Infrastructure

Dourish and Bell (2011) put a lot of analytic weight on the concepts of 'messiness' and 'infrastructure' in their socio-cultural analysis of technology in the twenty-first century. The starting point in their critique of ubicomp is sound and we do not take issue with it. Clearly we already live in a world in which ubiquitous computing resides. We are sympathetic, too, to the idea that technology, society and culture are inextricably entwined and that the entwining is provided for through the ordering of real world activities. As Harvey Sacks put it decades before with reference to the telephone, for example,

> Here's an object introduced into a world around 75 years ago. And it's a technical thing which has a variety of aspects to it … Now what happens is, like any other natural object, a culture secretes itself onto it in its well-shaped ways. It turns this technical apparatus which allows for conversation, into something in which the ways that conversation works are more or less brought to bear … … … This technical apparatus is, then, being made at home with the rest of our world. And that's a thing that's routinely being done, and it's the source for the failures of technocratic dreams that if only we introduced some fantastic new communication machine the world will be transformed. Where what happens is that the object is made at home in the world that has whatever organisation it already has. (Sacks 1992)

Sacks' point is that we need to be wary about seeing technology as radically transforming the social world. The invention of nuclear power did not transform the world; rather it was subjugated to the already organised affairs of the world. It became a device through which to threaten or retaliate against other nation states. Certainly one state could now annihilate more people, if not the entire world, in one go, but it was brought into the world as part of the existing military and political organisation of social life. It also became a device through which power could be generated, but it was built into existing infrastructures and economies of power production and consumption. The telephone, mobile phones, and mobile computing certainly provide for people to do certain things in different contexts to those they may have previously been done, but they are brought into the social world as ways of doing the same old things, such as engaging in leisure pursuits or personal communication. A seventeenth century writer of love letters with a quill pen might not understand the medium of the iPad and its accompanying enabling technology, but they would recognise what someone was doing in expressing their ardour for a loved one through its use.

In short, Dourish and Bell along with Sacks and whole schools of sociological thought before them recognise that socio-cultural and technical matters are irremediably entwined with social action. However, although we share these sympathies we are concerned about the way in which concepts such as 'messiness' and 'infrastructure' are used to understand this entwining; not because we have a problem with the concepts of 'messiness' and 'infrastructure' per se, but because of the consequence that the appropriation of these everyday terms from the everyday world in which they are sensibly used has for understanding the orderliness of contemporary life. Ripped out of everyday contexts of use, these concepts are distorted and transformed (Ryle 1949, Wittgenstein 1992) in order to provide a *generalised ana-lytic account* of social order in the twenty-first century.

The concept of 'messiness' enters into Dourish and Bell's socio-cultural analysis and shapes the ethnographic studies of their students because the networked world in which we live is seen to be heterogeneous in nature and this makes it difficult to apprehend. 'Messiness' is, then, a defining feature of the contemporary socio-technical landscape and from this it follows that we need approaches that are capa-ble of handling this 'messiness' on a global scale if we are to get a handle on the orderliness of a massively networked world. It is for this reason that multi-sited research commends itself, enabling ethnographers to track salient connections across sites and tease out the underlying orderliness of an inherently 'messy' world. Another way of putting it is that in contextualising situated action multi-sited eth-nography enables the socio-cultural analyst to develop a *holistic* view that extends what anyone can see in the use of AutoCAD in an Indian design firm, for example, to the global connections and web of relationships that reach out beyond it. Thus, the warrant for ethnography turns upon its ability to *generalise* from specific cir-cumstances (from just this use of AutoCAD in just this design firm in just this loca-tion) to society at large and the socio-cultural nature of technology within a globalised world.

The notion of 'mess' then is being used to perform an analytic task: it is being used to enable the socio-cultural analyst to *make generalisations* about the world, and to clear up that mess by enabling us to see its ordered character. However, 'mess' is a term that is taken from the everyday world. In contrast to the use it is put to by Dourish and Bell as part of their analytic apparatus, in the everyday world it is not a description that is *omni-relevant*. Rather, its use in everyday life is occasioned and it is employed in ordinary ways. For example, on entering a child's room we might see and comment on the mess it's in, where we mean it is untidy. We might recount a story about a colleague who works in a mess, where we mean he works chaotically. An old friend might tell us that he is in a mess because his wife has left him, where he means that he is distraught. In everyday life 'mess' is used by mem-bers to provide a description of certain states of affairs and its use is occasioned: by entering a child's room, for example, or tittle tattling about colleagues, or catching up with an old friend. We do not mean that all children's rooms are untidy; we do not mean that all offices are chaotic, or that all people whose wives leave them are in a mess. 'Mess' is not used as an omni-relevant description in everyday life. Its applicability is provided for through the situated occasion of its use.

It is often the case when we describe something as a 'mess' that we are being pejorative. Our children can be sanctioned because their rooms are a mess, our col-league is not efficient because he works in a mess, our friend's wife caused his state when she left him and is to blame, etc. 'Mess', then, is used in our everyday lives not only to render situated descriptions but also to hold others to account. However, our children may not care that their room is a mess; our colleague is able to put his hand on any document he needs amidst the chaos; and our friend's wife left him because he was already messed up with drink. Thus to describe something as a 'mess' is to make a contestable statement: my room is not messy, it is cosy and lived in; I know where everything is in my office; I'm not a drunk, I just drink a bit more than she does. 'Mess' then is not a given feature of a scene, it is an *achieved feature* of action and interaction produced through occasioned practices of description which hold people, situations, and events to account and which are subject to dispute. Using the term 'mess' in everyday life is to provide an occasioned description which involves pointing out certain observable matters in order to substantiate them and ignoring others, which in their turn can be pointed to in order to contest and undermine the description.

We do not just use the term 'mess' to refer to local matters such as messy rooms, offices and marriages. We also use them to describe systems, technological, social, political and economic. We can perfectly well understand what someone means when they say there is messiness in the world, that they are saying that nothing is really cut and dried, there are grey areas, things are put on hold and the like. However, when we make these global descriptions they share the same characteristics as the description of local scenes. They are contestable: the opposition described the UK economy as being in a mess, for example, whereas the Government described it as promoting prosperity. Again such descriptions involve pointing to certain features and ignoring others. Descriptions of 'messiness' are then *occasioned descriptions* used to do *particular actions* such as chide, rebuke, denigrate, or provide for a social science enterprise to bring order to the mess, and the like, and they are, by virtue of them being achieved descriptions for an occasion, always contestable.

However, to use 'messiness' as a generalised analytic category of description is to *reify* the concept and transform its intelligibility in everyday use. It is to take a concept, the intelligibility and applicability of which resides in everyday contexts of use, and make it into an omni-relevant, *situation and cohort independent* description. In its reified state it is applied to the world in order to make sense of it, and inevitably there is a gap between its analytic and ordinary use. The analytic use configures the socio-cultural lens and inevitably *distorts* that which it brings into view, turning an occasioned, situated description done for particular purposes into a generalised form of account. This practice of generalised description consequently leads us to view the social world in terms of the analytic *workings of the generalisation*, rather than in terms of the ordinary workings of culture and society. If we look at the world through another lens, conspiracy, for example, then the world is not a messy place but one that is ordered unbeknown to us for the purposes of a coherent ruling elite whose presence is everywhere but rarely seen. Juxtaposed against the messiness of the social world, the social world is, instead a regulated, regimented one in which there is the illusion of the messiness of freedom, for example. It is not then just that messiness is a distorting lens (conspiracy theory is just as distorting, for example), but that distortion is an inevitable feature of this fundamental social science descriptive practice; i.e., ripping everyday language out of the occasioned contexts of its ordinary use and repurposing it to furnish generalised accounts. So, then, if faced with two different cultural interpretations of the meaning things have in the world, and we do not mean this should be taken cavalierly, just take your pick, because for every example of messiness that can be given to substantiate its legitimacy as a cultural lens, an alternative example undermining it *can* be given.

The concept of 'infrastructure' is also put to work by Dourish and Bell alongside multi-sited ethnography to enable them to 'sort out the relationships of the local to the global' (Marcus 1995). The concept itself is not drawn from Marcus's writings but Susan Leigh Star's 'call to study boring things' (Star 1999). One such thing is 'infrastructure', which Star suggests is implicitly involved in many ethnographic studies of computing systems and whose explication is seen to be directly relevant by Dourish and Bell to developing our understanding of social order in today's massively networked world (though why infrastructure is boring misses us).

> People commonly envision infrastructure as a system of substrates – railroad lines, pipes and plumbing, electrical power plants, and wires. It is by definition invisible, part of the background for other kinds of work. It is ready-to-hand. This image holds up well enough for many purposes – turn on the faucet for a drink of water and you use a vast infrastructure of plumbing and water regulation without usually thinking much about it. (Star 1999)

Infrastructure is just about *everywhere* and thus a phenomenon we can tap into just about *anywhere*. While unequally distributed it is nonetheless pervasive and consists not only of technological characteristics (reservoirs, filtration plants, pipes, faucets, etc.) but also social and cultural characteristics (washing clothes, bathing, cleaning vegetables, etc.) which embed the technology in everyday life. Infrastructure cannot therefore be reduced to technological characteristics; it is not just electrical power, hardware platforms, software architectures, etc. It consists of technological characteristics *and* socio-cultural characteristics. Indeed infrastructure is analytically, for Star and others drawing on her work, the *relationship* between technological and socio-cultural characteristics.

Star's reflections on infrastructure construe it as an inseparable part of human relationships and their organisation, possessed of a number of distinctive properties. Infrastructure is 'embedded' within other structures, social arrangements, and technologies. It is 'transparent' or invisible in use. It has 'reach or scope', which is to say that it extends beyond a single site. It is 'learned as a part of membership' and is, as such, taken for granted by the people whose lives are enmeshed with it. It 'links with conventions of practice', i.e., it is enmeshed in everyday life through a community of practice. It 'embodies standards' and thus plugs into other infrastructures in a standardised fashion. It is 'built on an installed base' and thus predicated on legacy systems. It becomes 'visible on breakdown' and it is 'fixed in modular increments', which is to say that while potentially global it is configured and reconfigured locally. Elaboration of these properties through multi-sited ethnography enables the analyst to contextualise situated action. To see and point out, as Dourish and Bell (2011) put it, the infrastructures that 'lie below or beneath the surface' of human interaction and technology use: how post-its in an Indian design firm are not just bits of paper but 'an infrastructure embedded in other infrastructures' (particularly 'distribution infrastructures' and 'infrastructures of global finance'), for example, or how the adoption and use of AutoCAD by Indian designers turns upon 'a built on installed base' that lends professional credence to their work even though it comes at great expense (Irani et al. 2010).

Dourish and Bell, et al., put Star's notion of 'infrastructure' to work to sort out the 'messiness' of a globally connected world and the relationships between people, places and technology made visible through multi-sited ethnography. However, just as we have attempted to describe with respect to the concept of 'messiness', there is an issue that needs to be made visible with respect to the kind of descriptive practice this appeal to 'infrastructure' is wrapped up in. There is an old social science 'two step' going on between the particular and the general here. It involves the move that we saw with regard to Malinowski's ethnography, made visible by Geertz, with the particular being used as a site for viewing the general. That is, the particular is taken as the product of the operation of the general. Put another way the 'macro structure' is providing for the 'micro instance'. In this respect the particular is taken as evidence for the general, it provides data that indicates the existence of the general structure. It is a step made widely by social scientists, but the point of note about this descriptive practice is that it is also widely used across society at large. It is not a social science method per se, but a method of *common-sense reasoning* broadly employed in society by all manner of people to understand the orderliness of social affairs, social scientists included. It was first described by Karl Mannheim (1952) and subsequently elaborated by Garfinkel and is called '*the documentary method of interpretation*'. Garfinkel (1967) tells us that it,

> ... consists of treating an actual appearance as 'the document of', as 'pointing to', as 'standing on behalf of' a presupposed underlying pattern. Not only is the underlying pattern derived from its individual documentary evidences, but the individual documentary evidences, in their turn, are interpreted on the basis of 'what is known' about the underlying pattern. Each is used to elaborate the other.

We are all familiar with this method of accounting for occurrences in the everyday world. For example, racially prejudiced descriptions are often done by accounting for the actions of an individual by invoking their race as underlying their behaviour: 'he is doing that (the particular) because that is what people-like-him (the underlying structure) do'. In accounting for the particular through invoking an underlying structure we make visible the imputed structure, and provide yet another example that can be drawn on to elaborate the structure. Of course it is not just racist accounts of behaviour that can be put together in this way, the method is employed ubiquitously, but when it is used to construct social science accounts do not be blinded to it because of the seeming import of the thing it accounts for; look through the substantive argument and it is possible to see the account is put together *in the same way* in which common-sense descriptions of the world are put together.

A perspicuous example of the use of the documentary method of interpretation at work in social science is provided by Philips et al. (2012) in their postcolonial elaboration of the MIT Media Lab project 'One Laptop Per Child' (OLPC) and development of the XO or $100 computer. As part of their elaboration two photographs are juxtaposed: one (placed on the left) showing two girls using XO computers, the other (placed on the right) showing the XO assembly line. The authors ask,

> What are the conditions of possibility of this moment? The OLPC came to these two girls in part through the much publicised efforts of Nicholas Negroponte [Media Lab founder]

and open source coders, through the navigation of media and social networks, through sometimes antagonistic negotiations with software and hardware producers, and a dense assemblage of other forces and actors. In the second image, we see a rarer peek into the assembly lines of computing in a photo that stages the celebration of the XO's departure from design phases into manufacture and deployment ... The photo on the right is the indication of the standing reserves of feminised Asian labour that manufactures the XO laptop, like many of the world's computers. The women's labours are part of the conditions of possibility of the girls' use of the XO. Such labours are hardly attended to in ICT4D or HCI. Infrastructured, the women's labour recedes into the background of consciousness to be taken for granted in use.

Thus an actual appearance – the two girls using XO computers – is treated as 'the document of', as 'pointing to', as 'standing on behalf of' a presupposed underlying pattern – *infrastructure* – which is itself interpreted on the basis of 'what is known' about the underlying pattern: that standing reserves of feminised Asian labour make the world's computers and this is taken for granted or 'learned as part of membership' in Star's terms. In other settings, we see other underlying properties of the pattern – e.g., the 'embeddedness' of post-its or 'built on installed base' that design work in India trades upon. We see, in other words, large scale if not global infrastructure at work *in* situated action.

Philips et al. elaborate 'tactics' for observing and analysing infrastructure and 'tracing the long networks' that enable the technological formations that today furnish the conditions of situated action's very possibility. These tactics are part of an array of contextualising practices that social scientists exploit to make the documentary method of interpretation work. However, when the documentary method of interpretation is appropriated by social science from the everyday world in which it is used as a mundane way of accounting for the structure of social action, there are problematic consequences with respect to its deployment.

> The documentary method of interpretation is a convenient gloss ... The gloss is convenient and somehow convincing. It is also very powerful in its coverage; too powerful. It gets everything in the world for ... analysts. Its shortcomings are notorious: in any actual case it is undiscriminating and just in any actual case it is absurdly wrong ... ... in any case where [it is] administered as prescribed codes the result can be lucid, perfectly clear analytic ethnographic description, but the description will have missed the subject matter, its probity, and the point of the description, with no accompanying sign that [it is] misunderstood. (Garfinkel 2002)

Garfinkel is describing how the documentary method of interpretation inevitably looses the details of the particular situation it is accounting for and thus fails to describe social order *in any actual case* even though that is its intention. This gloss is the result of 'prescribed codes', whether they are codes that the analyst develops from the ground up (Glaser and Strauss 1967) or pre-existing codes, such as those furnished by, in Dourish and Bells' case, Star ('learned as part of membership', 'embeddedness', 'built on an installed base', etc.). These codes or categories are analytic devices that the sociological researcher uses to grab onto little bits of the real world in an attempt to make the analytic category or construct out to be an actual 'real-worldly' phenomenon that anyone can now see even though it usually 'lays beneath' everyday experience.

The documentary method of interpretation thus enables the socio-cultural researcher to make something that is imputed to be 'there', but which is said to be usually unobservable, visible and plain to see. It is used to provide empirical demonstrations of social structures posited *by the social scientist*. The demonstration turns upon the display of observable features of the world within an analytic account (e.g., the 'embedded' character of post-its in an Indian design firm) as indicators of the underlying construct (e.g., 'infrastructure'). Thus, the underlying construct (what lies beneath situated action) is made visible through the act of *sociological indication*; its visibility is made possible by treating, for example, the post-it note as data for the demonstrable existence of infrastructure. The post-it note is then turned into something other than what it is to those who produced it (for whom it is, after all, just a post-it); it is turned by the anthropologist or sociologist into an *indicator* of an underlying social structure.

Sociological indication can be done in wide variety of ways, even statistically, but in the case of ethnography it is done through 'exampling practices' (observations, anecdotes, postcards from the field, juxtaposition of photographs, etc.). Exampling practices indicate, point to, the underlying construct – e.g., infrastructure. It makes out that the underlying structure that is pointed to is 'really there'. However, as Baccus (1986) reminds us,

> ... indicators ... are indicative of the construct *but are not equivalent to it* ... What relation, then, does the construct have to real-worldly phenomena, to real-world events? It has none ... [the] analytic ... construct has a relation only to the data providing its empirically demonstrable existence as world sensible, as real worldly but that data is *not* the world's events ... (our emphasis)

In other words, in Dourish and Bell and the work of others we have referred to, we see the underlying socio-technical *construct* of infrastructure – which is essentially a theoretical construct in their discourse – being made 'real worldly', or more accurately being made out to be 'real worldly', made out to be 'really there' in the ways that the social scientist says it is.

The achievement of this kind of 'constructive analysis' is to *make social theorising real worldly*, that is, to make out that what essentially exists only in theory is a real feature of the world. This achievement is done through sociological indication, accomplished through common-sense practices of exampling, which provide for the visibility of underlying analytic constructs such as infrastructure:

> The constructive analytic theoretician's real accomplishment is not finding indicators to reference an unobservable but is the establishment of that unobservable and those indicators as 'real' objects in the world. (ibid.)

Sociological indication is a constituent feature of the documentary method of interpretation. It allows the sociological researcher to treat actual appearances as 'the document of', as 'pointing to', as 'standing on behalf of' a presupposed underlying pattern (e.g., infrastructure) and to render that pattern as if it was a feature of the real world: each is used to elaborate the other and to make underlying theoretic constructs into visibly 'real' objects in the world.

It is for this reason that Garfinkel tells us that the documentary method can and does produce 'powerful, lucid, clear, and convincing' descriptions of society and social order, which are, however, 'absurdly wrong' (Garfinkel 2002). Accounts of social order developed through the documentary method of interpretation stand on sociological indication and the problem with that, as Baccus points out, is that indication *does not* have a relationship to the real world; it only has a relationship to the construct it props up and makes world sensible. What of the examples – the 'data' – that make the underlying construct visible? Surely they are real? Surely they provide an empirical relationship between the construct and the world? No, for again as Baccus makes clear, such data *is not* the world's events. What she means here is that, for example, the post-it note that is treated as data pointing to the underlying concept of infrastructure is *not* data, not something that points to infrastructure *in itself*; in itself it is just a post-it. Treating it as data indicating the existence of an infrastructure is to ignore what it is in the world: a summary of an idea, a reminder of a job to do, a memo to self, etc. To ignore this is to ignore the social thing that produced it: the brainstorming session, for instance. Where is the orderliness of *that* work? In its place stand the constitutive concepts of infrastructure: 'builds on an installed base', 'learned as a part of membership', 'links with conventions of practice', etc. In this and the other infrastructure examples we have considered, the real world, real time orderliness of action and interaction is *glossed over*, with the particular things that people do and the organised ways in which they do them being selectively treated to *prop up* generic social science descriptions of the social order.

The consequences, then, of using the documentary method of interpretation for doing social science is that ordinary, perfectly understandable actions in the everyday world, such as sticking a post-it note on a board as part of a design brainstorming session, are turned into ethnographic 'data' to fuel the job of sociological indication. These common-sense practices gloss over and ignore the lived details and interactionally embodied organisation of the situated action being studied. Instead *remnants* of situated action are drawn upon methodically to breathe life into abstract social structures that would not exist without the act of sociological indication and the interpretation of patterns. Multi-sited ethnography thus has to be questioned as a solution to the problem of getting to grips with the socio-cultural character of technology in a massively networked world. Not only is it shot through with and trades upon common-sense practices of reasoning and accounting for social order, it reinstates the traditional role of anthropology and sociology as providing top-down structural accounts of social order, and in doing this reifies and distorts the orderliness of actual occasions and events.

The reification and distortion turns upon continued misunderstanding in the social sciences about the relationship between agency and structure, the relationship between culture and society and individual action and interaction, and the relationship between the macro and the micro. Hence the idea, for example, that multi-sited ethnography will bridge the gap between micro matters found in a single locality and macro matters found across localities. We have argued that this divide between structure and agency – between world systems and situated action – has been greatly exaggerated in the social sciences, mainly because the agency side has been misrepresented. It is *within* people's everyday lives and everyday interactions that so called 'macro' matters – such as 'society', 'culture', 'infrastructure' and the like – are brought about. The social order is an observable feature of situated action, it is part and parcel of social action, not something that 'lays beneath' it and that requires contextualisation by the socio-cultural interpreter to make it visible. The agency side of the argument does not ignore macro issues then, but understands them as situated achievements rather than matters that lie underneath interaction and shape it. Treated essentially as exercising external 'constraint' on situated action, the macro is misconceived by proponents of the structure side of the divide, in that they see social structure as an omni-relevant matter rather than a situationally occasioned and produced one (Coulter 1982).

These are complex issues and even in book format they are difficult to deal with, as they should perhaps be dealt with in their own right, not invoked as we are doing here to discuss ethnography in design. However, we are trying to balance a description of the problematics of social science description with the concerns of design. While the problems of social science description are not problems of design per se, we are trying to make it visible to systems designers who take the social seriously that what it is being offered by the call for 'new' ethnographies to advance ubiquitous computing is deeply problematic, and for a number of reasons: (1) 'New' design ethnographies are not new at all, but a call for design to pick up on traditional ways of doing social science description; (2) Traditional ways of doing social science description are problematic because despite their seemingly lofty appeals and worthy subject matters they are of the *same* order of account that *anyone* can give; (3) Like lay descriptions of social order they are built upon common-sense methods of reasoning and account; (4) As a resource for design they stand alongside other common-sense ways of interpreting culture and society, which means that if a designer wants to understand such matters as the meaning that technology has in society, or how technology is embedded into different cultural milieus, they do *not* particularly need ethnography and its paraphernalia to tell them; (5) In ignoring common-sense methods of reasoning and account, while actually using them in unacknowledged ways, 'new' ethnographies consequently miss how social life is actually ordered by those who are party to it; (6) It follows that any design enterprise based on such descriptions will miss out on the real world, real time orderliness of action and interaction too.

In making this argument we will inevitably be accused of not understanding ethnography; of failing to appreciate that it is essentially a theory-laden and interpretive business and that it cannot be otherwise. Concomitant to this we will undoubtedly be charged with peddling our own theory of the social, and that this theory is a realist, even a *naïvely* realist, one that ignorantly emphases the empirical while ignoring the reflexive constitution of the ethnographer's observational practices and their impact on that which is observed. In short, we will be charged with peddling an outmoded version of ethnography that is not only unsuitable for studying contemporary life, but shows an unpalatable ignorance of contemporary ethnographic practice within the social sciences and its salience to systems design. We turn next to address these matters, particularly towards the ways in which they are *irrelevant* for ethnomethodological studies of the everyday world and irrelevant *for systems design.*

References

Adorno, T., & Hockheimer, M. (1944). *Dialectic of enlightenment.* New York: Social Studies Association.

Baccus, M. (1986). Sociological indication and the visibility criterion of real world social theorising. In H. Garfinkel (Ed.), *Ethnomethodological studies of work* (pp. 1–19). London: Routledge and Kegan Paul.

Bell, G. (2001). Looking across the Atlantic: Using ethnographic methods to make sense of Europe. *Intel Technology Journal Q3.* http://dl.acm.org/citation.cfm?id=1067862

Bell, G. (2006). No more SMS from Jesus: Ubicomp, religion and techno-spiritual practice In: *Proceedings of the 8th international conference on ubiquitous computing* (pp. 141–158). Newport Beach: Springer.

Button, G. (2000). The ethnographic tradition and design. *Design Studies, 21,* 319–332.

Coulter, J. (1982). Remarks on the conceptualisation of social structure. *Philosophy of the Social Sciences, 12*(1), 33–46.

Dourish, P. (2004). *Where the action is: The foundations of embodied interaction.* Cambridge, MA: MIT Press.

Dourish, P. (2006). Implications for design. In: *Proceedings of the conference on human factors in computing systems* (pp. 541–550). Quebec: ACM.

Dourish, P., & Bell, G. (2011). *Divining a digital future: Mess and mythology in ubiquitous computing.* Cambridge, MA: MIT Press.

Dourish, P., & Button, G. (1998). On 'technomethodology' – Foundational relationships between ethnomethodology and systems design. *Human Computer Interaction, 13*(4), 395–432.

Durkheim, E. (1897). *Suicide: A study in sociology.* Paris: F. Alcan.

Falzon, M. (2009). Introduction. In: *Multi-sited ethnography: Theory, praxis and locality in contemporary research.* (pp. 1–23). Farnham: Ashgate.

Garfinkel, H. (1967). Common-sense knowledge of social structures: The documentary method of interpretation in lay and professional fact finding. In: *Studies in ethnomethodology* (pp. 76–103). Englewood Cliffs: Prentice-Hall.

Garfinkel, H. (2002). Central claims of ethnomethodology. In: *Ethnomethodology's program: Working out Durkheim's aphorism* (pp. 91–120). Lanham: Rowman and Littlefield.

Garfinkel, H., & Sacks, H. (1970). On formal structures of practical action. In J. C. McKinney & E. Tiryakian (Eds.), *Theoretical sociology: Perspectives and developments* (pp. 160–193). New York: Apple-Century-Crofts.

Glaser, B., & Strauss, A. (1967). *The discovery of grounded theory: Strategies for qualitative research.* Chicago: Aldine.

Irani, L., Vertesi, J., Dourish, P., Philip, K., & Grinter, R. (2010). Postcolonial computing: A lens on design and development. In: *Proceedings of the SIGCHI conference on human factors in computing systems* (pp. 1311–1320). Atlanta: ACM.

Latour, B. (1991). Technology is society made durable. In J. Law (Ed.), *A sociology of monsters* (pp. 103–131). London: Routledge.

Mannheim, K. (1952). On the interpretation of weltanschauung. In: *Essays on the sociology of knowledge* (pp. 53–63). London: Routledge.

Marcus, G. (1995). Ethnography in/of the world system: The emergence of multi-sited ethnography. *Annual Review of Anthropology, 24,* 95–117.

Marcus, G. (1999). An introduction. In G. Marcus (Ed.), *Critical anthropology now: Unexpected contexts, shifting constituencies, changing agendas* (pp. 3–28). Santa Fe: SAR Press.

Philips, K., Irani, L., & Dourish, P. (2012). Postcolonial computing: A tactical survey. *Science, Technology and Human Values, 37*(1), 3–29.

Plowman, L., Rogers, Y., & Ramage, M. (1995). What are workplace studies for?. In: *Proceedings of the fourth European conference on computer supported cooperative work* (pp. 309–324). Stockholm: Kluwer Academic Publishers.

Ryle, G. (1949). *The concept of mind.* London: Hutchinson.

Sacks, H. (1963). Sociological description. *Berkeley Journal of Sociology, 8,* 1–16.

Sacks, H. (1992). A single instance of a phone-call opening; caller-called, etc. In G. Jefferson (Ed.), *Lectures on conversation* (Vol. II, Part VIII, Spring 1972, Lecture 3, pp. 542–553). Oxford: Blackwell.

Star, L. (1999). The ethnography of infrastructure. *American Behavioural Scientist, 43*(3), 377–391.

Weiser, M. (1991). The computer for the 21st century. *Scientific American, 265*(3), 94–104.

Williams, A., & Irani, L. (2010). There's methodology in the madness: Toward critical HCI ethnography. In: *Proceedings of the SIGCHI conference on human factors in computing systems – extended abstracts* (pp. 2725–2734). Atlanta: ACM.

Williams, A., Anderson, K., & Dourish, P. (2008). Anchored mobilities: Mobile technology and transnational migration. In: *Proceedings of the conference on designing interactive systems* (pp. 323–332). Cape Town: ACM.

Wittgenstein, L. (1992). *Philosophical investigations.* Oxford: Blackwell.

Zimmerman, D., & Pollner, M. (1970). The everyday world as a phenomenon. In J. Douglas (Ed.), *Understanding everyday life* (pp. 80–103). Chicago: Aldine Publishing Company.

Chapter 5
Interpretation, Reflexivity and Objectivity

Abstract We have argued that 'new' approaches to ethnography in systems design return ethnography to its old remit of providing interpretations of and giving meaning to social and cultural matters. Something that features strongly within calls for 'new' approaches is the fundamental assertion that observations are always theory laden and that ethnography is, accordingly, inherently a matter of interpretation. In this chapter we examine this proposition and note that the descriptive practices for seeing and recognising human actions do not belong to or derive from professional sociological theorising, but reside in the doing of the actions themselves. Theory, in that case, turns out to be not so much a necessary way of observing the social world but of *re-describing* its observable characteristics for social science purposes. The job of re-description is also marked by an academic concern with reflexivity and the questions of objectivity and realism. Here there is a push to problematise the relationship between the ethnographer and the field of study with which they are engaged: to problematise how it is that ethnographers can be said to know and understand the world, and how they orient themselves to the factual and objective character of the social phenomena they are observing. For both of these matters the critical error lies in constituting these as *the fieldworker's problem*.

5.1 Observation and Interpretation

Seen and treated as an exemplar of traditional social science approaches to ethnography, Dourish and Bell's (2011) methodological orientation, and the problems we have seen that accompany it, turn upon the fundamental *assertion* that "observations are always theory laden" and that ethnography is, therefore, "inherently interpretive". As Lynch (1999) puts it,

> … 'theorising' in this context [means] the work of constructing intellectual genealogies that commemorate notable authors and foundational writings. It is part of a broader effort to index empirical investigations to bodies of literature. The work of indexing is facilitated by scholarly efforts to identify abstract themes and topics, formulate propositions and postulates, articulate common problems, and ascribe assumptions and presuppositions to authors and schools. This work is more than a matter of encoding and decoding a literature. It also has to do with methodology: the use of criteria, decision rules, and models which tie research designs to scholarly traditions. The point of such endeavours is to isolate funda-

© Springer International Publishing Switzerland 2015
G. Button et al., *Deconstructing Ethnography*, Human-Computer
Interaction Series, DOI 10.1007/978-3-319-21954-7_5

mental precepts and to construct intellectual histories for one or another literary tradition of social thought.

It is plain to see in our elaboration of Dourish and Bell's work in the previous chapter that they are deeply engaged in theorising the social, and the suggestion that accompanies this effort is that it *cannot* be otherwise because all empirical investigations – all observations – are always theory laden, inevitably coloured by some literary tradition.

The idea that observation is theory laden is not a particularly new one; it was initially developed by philosopher of science Norman Hanson in 1958. Today it is deeply entrenched in the social sciences and underpins a broad range of otherwise diverse viewpoints. The idea suggests that it is impossible to see something – anything at all – without making use of a theory of some kind to recognise it. The suggestion derives from Hanson's reflections on arguments about the authority of scientific claims. Basically the argument goes that anchoring scientific claims in sensory experience or 'observation' provides an evidential justification that underwrites their authority. Hanson suggested that this was far too simplistic a view of science and the nature of observation; that there is in effect a 'praxiology' to perception:

> Pierre Duhem writes:
>
>   Enter a laboratory; approach the table crowded with an assortment of apparatus, an electric cell, silk-covered copper wire, small cups of mercury, spools, a mirror mounted on an iron bar; the experimenter is inserting into small openings the metal ends of ebony-headed pins; the iron oscillates, and the mirror attached to it throws a luminous band upon a celluloid scale; the forward-backward motion of this spot enables the physicist to observe the minute oscillations of the iron bar. But ask him what he is doing. Will he answer 'I am studying the oscillations of an iron bar which carries a mirror?' No, he will say that he is measuring the electric resistance of the spools. If you are astonished, if you ask him what his words mean, what relation they have with the phenomena he has been observing and which you have noted at the same time as he, he will answer that your question requires a long explanation and that you should take a course in electricity.
>
>   The visitor must learn some physics before he can see what the physicist sees. Only then will the context throw into relief those features of the objects before him which the physicist sees as indicating resistance. (Hanson 1958)

It might otherwise be said that 'seeing or 'observing' is entwined with some 'scheme of interpretation', some way of making sense of what is seen. Hence the suggestion that observation is always theory-laden.

Now the idea that people use schemes of interpretation is one that ethnomethodologists have themselves used to account for the ways in which they see and recognise the actions and interactions around them and detect the orderliness of their individual and collaborative endeavours (e.g., Sharrock and Button 1991). So how could we object to the suggestion that observation is always theory laden? Well, as Hutchinson et al. (2008) remind us, if observation is always theory laden then so too must be description (as a theory is a description), and this is where things get problematic. In short, the descriptive practices for seeing and recognising some action, for observing and accountably identifying it as the thing that it is – e.g., 'measuring the electrical resistance of spools' – do not belong to or derive from professional sociological theorising, but from the social settings within which the action occurs. Thus, the practices for *correctly* observing and describing action – for seeing and accountably recognising any action for the action it is – are *built into* the action being observed. Yet professional sociology, anthropology and the social sciences more generally systematically ignore mundane descriptive practices for seeing and recognising or 'observing' action. As Hutchinson et al. put it,

> Professional sociology [etc.] does not provide an extensive re-classification of things that people are doing. That is, they have no substitutes for commonplace descriptions such as 'standing six places from the front of the bus queue' or 'scoring an equaliser in injury time' … Professional sociologists do not want to change or contest these descriptions, but want to argue, instead, about the understandings that attach to these actions when they are considered from the point of view of … some postulated social system …

Theory, then, is not so much a way of observing the world but of *re-describing* its observable characteristics; theory provides a scheme for doing the job of re-description and arriving at disciplinary interpretations of action and interaction. In doing so it leaves 'commonplace descriptions', which are part and parcel of the action and interaction observed, intact but untouched. Thus the mundane descriptive apparatus that people use to make action and interaction observable and reportable or accountable to one another in the very course of doing it is set aside, along with the orderliness that accompanies their accountable doings.

This begs an important question for systems design, and one that drives our objection to the uncritical acceptance of what Lynch (1999) calls, "much abused slogans from the philosophy of science". The question is this: whose theory – i.e., whose scheme of interpretation, whose way of accounting for the orderliness of everyday life – is to be used? The first order scheme that is part and parcel of the settings observed through fieldwork and the action that accountably takes place there, or the second order re-description that puts the fieldworker's in its place? The two forms of description are not at all the same: one is wrapped up in and elaborates the orderliness of action from the point of view of those who are party to it and within which the notion of 'theory' is rarely operative, the other elaborates the orderliness of action from an *essentially abstract* point of view that does possess the properties of a theory as outlined by Lynch above. The uncritical acceptance of the 'theory-ladeness of observation' masks the substitution of members' ways of seeing, recognising and thereby accounting for the orderliness of social life for the social theorists'. The substitution trades on the widespread abuse of the meaning of 'theory-laden' – it does not mean that theory as it is understood in the social sciences is a necessary part of observation. It means, as Hanson's use of Duhem's example makes perspicuous, that "there is more to seeing something than meets the eyeball" (Hanson 1958); that there is a 'praxiology' to perception, which locates seeing in the *recognisability* of the action being observed (Coulter and Parsons 1990).

The 'praxiology of perception' is part and parcel of membership competence. It consists of the taken for granted knowledge of everyday practice (i.e., of what is done in a everyday life and how it is done) that Duhem's visitor, like the sociological theorist qua theorist, does not possess. Taken for granted knowledge furnishes a setting's members with situationally-relevant schemes of interpretation. These schemes are rooted in and provided for through the mundane practices that members use to both conduct *and* recognise action. They are drawn upon to make correct observations of action and are situated, not in a literary tradition of social thought, but in the settings they elaborate, and in the doing of the actions themselves. Ethnomethodology's injunction is that the ethnographer take the schemes of interpretation that people employ to see and recognise a setting's features seriously. This seriousness is reflected in the requirement that the fieldworker develop 'vulgar competence', i.e., that he or she master just how it is that a setting's members see and recognise just what is going on around them (Garfinkel and Wieder 1992).

In saying this it might be argued that the ethnomethodologist must be making use of a theory to develop vulgar competence and their analyses of social order. As Hutchinson et al. (2008) tell us, those who are wedded to abusing philosophical slogans will insist that those of us who deny having and using a theory to observe and describe action must have one; that it *cannot* be helped no matter what we say, and that if we deny having a theory it can only mean that our actual theory is implicit or tacit: we obviously have a tacit theory about the praxiology of perception, for example. Nonetheless, the praxiology of perception does not provide *us* with a scheme of interpretation – let alone a scheme of interpretation rooted in a literary tradition of scholarly thought – but rather *orients us* to the practices that *members use* to see and recognise the orderliness of what is for them an obstinately familiar world. At best, the praxiology of perception is a presupposition, one of many that define ethnomethodology's program (Garfinkel 2001), but it and they do not constitute a theory of the social. As Lynch (1999) puts it,

> ... it may seem reasonable to suppose that ethnomethodology *must* have some sort of coherent theory behind it ... [However] Garfinkel and Sacks, in different ways and with differing success, undertook to initiate a practice that was fundamentally different from existing social science methods. They de-emphasized abstract theory and scholarship, and stressed the necessity to *do* studies. Their notions of practice differed from the currently fashionable interest in the social sciences with devising theories of practice, because *practice* was not just a topic of explanatory interest, it was the primary basis for attaining an ethnomethodological mastery.

Ethnomethodology's presuppositions, along with its policies and methods, do not constitute a theory in the sense that a literary tradition is drawn upon to interpret what is observed. Rather, they are "administered and used locally as an instruction" to uncover the orderliness of everyday life in the course of *doing* observational studies (Garfinkel and Wieder 1992).

This, then, throws into doubt the idea that ethnography is 'inherently interpretive'. When social scientists say this it is important to appreciate that they do not use the word 'interpretation' in its ordinary sense – i.e., in the sense that *anyone's* description may be said to provide an account of what they see. Rather, the social scientist as scientist means that observation is always grounded in some theory of the social. This, however, is not *always* the case. Indeed most schemes of interpretation operative in the world are not organised in terms of *literary traditions in social science*, but in terms of the real world practices that provide for the situated observability of a setting's work. This means, as Coulter and Parsons (1990) remind us, that "only some observations are theory laden" and that while an ethnographic account might be an interpretation in the ordinary sense of the word, where this effectively means that it provides 'just another point of view', it need not be so in the rarefied sense meant by social scientists: this rarefied kind of interpretation is not *necessarily* an inherent feature of ethnographic work.

But surely ethnomethodological accounts are second order accounts and thus offer essentially abstract interpretations just the same as mainstream social science accounts do? No, ethnomethodological accounts are of an entirely *different* order. They do not seek to re-describe a setting's features but to explicate through the production of 'corrigible sketch accounts', or detailed depictions of action and interaction being done, the lived work of a setting (Garfinkel and Wieder 1992). In ethnomethodological terminology, these sketches provide 'praxiological' accounts that make the activities done by members in a setting and (importantly) how they are done 'instructably observable' – i.e., see-able and recognisable in the same terms that they are for members. They are, therefore, corrigible – members can point out mistakes and identify corrections – and are as such open to revision. The same cannot be said for traditional ethnographic accounts as the work of a setting and the practices that members use to conduct, see and recognise it are supplanted by theoretical interpretations: the work through which action and interaction is achieved as that which it recognisably is for a setting's member has *not* been explicated by traditional ethnographic accounts. The orderly work of the streets, as it were, is surplus to the theoretical re-description of everyday life.

Now for all this talk of interpretation it is worth pointing out that people do not go around the real world with pre-existing interpretive schemas in their heads that they overlay onto words or bodily movements; rather the meaning of action is visible in its doing. Take an ordinary run of the mill workplace in the morning by way of example. Jim walks through the door of the kitchen to make a cup of coffee before starting work. He encounters John, who was there before him and who on seeing Jim says, "Morning Jim". Jim responds, saying "Morning John". In doing this Jim has *not* interpreted John as greeting him, he has not gone through some indefinable cognitive process of interpretation to make what John has said 'a greeting', as if he could come up with another interpretation such as John being humorous that would stand alongside the greeting. First, Jim recognises John's utterance as a greeting in it being done *as* a greeting – John uses a standard greeting term in his culture, situated in an 'initial turn position' in a sequence of interaction that provides for Jim to return a greeting (Schegloff 2007). Second, any sense that Jim has of John being humorous turns upon Jim *first* being able to find that John has greeted him. In any case, even here, this seems to stretch what we ordinarily mean by interpretation. We might rather say that Jim employs the "hearer's maxim" (Sacks 1992) and recognises the humour in John's greeting through the contextual character of their interaction – they go through this ritual every morning, John knows that Jim was out late last night, John has a twinkle in his eye and a knowing lopsided grin on his face, for example.

Simply put, actions are recognisably produced to be the things that they are. They are produced to be accountable – observably and reportably just 'this' (Garfinkel 1967). If they were not then how could the very phenomena of sociality be possible? How could Jim respond to John in a recognisably appropriate way? Jim and John are not interpreting their words and bodily movements through some theory that endows their actions with meaning. They are *doing accountable actions* and doing them through the practices whereby such things are recognisably done in their culture, which means that other members of the culture can recognise what is being done too. Jim and John's exchange of greetings is taken from a recording that an ethnographer (one of the present authors) made, and as a member of the same culture the ethnographer was just as able to recognise an exchange of greetings when it was done as the participants themselves. Like Jim and John the ethnographer did not require a body of literature, a theory of action, to see what was being done for what it was.

This takes us back to Hanson's quotation of Duhem's physics experiment. The recognisability of what the physicist is doing – 'measuring the electric resistance of the spools' – does not turn upon the visitor's interpretation of his actions, but upon his *competence* (or lack of it) in the culture of experimental physics. As Duhem puts it, "the visitor must learn some physics before he can see what the physicist sees." We would argue that the same applies more generally. That the fieldworker needs to learn how the people he or she studies see and recognise action and interaction, and that vulgar competence is an essential condition of ethnography, *not* theoretical interpretation. One might wonder then, if theoretical interpretation is not a necessary, why it is that anthropologists, sociologists and social scientists more generally persist with what appears to be such a perverse practice? What is it about mainstream social science that compels social scientists to keep making the same mistake? Why would the ethnographer set the explication of practice aside and choose instead to re-describe the world through theoretical interpretation? It is towards understanding the predilection of some ethnographers to keep on ignoring the inherently accountable organisation of everyday life, in favour of reflecting upon their own descriptive practices, that we turn next.

5.2 Reflexivity in Ethnographic Observation

Reflexivity has become a key idea in many quarters of contemporary social science, it has certainly (re)defined it over the last generation. Dourish and Bell (2011) put it as follows,

> There is, of course, more to ethnography than its ability to ground conversations in daily lived reality. It also has attendant to it a set of theoretical practices that have to underpin critical self-reflection. By this we mean the ability to talk about one's biography, location, and subjectivity, and the ways in which they might shape the identification of research problems, projects, and participants. While we would hate to see ubicomp practitioners and the field more broadly suffer through the 'crisis of representation' that has beset

anthropology, in particular, for the last twenty-plus years, there is much to be learned from that process, and a small dose of critical reflection about subjectivity, positionality, and voice would go a long way.

Dourish and Bell also point out that such critical self-reflection is largely absent in contemporary systems development, but that developing an appreciation of it is important to the interdisciplinary mix.

> To understand the ways in which ethnography figures within and without ubicomp is to understand not just its methods but also its methodologies and larger epistemological concerns with reflexivity … (Dourish and Bell 2011)

We agree, but not for the same reasons. What for Dourish and Bell is a source of illumination is, for us, a primary source of obfuscation. Reflexivity as it is largely understood in mainstream social science guarantees the systematic ignorance of the already accountable organisation of everyday life. Academic reflexivity is blind to the *incarnate reflexivity* that is 'built in' to everyday accounts as a methodological matter constitutive of recognisable social settings, scenes and events. It is towards understanding why and how academic reflexivity – the kind of reflexivity that Dourish and Bell champion – achieves and guarantees this ignorance that we turn our attention below.

The impetus towards critical self-reflection was occasioned, as Dourish and Bell point out, through what is described as the 'crisis of representation'. This afflicted not only anthropology but cut through the social and human sciences as well. It's origins and implications for ethnographic work are outlined by George Marcus and Michael Fischer in their critically acclaimed book *Anthropology as Cultural Critique*. Marcus and Fischer locate the crisis in the failure of the post-World War II 'positivist' paradigm that sought to develop an objective science of Man and was characterised by total or 'grand' theories of society. Academic dissatisfaction grew with these overarching theories during the 1960s and 1970s, in light of their failure to provide realistic and accurate representations of the conflict and social changes that were occurring (most notably in America) at the time. The dominant positivist paradigm could not handle what Marcus and Fischer (1986) call the 'messier' side of social action, and so confidence in it waned and the so-called crisis of representation emerged and took a widespread hold on the human sciences. At its heart lay uncertainty about Marcus and Fischer termed 'adequate means' of describing social reality. Our examination in Chap. 3 of the way in which two different grand theories of social life, a functionalist theory and a conflict theory, give rise to different descriptions of the cultural milieu in the same environment, is an example of the type of problem encapsulated for anthropology by the terms 'crisis of representation' and 'adequate means' of description.

Seen from the perspective of anthropology, uncertainty centred on the ethnographic account:

> Ethnography is a research process in which the anthropologist closely observes, records, and engages in the daily life of another culture – an experience labeled as the fieldwork method – and then writes an account of this culture … These accounts are the primary form in which fieldwork procedures, the other culture, and the ethnographer's personal and theoretical reflections are accessible to professionals and other readerships. (ibid.)

The cause of the uncertainty lay in the largely unexamined incorporation of the 'generalist orientation' that underpinned positivism in descriptive practice, which resulted, for example, in Malinowski's functionalist account of the Kula ring as we discussed in Chap. 3. In other words, and somewhat ironically as we shall see, the uncertainty revolved around a concern with bringing general theories of society into the description of particular social occasions and events. This occasioned a new kind of holism marked by a shift away from developing total theories of society to understanding 'mental culture' – i.e., what it means to be a member of a particular culture. The shift recast interpretive anthropology as a relativistic enterprise in which the ethnographer acts as a cultural interpreter of local systems of meaning to provide a "jeweller's eye view" on the world. It was accompanied by a pervasive and highly self-conscious interest in the *writing* of ethnographic accounts – the primary form of access that others have to those local systems and the ethnographer who studied them. This 'highly self-conscious interest' (or critical self-reflection) in the production of ethnographic texts is what constitutes academic 'reflexivity', and to our minds it creates a confusion with respect to what it is that is of interest in the ethnographic undertaking.

Academic reflexivity places *the fieldworker*, not the people he or she is studying and the naturally accountable organisation of their day-to-day activities, *at the centre* of the ethnographic enterprise. It is marked by methodological interest in the communicative processes by which the fieldworker gains knowledge of his or her subjects, and thus becomes the pivot-point around which issues of *validity* turn.

> The validity of ethnographic interpretation came to rest on fuller understandings and dis-
> cussion of the research process itself … and the epistemological groundings of such
> accounts. (Marcus and Fischer 1986)

This, of course, may seem like an entirely reasonable matter. After all any science or rigorous means of inquiry must be able to account for how it knows the world – its methods as it were – but academic reflexivity reframes what is perceived as a positivistic expectation that an objective account of methods be provided by relocating epistemology in the fieldworker's accountable relationship with his or her subjects. In place of a conventional understanding of methods, the focus shifts to understanding how it is that interpretations are constructed by the fieldworker from the interpretations of his informants. This leads to the kind of claims made by Williams and Irani (2010), for example, that ethnography respecifies criteria of rigour by relocating it in "reflexive accounts generated by the body as an instrument of knowing" – the body in question being the ethnographer's, situated in the field (Conquergood 1991), hence our argument that academic reflexivity places the fieldworker and not the people he or she is studying at the centre of the ethnographic enterprise.

Academic reflexivity refocuses attention on the process of interpretation that *the ethnographer* engages in and develops to understand social life. This is seen as a challenging but essentially unproblematic move by Marcus and Fischer:

> [It] does not mean that the traditional rhetorics and task of anthropology to represent dis-
> tinctive and systematic cultural forms of life have been fundamentally subverted … Rather,

its traditional task is now much more complicated, requiring new sensibilities in undertaking fieldwork and different strategies for writing about it.

These 'new sensibilities' revolve around and focus attention on the ethnographic process of interpretation, and 'different strategies of writing' provide for the local elaboration of that process and the accountable relationship it enabled the ethnographer to foster with his or her subjects – in short, how it is that the ethnographer came to 'know' other cultural forms of life. By way of example, Marcus and Fischer elaborate 'defamiliarisation' strategies (see Bell et al. 2005) and Van Maanen (1988) elaborates 'confessional' and 'impressionistic' strategies (see Rode 2011), but reflexive strategies of writing are today diverse and ever developing, driven by broad theoretical interests in the social sciences. If they share anything in common apart from an analytic commitment to critical self-reflection then it is their avowed counter-position to what Van Maanen calls "realist tales".

Realist tales are described as flat and dry in comparison to their reflexive counterparts, focusing on regular and often-observed activities in a setting and making use of quotations from the setting's members to convey to readers, as Van Maanen puts it,

> … that the views put forward are not those of the fieldworker but are rather authentic and representative remarks transcribed straight from the horse's mouth.

Ethnomethodology is cited as a "realist mode" of ethnography, which seeks to elaborate the perspective and practices of a setting's members and in whose accounts the author of the text (thus) disappears from view. Van Maanen argues that realist tales trade on the assumption that what the fieldworker saw and heard in the field is more or less what anyone else would see and hear. However, academic reflexivity challenges the assumption that there is in effect an objective reality that is knowable independent of the particular observer, and takes it instead that what is seen and heard and what therefore comes to be known is always dependent *on the observer*, on the ethnographic self towards which so much critical reflection is therefore directed.

In an attempt to educate designers as to how to read and interpret ethnography, Dourish (2014) puts it like this,

> What does it mean to suggest that the self is an instrument of knowing? It requires us to imagine that the process of ethnographic fieldwork – going places to see what happens – is not merely a question of traveling to the places where things happen in order to witness them but is more about the insertion of the ethnographer into the scene. That is, if we think about ethnography's primary method as participant-observation, then it directs our attention towards the importance of participation not just as a natural and unavoidable consequence of going somewhere, but as the fundamental point. This, in turn, suggests that question that often arises in interdisciplinary investigations – "doesn't the ethnographer alter things by being there?" – is ill-founded on the face of it. That is, the ethnographer absolutely alters things by being there, in exactly the same way as every other participant to the scene alters things by being there; indeed, there is "no there" without the participation of whatever motley band of people produce any particular occasion …

This reflexive view on the world suggests that knowing very much turns upon the ethnographer's interventions in the world and the relationships he or she develops with 'whatever motley band' they are studying during the course of those interventions. Academic reflexivity is all about explaining the nature of that intervention – i.e., the process whereby an interpretation of the motley band's cultural forms of life was constructed in and through fieldwork – and in this respect reflexive writing strategies have two distinctive purposes.

In the first instance these strategies are intended to help the reader validate an ethnographic account. They provide, as Marcus and Fischer (1986) put it, "readers with ways of monitoring and evaluating the sources of information presented." It is notable that these strategies are not members' strategies but anthropological strategies extraneous to the actual situations they offer interpretations about. Nonetheless, an ethnographer who fails to demonstrate academic reflexivity in his or her writing is going to find their account invalidated by the professional anthropological community. In the second instance, and arguably in reaction to those of us who might argue against what is essentially an *idealist* position and suggest that there is for society's members a world out there that anyone can go and see and hear, and that what they see and hear does not necessarily depend on the theory-ladeness of observation, nor does it necessarily mean that they will alter what goes on in the course of seeing and hearing it, then reflexive writing strategies are purposed with the problem of understanding what has been seen and heard. Thus, even if the interpretive anthropologist were to concede that there is an objective reality out there that can be realistically described – which of course is never going to happen – there would still remain the problem of working out what it *means*. As Van Maanen (1988) puts it

> … it is no longer adequate for the fieldworker to tell us what the native does day in and day out. We must know what the native makes of all this as well.

Understanding the meaning of specific cultural forms of life is, for Marcus and Fischer, a challenging matter. The challenge consists in responding to critiques of relativism that sideline ethnographic studies for failing to connect local cultural forms of life to larger social organisational matters. The challenge for the interpretive ethnographer in working out the meaning of local cultural forms of life thus becomes one of working out, as Marcus and Fischer put it,

> … how to represent the embedding of richly described local cultural worlds in larger impersonal systems of political economy.

Understood as a representational problem this *problem of generalisation* is, again, seen as an issue of textual construction and Marcus and Fischer suggest that 'world-system theory' may be used as a means of building some vision of larger world-historical trends into ethnographic accounts (Dourish and Bell, as we have seen in chapter four, invoke the idea of *infrastructure* to do the same job). They also suggest that this will involve a radical reworking of the grounding assumptions by which anthropologists have conceptually constructed their subjects, one that recasts the subject of ethnographic inquiry from a setting inhabited by members to 'the system' (be it infrastructure or whatever other 'world-historical' motif is at hand at the time) and how it spans different cultural locales and even different continents.

> ... the point of this kind of project would be to start with some prior view of a macro system or institution, and to provide an ethnographic account of it, by showing the forms of local life that the system encompasses, and then proposing novel or revised views of the nature of the system itself, translating its abstract qualities in more fully human terms.

What we end up with, again, is the idea of multi-locale or multi-sited ethnography and the invocation of socio-cultural theories to 'contextualise' fieldwork, as we examined in the previous chapter.

Interpretive anthropology has come full circle then, first eschewing general theories of the social and adopting a relativist stance and then adopting general theory in order to avoid its studies being marginalised. Marcus and Fischer along with other interpretive anthropologists and those who draw on their work in other contexts obviously do not recognise the irony, seeing the reflexive approach as one that provides 'bottom up' views of the social rooted in the so-called 'messiness' of social action, in contrast to the overarching top down theories that sparked the crisis of representation in the first place. Nonetheless, any and every attempt to locate local order in 'visions of larger world-historical trends' inevitably obliges the ethnographer to engage in generic practices of sociological theorising, no matter which way round the theorising is construed of. The result (as we have seen in our discussion of infrastructure in Chap. 4) is that ethnography is thus purposed to render theoretical constructs real-worldly, at the expense (as we have seen in Chap. 3) of the action and interaction that actually goes on, on the ground and understanding its naturally accountable organisation, not that interpretive ethnography can handle that either.

Critical self-reflection or academic 'reflexivity' inevitably reduces the study of social action to the study of how it is that ethnographers can be said to know and understand the world. With it, the problem of adequate description of the social becomes a problem of writing texts that 'embed' the ethnographer's interpretation of social action in 'larger impersonal systems'. Now, from the point of view of systems design we might think, though of course we might be entirely wrong, that designers might feel somewhat cheated if what they got when they hired an ethnographer to inform the development of a computing system in some way was not an understanding of the social action the system was being designed to support, but an intellectual account of how the ethnographer went about interpreting what he or she saw and heard in the field and what that means in terms of the broader world-system that the people studied live in. A designer might, by way of example, take a look at Paul Willis's *Learning to Labour* (1977), a study of the schooling of working class males in the UK that Marcus and Fischer are fond of citing as in many ways exemplary and a designer might ask, were they to be tasked with building a computing system to support teaching and learning in this context, whether or not an interpretation of the local culture and its relationship to capitalism would help them build a computing system? What would they be building a system to support? What teaching and learning activities would the system support? Try as they might when they read the text they would not find an answer to these kinds of questions. These sorts of questions reflect of course, as we have previously noted, the sort of empirical interest in ethnographies of work as a means of furnishing requirements for systems, which have been strongly criticised by proponents of 'new' approaches to ethnography. Nevertheless they are the sorts of questions that actual systems designers have asked in the past and continue to ask as they seek not only to understand the contexts in which systems will be placed, but also to build systems that fit into them.

Despite the pervasive nature of academic reflexivity as a fundamental mode of inquiry and representation in the social and human sciences, its ability to handle practical matters – both of the accountable organisation of everyday life and the building of systems rooted in the social – begs questions as to the appropriateness of such an approach *in* and *for* systems design. Interpretive anthropology, as any other form of reflexive inquiry, is built on an inherent cognitivism that places the ethnographer at the centre: it's all about how 'I' conducted 'my' study and connect 'this' local situation to 'these' world-systems. It should be no surprise then that academic reflexivity *makes* ethnography into an inherently interpretive enterprise that can do nothing else but ignore the accountable organisation of everyday life, as there is little room in the interpretive ethnographer's *egocentric* world for anything but his or her own methodological ruminations. Even if everyday life were to smack the interpretive anthropologist in the face, the resulting account would still be about the ethnographer and how he or she interprets the meaning of any such action: as Garfinkel and Wieder (1992) put it, "eyeless in Gaza."

Nevertheless, it seems plain to mainstream ethnographers that ethnographic knowledge turns upon 'the body as an instrument of knowing', or the fieldworker 'being there' in more prosaic terms, and that academic reflexivity is, as Marcus and Fischer put it,

> … a means of attacking the naïveté of those who think cultural transmission can occur without mediation or interpretation, that ethnographers can merely be scribes …

There are, however, a number of confusions built into the idea of the body as an instrument of knowing, the role and effect of the ethnographer's participation, and the idea that understanding how participation gets done elaborates that which is participated in. Really all of these emanate from the way that the social sciences have *since their inception* understood their task to be one of *re*-interpreting what everyone knows about social life in terms of theoretical schemas, including the schemas of self-reflection. The first confusion here concerns the importance of 'particular cohort production' – i.e., that what is going on in the social world turns in some way on who is party to its production, and how they are party to it. In a sense it is taking the idea of addressing the actor's point of view to absurd lengths, and illustrates the problem of rendering the actor's point of view in terms of the actors themselves (Davies 1999). Ethnomethodology has respecified the actor not in terms of *who* they are but in terms of *what* they are accountably doing, not in the sense of what it is that they can be said to be doing, how their action can be interpreted if you like, but in terms of *how* they are doing that which they are recognisably doing (Czyzewski 1994). This is a radical re-orientation of the social science enterprise, an enterprise that in the hands of interpretive anthropology arrives at the absurd position that the interest is in the ethnographer and their study practices above the social world to which those practices are applied. Ethnomethodology's respecification of social science radicalises the very idea of the actor's point of view (Sharrock and Button 1991). An example might help, and we turn to a branch of ethnomethodology, conversation analysis, to make it.

It might be supposed that given the emphasis on situated action in ethnomethodological studies which have been done for design purposes that ethnomethodology places importance on the 'here and now', the context, the setting in which actions and interactions take place. This would be correct, but only in as much as it emphasises how social matters are ordered and organised as *local* achievements. This is not to say that the practices or methods involved in the local achievement of order are dependent upon who is involved. In the social sciences who people are typically matters for its descriptions, where the 'who' can be provided for by a particular social theory or methodology. For example, in conflict theory people are identified by their relationship to power; theories of patriarchy stress the gender identity of the person; or in methodological terms the 'who' is prescribed by the method, as with academic reflexivity where the identity of the author as, for example, an ethnographer, assumes importance. However, in a seminal paper on the 'systematics' of turn-taking in conversation Sacks et al. (1974) provide a powerful example of the ways in which the methods people use to order and organise their actions and interactions can cut across the identity of persons, that they can be *cohort independent*.

Thus Sacks et al. demonstrated that the orderliness of an exchange of turns in conversation is not dependent on *who* is involved. For instance, an exchange of greetings is in part organised in terms of 'adjacency pairs' – e.g. "Good morning." "Good Morning." – as a recognisable feature of turn-taking (Schegloff 2007) *irrespective* of the fact that it involves, for example, the headmaster of a school and a pupil or even a random selection of pupils, though it can accommodate just who is involved (e.g., "Good morning Jones.", "Good morning Headmaster."). Specifying just who is involved is not a requirement of conversational exchange, however, any more that specifying just where it takes place is. Thus, at the same time as turn-taking in conversation was shown to be cohort independent, it was also shown to be *setting independent*. The methodical ways in which people conduct talk cuts across different social environments then, such as conversation being carried out on an airplane, or at work, or in a restaurant, etc.[1]

None of this is to say that personal attributes and settings are not important for the organisation of human action and interaction. It is to say that their relevance is an occasioned matter, that they are made visibly relevant in peoples' actions and interactions. In other words, the relevance to a description of interaction in terms of its occurrence in a particular setting, or its being done by a person to whom a personal attribute may be assigned, resides in the action or interaction itself, not in some sociological characterisation underpinned and motivated by a particular social theory or methodology. Thus, for example, the relevance of the fact that talk is taking place in a court of law resides in the way in which people organise taking turns

---

[1] It is telling in this respect that some of the early material used by Sacks was gathered from therapy sessions and was used to describe how, for example, stories are constructed, not how 'therapy talk' is done (see Sacks' *Lectures on Conversation*).

at talk in courts of law, which often displays different characteristics to the organisation of turns at talk in casual conversation, and in the selection of the terms used to refer to persons (e.g., the witness, defense counsel, your honour, etc.), not in a sociological theory of power and the judiciary.

The point is that it is not so much the persons involved, the actors, that are of concern in conversation analysis but rather the methodical practices employed by people to order action and interaction as conversation; it is not 'the actors' that conversation analysis strives to address. Schegloff takes this point up in a response to Stivers and Rossano's (2010) description of initial turn-taking sequences, which they account for in terms of the way in which actors impose normative obligations on one another. However, conversation analysis, as Schegloff (2010) describes it is not concerned with what people do as actors but *how* they do what they do and how it is possible to gain an understanding of *how* they do what they do through an examination of their actions and interactions. It might appear that the difference is slight, and Stivers and Rossano might wonder at the force of Schegloff's problem. However, much turns on the difference between describing things in terms of *the doer* or *the doing*.

Starting off analysis from the actor's point of view means that issues such as who the actor or actors are might be relevant and what 'they' in this instance may require from particular 'others'. However, as conversation analysis has made perspicuous, the organisation of conversation cuts across issues of who – the organisation of talk in action and interaction is *independent of particular actors*. Thus it is not an actor that exerts a normative obligation on an interactant, it is the organisation of talk (just try breaching the situation next time someone you know greets you, try ignoring them and see what happens). Garfinkel, as we mentioned above, described how actions are done so as to be accountable, that is they are done so as to be recognisable as what they are, and this recognisability resides in the organisation of the action *not* in the person performing that action. It might otherwise be said that the orderliness of action is not a personal property. While individuals use the organisation of action to get the activities they are involved in done, the organisation is not *reducible* to individuals: you do greetings as they are recognisably done in your culture just like the next man or woman, you queue in the way in which queuing is recognisably done by the others around you, you drive in much the same way as well, and so on. You do things in the way in which everyone else does them because that is what your culture provides for and equips you with: methodical practices for producing and recognising action and interaction (Sacks 1984). Schegloff (2010) sums up what is of interest then in quoting Goffman,

> ... not persons and their moments, *but the organisation of those moments*. (our emphasis)

The second confusion raised by academic reflexivity concerns the very idea of reflexivity itself. It is a confusion introduced by the social sciences in the appropriation of the notion of reflexivity *from the everyday world*, where it is an indispensable part of the way in which members order action and interaction. In that appropriation the way in which reflexivity works and how its workings are used in the everyday world is *lost*. Garfinkel (1967) described reflexivity not as reflective state, self-critical or otherwise, but as an incarnate feature and inherent property of the practical organisation of everyday life; a constitutive feature of account-able action. The hyphen here is not accidental, it emphasises that action is done in such a way that members can recognise *and* describe it as the particular thing that it is. A simple example will hopefully clarify the point. Andy is walking out of the office; Graham and Peter are walking in. Graham knows Andy and says, "Hi Andy." Andy looks at Graham, makes no response and walks on by. Graham turns to Peter and says, "He snubbed me. He didn't even acknowledge I was there, let alone say hello!" Now any wide-awake member of society will see the snub in this. It is an ordinary if uncomfortable occurrence and while the whys and wherefores of it may not be apparent, that Graham has been snubbed by Andy is plain to see. What the ethnomethodological preoccupation with reflexivity would also have us see is *that* the snub can be and is an account-able matter for Graham and anyone else witnessing it *is* provided for by the methods implicated in its production: there is a reflexive relationship between recognising *what* was done and *how* it was done.

To unpack this we can see that one way in which a snub can be done is through *not doing something*, and quite visibly not doing it. Thus, the snub in this case has been done by Andy not doing what was provided for in Graham's initial greeting, which is to return it. As Schegloff (2010) would put it, the snub is done by a return greeting being 'noticeably absent'. The account "He snubbed me. He didn't even acknowledge I was there, let alone say hello!" brings to notice the absence of a return greeting and is, as such, tied methodically to the snub's production, to the not doing of that return greeting. The account is a constitutive part of the act then, not in the sense that it interprets what is being done, but in the sense that there is a *methodical relationship* between the *accounts* that members provide in the course of action and interaction and the *production* of recognisable social scenes and events (e.g., the witnessable doing of a snub). Thus, reflexivity in everyday life speaks to the entwined or interdependent relationship between action and its account-ability. This relationship is given and used by members in methodical ways, as Andy's snub was given to Graham in the above example in the noticeable absence of a return greeting. Reflexivity as a members' matter stands in stark contrast to reflexivity as used by the social sciences then. In everyday life it speaks to the methodical relationship between members' accounts and the settings, scenes and events they make observable (Garfinkel 1967), whereas in the social sciences the idea of reflexivity is used by to license reflection on one's investigative practices and theoretical interpretations of action.

The reflexivity of accounts in everyday life also makes it plain to see that members' are skilled *analysts* of the social order. They not only know how to put their actions together in methodical ways so as to provide for the recognition of their actions, they also know how to 'see' and 'read' those methodically assembled actions; hence Graham being able to account for what Andy did in not returning his greeting. This brings us full circle back to the matter of praxiology. The reflexivity of accounts invites the ethnographer to develop mastery in the methodical practices that members use to see, recognise and understand the social world. The reflexivity of accounts puts in place of the self-conscious ethnographer and the ethnographer as scribe an *apprentice* model of fieldwork (Lynch 1999); a model that puts emphasis on the ethnographer developing vulgar competence in the activities being investigated and the sketching out of praxiological accounts. These accounts provide both the ethnographer and the reader with 'tutorials' elaborating a setting's distinctive features – its local cultural forms of life if you will – and how they are made accountable in the methodical achievement of the situated interactional work that provides for their observability. This, in turn, elaborates the practices that reflexively provide for the recognisable orderliness of a setting's work.

While the tutorials may be viewed as interpretations in the ordinary sense of the word, that is, as 'just another' perspective on the social, they do not need to be 'contextualised' or embedded in larger impersonal systems in order to convey their meaning and generalise the results. On this view, the meaning of action is embedded in its accountability – in the observable and reportable sense it has for members as they go about doing, seeing, recognising and reasoning about action. Meaning is, then, *built in* to action and the methodical ways in which it is built in provide for the generalisation of ethnographic results, not as reflexive interpretations embedded in larger impersonal schemes but as praxiological accounts that *display* the practices that members use to recognisably assemble their activities as accountable affairs in society (Sharrock and Randall 2004). The generalisations provided by praxiological accounts are not of the same order as those provided by generic practices of sociological theorising then. Generic practices of sociological theorising do generalisation by extrapolating, through theoretical means of interpretation as elaborated in Chap. 4, from some specific activity or cultural form of life to broader world systems. Whereas praxiological generalisations operate by describing the practices that members use to see and recognise what Sharrock and Randall call 'the regularities' of everyday life. Practices, in other words, that enable *members* to detect and analyse the orderliness of action (e.g., to see and recognise what Duhem's experimenter is doing) and which elaborate that order in being reflexively implicated in its naturally accountable production (Crabtree et al. 2012).

The rub then with respect to reflexivity is that the social sciences have appropriated an ordinary feature of social life to do ethnography, but in that appropriation they have made reflexivity into a disciplinary matter as opposed to a members' matter; a matter for intellectual consideration, rather than a practical matter bound up with the organised conduct of social life. The base assumption that witnessing something involves mediating it by being there and interpreting it through a theory leads to a dilemma of not being able to touch the thing mediated because it only exists in its interpretation. In these terms there is, as Dourish puts it, "no there" there, nothing that exists independently of the ethnographer. There is only that which is constituted through participation. Hence the necessity for reflexive examination of the ethnographer's mediating and interpretative practices, for that is all there is. Thus all ethnography can be is a reflection on how *it* engages with the world and what *it* finds in that engagement.

Nevertheless, and putting the absurdities of idealism aside, just by being in the world it is obvious to any wide-awake member of society that the world is full of 'heres' and 'theres' and full of things taking place within them. The world is like that for the interpretive ethnographer when he or she takes his or her academic hat off, just as it is for anyone else. They are snubbed; they snub. They misunderstand; they are misunderstood. They do *things* to other people and they have things done to them. And they do the things that they do in recognisable places, 'here' and 'there'. It does not take an act of interpretation based on some social theory to recognise action in the world. A spouse packing their bags, banging doors and remaining steadfastly mute as they walk out does not require some theory to be used to interpret that they are leaving home; it is plain to see that they are leaving in the doing of these things. Is the interpretive ethnographer going to stand and reflect on how their theory enables them to interpret this, or are they going to breakdown in tears or shout out "come back" or "good riddance"?

None of this is naïve realism; it is understanding that society's members live in a world of 'heres' and 'theres' animated by the things they do *independently* of the interpretive ethnographer's imagination. Ethnomethodology respecifies understanding of the world as residing in members' analyses of it, analyses provided for through *their* reflexive practices, which are constitutive of the world.[2] The point of note here is that, understood in these terms, the ethnographer is not merely a scribe noting down what they see, or an interpreter constituting 'heres' and 'theres' in the world through a mediating social theory. Rather, the ethnographer is being instructed in the 'heres' and 'theres' of the world by those doing the things that accountably animate the specificities of social life and make them demonstrably real and concrete. Such things, such specificities, such settings, scenes and events that actually make up the social world we live in, may and indeed will be done by some 'motley gang'. However, what is done *does not* turn on the gang's personnel, but on the organising methods of action and interaction the gang observably and reportably employ to get their business 'here' and 'there' done.

A last point here with regard to the significance of the reflexivity of action. Whenever we give an example we turn to simple, what some might call trivial, examples, such as greetings'. We can understand how it might appear that questions regarding the larger social system in which local actions and interactions could be seen to take place in, or questions as to the meaning that technology has in a culture, may seem to the designer, as indeed they seem to the mainstream social scientist, to be ones that are more important than people saying hello to one another, or not saying hello as the case may be. However, we need to bear in mind what is at stake here. In describing the snub, for example, we are not merely describing what happened between Andy and Graham, but are using what happened between them to make visible that the real world intelligibility of members' accounts in general is provided for through particular methodical practices which organise the social world. Thus, in the snub we view a particular *ordering mechanism* at work: not doing something that has been provided for. It would be short-sighted to see any such a mechanism as trivial, for indeed wars have been accounted for in these terms.

---

[2] This, of course, is a strong claim to make, especially with regards to the world of 'natural facts'. See Garfinkel et al. (1981) for a detailed explication of the point.

At 11.15 on 3rd September 1939, Neville Chamberlain, the then Prime Minister of Britain, declared war on Germany in the following statement:

> This morning the British Ambassador in Berlin handed the German Government a final Note stating that, unless we heard from them by 11 o'clock that they were prepared at once to withdraw their troops from Poland, a state of war would exist between us. I have to tell you now that no such undertaking has been received, and that consequently this country is at war with Germany.

Here, Chamberlain is making it visible that something that was provided for – word that the German Government was prepared to withdraw their troops from Poland – was noticeably not done. Social mechanisms of action and interaction may be used to do things we might characterise as trivial, but they might also be used to do things considered momentous. Schegloff's quotation from Goffman is again apposite:

> ... not persons and their moments, but the organisation of those moments.

5.3 Objectivity and Realism

The interpretive anthropologist, like most mainstream social scientists, is likely to insist that praxiological accounts are nothing more than realist tales and that we are, despite our objections, naïve realists who would perpetuate an outmoded 'objective' program of research. Merritt (2011), by way of example, insists that,

> Crabtree, et al., believe that ethnography in HCI research should only be used according to the former status quo ... [they] argue for objective, empirical observations for use in HCI design ...

The issue of objectivity and the idea that social reality is independent of the descriptions that can be given of it have troubled social science from its very beginnings. However, those troubles are ones that arise for the social sciences in the ways in which they have developed an understanding of what it is to do social science, and they become ones that are omni-relevant. This contrasts with the ways in which objectivity and reality are spoken about in the everyday world, where neither are omni-relevant matters, but occasioned ones.

We can and do perfectly well use the words 'objective' and 'reality' as everyday matters without a problem. Someone's wife really did leave him, for example, and while he is a friend we are trying to be objective about it because it has to be said, he really did give her a hard time. Problems in the use of these words arise when the social sciences, as we have seen that they do with other words, appropriate them for the purposes of doing social science. Since social science descriptions of what is really going on in the social world are often at odds with descriptions that people might give of their own doings, and at odds with each other, some way of *legitimising* those descriptions has been sought. Initially this was done through the use of positivist methodologies, which were deemed to be 'objective' in mimicking the natural sciences, but as these began to be questioned ideas associated with the view that reality is socially constructed, and thus available to reflexive inquiry, came to the forefront. Although they can be juxtaposed against one another, neither positivistic objectivity nor constructionist reflexivity guarantees insight into social arrangements. As Lynch writes,

> … attempting to *be* reflexive takes one no closer to a central source of illumination than attempting to *be* objective … *Ordinary* and *occasional* virtues and difficulties can be ascribed to thinking about what one is doing … but reflexivity *in general* offers no guarantee of insight or revelation. (Lynch 2000)

Egon Bittner, writing some time ago in 1973 elaborates difficulties in both the positivist position and reactions to it, providing substance for Lynch's later remarks.

> For many years … strict compliance with certain canons of objectivity alone guaranteed the attainment of all objectives of rational inquiry. Clearly this is no longer the prevailing view … Quite the contrary, in some quarters objectivity has fallen into ill repute and is explicitly denounced … even where the criteria of objectivity are adhered to … much less is made of it than used to be the case. But neither contempt nor neglect will make the problem of objectivity disappear and sociologists cannot – must not – divest themselves of the responsibility for rendering an accounting of the way in which they try to do justice to the realities they study. (Bittner 1973)

Now Bittner's insistence could be taken as an invitation not only to sociologists but to other social scientists as well to engage in academic reflexivity: to render an account of the ways in which *we* try to do justice to the social realities that *we* study. The reader might take the invitation to be underscored given Bittner's critique of the "naïve realism" built into the positivist paradigm that was dominant in the 1960s, which essentially sought to impose a model of natural scientific inquiry on the study of the social and which lives on today in quantitative modes of inquiry.

However, on closer inspection Bittner is not simply arguing that what makes positivism naively realistic is a misplaced analytic commitment to the rationality of natural science, but the unexplicated predication of the objective study of society on what *anyone knows about it.*

> … naïve realism … entails the belief that the knowledge normally competent, wide awake adults have of the world around them, about the society in the midst of which they live, and concerning human affairs *is*, despite its ambiguity, uncertainty, and incompleteness, an adequate beginning point for more systematic study aimed at the removal of these inadequacies … … … Although … the proverbial man on the street has motives in seeking information that differ substantially from the motives that move scientific curiosity … naïve realism … meant the unexamined acceptance of the reality of the world of everyday experience as a heuristic fact …

Positivism is naively realistic then not so much because it adopts the model of natural science but because it is based in unexplicated ways on common-sense reasoning (something we have encountered in previous chapters and which we will elaborate on in more depth in Chap. 7). This means that dispensing with the objectivity of natural science does not of itself *dispense with naïve realism* because what anyone knows about society remains the unacknowledged bedrock of interpretive approaches to social science as well as positivistic ones.

Interpretive programs and the idealist critiques that underpin reflexive arguments against objectivity are consequently as problematic as the programs of positivism, as they offer no guarantee that naïve realism will be dispensed with either.

> ... the fieldworker ... forever confronts 'someone's social reality' ... when he dwells on the fact that this reality is to 'them' incontrovertibly real in just the way 'they' perceive it, he knows that to some 'others' it may seem altogether different, and that, in fact, the most impressive feature of the social world is its colorful plurality. Indeed, the more seriously he takes this observation, the more he relies on his sensitivity as an observer who has seen first hand how variously things can be perceived, the less likely he is to perceive those traits of depth, stability, and necessity that people recognise as actually inherent in the circumstances of their existence. Moreover ... he renders them in ways that far from being realistic are actually heavily intellectualised constructions that partake more of the character of theoretical formulation than of realistic description.

Bittner's commentary is anything but an invitation to academic reflexivity as a fundamental mode of inquiry and representation. Rather, he problematises positivistic and interpretive approaches in equal measure. You can no more understand someone else's social reality through the imposition of a natural scientific model than you can by rendering theoretical 'formulations' or interpretations of it.

Bittner's is not a critique of objectivity per se then, only of the positivist version of it and interpretive reactions to it. The problem is not one of getting rid of objectivity in social science research, but of figuring out what it might actually amount to.

> ... it still remains to be made clear what objectivity in sociology might consist of, if it were to take full account of the objects of social science inquiry in their actually given nature ... What then is left for a new start?

Bittner's comments stand the charge of naïve realism levelled at ethnomethodological studies on its head. It is not ethnomethodology that is naïvely realistic, the positivistic and reflexive social sciences are because they build in common-sense knowledge of society as a 'heuristic fact', assuming and using its commonly known features without understanding how those features are themselves brought about as organised features of everyday life. This is a familiar early charge of ethnomethodology against social science. The 'new start' that Bittner refers to involves suspending the common-sense perspective, or 'bracketing' it off in ethnomethodological terminology, to investigate its orderly properties and how members display and use them in their actions and interactions.

Ethnomethodology's intent in making this new start was and is to investigate the knowledge that normally competent people have of the world around them and the society in the midst of which they live. Not abstractly, but concretely in particular settings and in the conduct of particular actions and interactions that make up their affairs. Rather than trade in generic definitions of objectivity and reality, ethnomethodology sought, and continues in this vein, to understand what constitutes objective reality from the perspective of society's members *as they go about their daily business*. The production of praxiological accounts was and is a means of doing this, of describing what the members of the settings we investigate take to be objective features of their lives: the activities that take place in their world; the ways in which they are done and reflexively organised; the taken for granted knowledge the doing and organising relies upon; the schemes of interpretation this knowledge provides for; and the meaning those schemes of interpretation enable members to ascribe to society as an objectively accountable feature of *their social reality*. Objectivity and reality are then matters for members, just as reflexivity is a members' matter.

There are, of course, ethnographers working in an interpretive tradition that object strongly to the suggestion that interpretive forms of ethnography are no better equipped to provide empirical insight into social reality and the organisation of everyday life than positivistic approaches. Blomberg and Karasti (2013), for example, insist that interpretive approaches are just as capable as an ethnomethodological approach at understanding social reality as it is practically encountered and practically organised by the parties to it:

> … we do contest Crabtree et al.'s implication that interpretive ethnography is not focused on 'detailed empirical studies of what people do and how they organise action and interaction in particular settings'. To the contrary, as Geertz argues, ethnography is always tied to the details of the lived experiences of the people studied … … … we do not concur [then] with those who suggest 'new' … ethnographic approaches do not provide a valuable contribution to CSCW … On the contrary, we believe as the saying goes 'the proof is in the eating' …

Blomberg and Karasti's comments are not confined to Computer Supported Cooperative Work but apply to ethnography and systems design more generally. Their response to the kinds of arguments we have made about interpretive approaches is, however, itself problematic in two key respects.

First, and to be clear, Geertz does indeed argue that ethnography is always tied to the details of the lived experiences of the people studied:

> If anthropological interpretation is constructing a reading of what happens, then to divorce it from what happens – from what, in this time or that place, specific people say, what they do, what is done to them, from the whole vast business of the world – is to divorce it from its applications and render it vacant. A good interpretation of anything – a poem, a person, a history, a ritual, an institution, a society – takes us into the heart of that of which it is the interpretation. (Geertz 1973)

However, and as noted in Chaps. 2 and 3, Geertz *also* points out that the locus of an interpretive ethnographic study "is not the object of study". The object of study for Geertz is the imputed structural forces at play on people in the situations they find themselves. What people do in their situated actions is, then, a platform from which to view structural forces at work. Conflating Geertz with ethnomethodology's interests in empirical studies of situated action not only misunderstands ethnomethodology, it also misunderstands Geertz. Ethnomethodological studies treat situated action as a *topic* of investigation and focus on the explication of the orderliness of action and interaction as it is achieved by a setting's members. Interpretive ethnography on the other hand focuses on the interpretation of situated action and thus on how it is perceived as a *resource* for thinking "creatively and imaginatively" about the "mega-concepts" in social science (ibid.) – i.e., as a resource for sociological theorising. As Garfinkel and Wieder (1992) make clear the two are incommensurate and irreconcilable, which makes Blomberg's and Karasti's comments difficult to understand (unless of course they have not understood Garfinkel in the first place).

It is, perhaps, to counter our objections to interpretive ethnography that Blomberg and Karasti hold out what looks like an olive branch:

> As Randall et al. (2001) argue, '… what justification we have for arguing that any particular thing is 'going on' should be evident in the data and open for inspection.' Perhaps on this point ethnomethodological and interpretive ethnography can agree.

The evidential nature of social studies of course is something we agree with, just as we agreed with Dourish and Bell's (2011) emphasis on analysis. However, these particular calls place analysis in the hands of the social scientist, and (as discussed in detail in Chap. 4) the documentary methods of interpretation they use to evidence their claims. The social world that the social scientist seeks to analyse is itself reflexively produced in the analyses that members are doing of it as an ongoing and account-able feature of their actions and interactions. The reflexivity built into action and interaction contrasts with the reflexive way of seeing the world and accounting for its organisation that is manifest in interpretive anthropology. Academic reflexivity is not an analytic approach that elaborates how someone else's social reality is seen and recognised as an objective order of affairs constituted *in* everyday action and interaction. The alternative is to understand objectivity and reality as these matters are turned in member's accounts and the reflexive constitution of the social occurrences, scenes and events that make up and shape *their* world. Objectivity and reality in the social sciences has little to do with this, however, but rather with how these matters can be turned for the doing of social science. The distinction her is not theoretical but an easily – indeed an absurdly easily – visible matter: the objective world and social reality are manifest in member's (not social analyst's) actions and interactions. In the next chapter we examine how people interactionally constitute as an objective matter just *what* is going on in their actions and interactions, and how the 'interactional what' of social action is *missing* from mainstream social science accounts.

References

Bell, G., Blythe, M., & Sengers, P. (2005). Making by making strange: Defamilarisation and the design of domestic technologies. *ACM Transactions on Computer-Human Interaction (TOCHI), 12*(2), 149–173.

Bittner, E. (1973). Objectivity and realism in sociology. In G. Psathas (Ed.), *Phenomenological sociology: Issues and applications* (pp. 109–125). New York: Wiley Interscience.

Blomberg, J., & Karasti, H. (2013). Reflections on 25 years of ethnography in CSCW. *Computer Supported Cooperative Work: The Journal of Collaborative Computing, 22*, 373–423.

Conquergood, D. (1991). Rethinking ethnography: Towards a critical cultural politics. *Communication Monographs, 58*, 179–194.

Coulter, J., & Parsons, E. (1990). The praxiology of perception: Visual orientations and practical action. *Inquiry, 33*(3), 251–272.

Crabtree, A., Rouncefield, M., & Tolmie, P. (2012). *Doing design ethnography*. London: Springer.

Crabtree, A., Tolmie, P. Rouncefield, M. (2013). 'How many bloody examples do you want?' – Fieldwork and generalisation. In *Proceedings of the European conference on computer supported cooperative work* (pp. 1–20). Paphos: Springer.

Czyzewski, M. (1994). Reflexivity of actors versus the reflexivity of accounts. *Theory, Culture & Society, 11*, 161–168.

Davies, C. (1999). *Reflexive ethnography: A guide to researching selves and others*. London: Routledge.

Dourish, P. (2014). Reading and interpreting ethnography. In J. Olson & W. Kellogg (Eds.), *Ways of knowing in HCI* (pp. 1–24). New York: Springer.

Dourish, P., & Bell, G. (2011). *Divining a digital future: Mess and mythology in ubiquitous computing*. Cambridge, MA: MIT Press.

Garfinkel, H. (1967). *Studies in ethnomethodology*. Englewood-Cliffs: Prentice-Hall.

Garfinkel, H. (2001). *Ethnomethodology's program: Working out Durkheim's aphorism*. Lanham: Rowman and Littlefield.

Garfinkel, H., & Wieder, D. L. (1992). Two incommensurable, asymmetrically alternate technologies of social analysis. In G. Watson & R. Seiler (Eds.), *Text in context: Contributions to ethnomethodology* (pp. 175–206). London: Sage.

Garfinkel, H., Lynch, M., & Livingston, E. (1981). The work of a discovering science construed with materials from the optically discovered pulsar. *Philosophy of the Social Sciences, 11*, 131–158.

Geertz, C. (1973). *The interpretation of cultures: Selected essays* (pp. 3–30). New York: Basic Books.

Hanson, N. (1958). *Patterns of discovery: An inquiry into the conceptual foundations of science*. Cambridge: Cambridge University Press.

Hutchinson, P., Read, R., & Sharrock, W. (2008). *There is no such thing as a social science*. Farnham: Ashgate.

Lynch, M. (1999). Silence in context: Ethnomethodology and social theory. *Human Studies, 22*, 211–233.

Lynch, M. (2000). Against reflexivity as an academic virtue and source of privileged knowledge. *Theory, Culture & Society, 17*(3), 26–54.

Marcus, G., & Fischer, M. (1986). *Anthropology as cultural critique: An experimental moment in the human sciences*. Chicago: The University of Chicago Press.

Merritt, S. (2011). Toward improved ethnography for transnational HCI. In *Proceedings of the SIGCHI conference on human factors in computing systems*, workshop 30. Transnational HCI, May 8th, Vancouver: ACM. www.princeton.edu/~jvertesi/TransnationalHCI/Participants_files/Merritt.pdf

Randall, D., Marr, L., & Rouncefield, M. (2001). Ethnography, ethnomethodology and interaction analysis. *Ethnographic Studies, 6*, 31–44.

Rode, J. (2011). Reflexivity in digital anthropology. In *Proceedings of the SIGCHI conference on human factors in computing systems* (pp. 123–132). Vancouver: ACM.

Sacks, H. (1984). Notes on methodology. In J. M. Maxwell & J. Heritage (Eds.), *Structures of social action: Studies in conversation analysis* (pp. 21–27). Cambridge: Cambridge University Press.

Sacks, H. (1992). The baby cried. The mommy picked it up. In G. Jefferson (Ed.), *Lectures on conversation* (Vol. I, Part III Spring 1966, Lecture 1 (R), pp. 243–251). Oxford: Blackwell.

Sacks, H., Schegloff, E., & Jefferson, G. (1974). A simplest systematics for the organisation of turn-taking for conversation. *Language, 50*(4), 696–735.

Schegloff, E. (2007). The adjacency pair as the unit for sequence construction. In *Sequence organisation in interaction: A primer in conversation analysis* (pp. 13–21). Cambridge: Cambridge University Press.

Schegloff, E. (2010). Commentary on Stivers and Rossano: Mobilizing response. *Research on Language and Social Interaction, 43*(1), 38–48.

Sharrock, W. & Button, G. (1991). The social actor: social action in real time. In *Ethnomethodology and the human sciences* (pp. 137–175). Cambridge: Cambridge University Press.

Sharrock, W., & Randall, D. (2004). Ethnography, ethnomethodology and the problem of generalisation in design. *European Journal of Information Systems, 13*, 186–194.

Stivers, T., & Rossano, F. (2010). Mobilizing response. *Research on Language and Social Interaction, 43*(1), 3–31.

Van Maanen, J. (1988). *Tales of the field: On writing ethnography*. Chicago: University of Chicago Press.

Williams, A. & Irani, L. (2010). There's methodology in the madness: Toward critical HCI ethnography. In *Proceedings of the SIGCHI conference on human factors in computing systems – Extended abstracts* (pp. 2725–2734). Atlanta: ACM.

Willis, P. (1977). *Learning to labour: How working class kids get working class jobs*. Farnborough: Saxon House.

Chapter 6
The Missing What of Ethnographic Studies

Abstract In this chapter we look at how various kinds of ethnographic studies done within social science and systems design have tended to generate 'scenic descriptions' of action and interaction. Scenic description orients us to grossly observable features of action and interaction without examining the 'just how' of its doing, i.e., just how what was done was done so as to pull it off as the thing that grossly observable is. This concern with the *absence* of the lived orderliness of action and interaction is framed in terms of the discussion of 'work' as it is understood within ethnomethodological studies. The critical thing to note here is that 'work' is not restricted to what goes on in the workplace but is a *generic feature* of interaction. It draws attention to the fact that action and interaction, wherever it takes place, is always an *achievement*. The work of interaction is all too often missed in ethnographic studies, resulting in descriptions of human activity that have the character of 'X did this, and Y did that', without lifting the lid on *how* it is done as an organised interactional accomplishment. The problem here is that if ethnography resides at a scenic level of description, detailing merely observed behaviour that anyone can see, it can and will *misdirect* designers' understanding of the foundational relationship between ethnography and systems design and what designers can hope to take away from ethnographic studies.

6.1 Scenic Description

We have been examining the idea of ethnography as it developed in anthropology and have attempted to track through some of the consequences of rendering understandings of culture and society through theoretical interpretation. In doing so we have attempted to explain our concerns about the return to traditional anthropological practices introduced by 'new' approaches to ethnography in systems design, and the confusions about the nature of the social and its investigation that accompany them, which have been problematic within the social sciences since their inception. However, another closely associated social science – sociology – has also developed a strong ethnographic character, so much so that the boundaries between anthropology and sociology have become increasingly blurred and mainstream ethnography has come to reflect the innate tendencies of both disciplines. Like anthropology,

G. Button et al., *Deconstructing Ethnography*, Human-Computer
Interaction Series, DOI 10.1007/978-3-319-21954-7_6

ethnography in sociology has been mainly associated with disciplinary interest in culture and social structure. In turning to 'new' approaches to ethnography from the social sciences, we are also worried then about the way in which many ethnographies conducted for the purposes of systems design incorporate problematic characteristics associated with ethnography in sociology, particularly the production of *scenic* in distinction to *analytic* descriptions of human action (Button 2000).

While the call for 'new' ethnography is, in part, articulated by a break with empirical interest in the social that has been associated with design's engagement with ethnography to date (Dourish 2006), other approaches to ethnography hold on to the idea of empirical investigation but view this as involving matters other than those associated with previous 'studies of work'. Before we turn to these it is worth reminding the reader that we are not trying to legislate as to what aspects of the social systems design could or should be interested in, or how it should be interested in it. Rather, we are concerned to make visible what it is that systems design is buying into should it take up alternate approaches to ethnography. Our concerns here can be elaborated by considering the kinds of problems that have been encountered by sociologists in the study of work and occupations. As noted above, we have so far been examining how traditional anthropological approaches to ethnography are being tracked into design and the problems this raises. We will proceed in the same way with respect to our examination of more empirically-based approaches, first examining problems inherent in early empirical studies of work in sociology, and then finding those problems in ethnographies done for design purposes, both in work and non-work settings or under the auspices of work or non-work interests.

The history of sociology's interest in work has been crafted in the investigations of many and varied people and perspectives over a great many years. The different theoretical auspices they have laboured under and the different characterisations of the nature of work they have produced can be invoked for the purposes of presenting catalogues of, and introductions to, the sociology of work. Despite profound differences in perspective, there is sufficient similarity in the sociological orientation to the study of work to allow the following remarks made by Anslem Strauss and his colleagues (1985) to ring true.

> … remarkably little writing in the sociology of work begins with the work itself (except descriptively, not analytically) but focuses on the division of labour, on work roles, role relationships, careers, and the like. A concerted *analytic examination of work itself* ought to provide a needed corrective to more traditional approaches, which, however effective, still leave important issues untouched or unresolved.

An examination of Keith Grint's popular introduction to the sociology of work (Grint 1991) would seem to bear out Strauss et al.'s remarks. If the sociology of work were concerned with the 'work itself' then we might find in an introduction such as Grint's descriptions of work activity, how work is done, what distinguishes some work from other work, or what makes some work similar to other work in terms of how it is done, and the like. However, instead of introducing the sociology of work in these *analytic* terms, Grint introduces it in *definitional* terms by considering both sociological and cultural characterisations of work. Grint highlights problems in the definition of work. He points to the way in which work is traditionally defined in terms of paid employment within western industrial societies, and argues that such definitions can make some work invisible, such as the domestic labour of 'housework' which although unpaid is nevertheless work. Grint goes on to consider the classical theories of work presented by Marx, Weber and Durkheim, and the contemporary theories of post-modernism and actor-network theory. His final move is to then use work as a structure from which to view social stratification, examining phenomena such as conflict, class, gender, patriarchy, resistance, race, ethnicity, markets, and politics.

If we wanted a synoptic view of work from a sociological point of view then it is clear that work is treated as an *object for theoretical definition* and a vehicle for apprehending the varied structural forces postulated by sociology, as opposed to a *situated practical undertaking* that is available for analytic study. These remarks are not particularly intended as a criticism of Grint. Our point is that he does indeed do a commendable job of introducing the sociology of work, but that in so doing he provides a characterisation of what the sociology of work amounts to that bears out Strauss's remarks. The sociology of work is not so much about work itself but about the social and organisational conditions under which work, whatever that might be, is conducted and the social characteristics that may be attributed to cohorts who conduct it.

It is also the case that the particular conditions and the particular characteristics that any particular sociological study of work elaborates derive from the particular sociological theory under whose auspices the study is conducted. Thus, for example, Braverman's (1974) depiction of the dehumanising conditions of work results from his confronting Taylorism with a Marxist examination of monopoly capitalism, while Firestone's (1970) depiction of patriarchal subordination implicit in domestic labour derives from a radical feminist theory of cultural reproduction. The sociology of work would thus seems preoccupied with '*scenic*' features of work – i.e., observable and reportable features of the social world that are drawn upon to frame and set the stage upon which work is conducted. Gender distribution is, for example, a scenic feature of work. No doubt such a statement will raise some hackles. However, take the following example before crucifying us. Statistics on the number of women engineers may be used as evidence for a number of social inferences such as the way in which women are viewed in society, or the way in which particular types of work are viewed in society, or the challenges facing women in what are traditionally male roles, or the organisation of the education system, etc. All of these matters might be socially interesting and important in their own right, however, interesting as such inferences may be, they do not inform us as to what it is to *do*, for example, engineering work, whether it is done by men or by women. The doing of work is taken for granted and ignored, and it is in that respect that the personal attributes of the engineer, that they are a man, a woman, tall, short, black or white, heterosexual or GLBTI, is a scenic feature of the work of engineering.

One way in which Strauss's comments can be read – a 'lite' version if you will – is to read them not so much as a critique of scenic description but that the very *doing* of work could and should be a proper sociological topic. However, the difference between the sociology of work as it is depicted in (for example) Grint's rendition, and the sociology of work as gestured at by Strauss is, we believe, about more than extending the remit of the sociology of work. If it were just about extending the remit then it might be possible, on the lite reading at least, for sociologists to shrug their shoulders and permit the realisation of Strauss's ambitions within the arena of sociology's traditional concerns. It would be possible for the sociology of work to continue to spin out its definitions and theoretical formulations and to also take up Strauss's invitation to study the actual composition of work. On this lite reading, Strauss is not challenging the foundations of the sociology of work by putting the very ways in which it formulates an understanding of its subject matter into question. He is merely proposing a further domain of interest: the doing of work itself. However, a stronger reading of Strauss is possible if we consider the implications of scenic description – that the actual organised conduct of work is *absent* and *will always be absent* from such accounts. On this stronger reading, Strauss's comments may indeed be read as criticising the sociology of work, not merely providing it with further investigatory opportunities.

Though only gestured at in Grint's introduction, there is a body of investigations in the sociology of work, and one with which Strauss is strongly associated, that *has* attempted to address what it is that people actually *do*. This work originated in the 1920s and is primarily associated with the Chicago School of Sociology. To name the anthropologists and sociologists associated with the Chicago School is to make a roll call of some of the most influential researchers in the social sciences: Anderson, Burgess, Frazier, Hughes, Mead, McKenzie, Park, Sutherland, Thomas, Wirth, and Znaniecki, to name but a few. Their research marked a step change in ethnographic interest, shifting it from something preoccupied with non-western societies and cultures to focus on life much closer to home. The Chicago School took the city as its subject matter, and through numerous extensive and detailed ethnographic examinations of urban life subjected the city to an order of examination previously reserved for 'other' societies and cultures. Indeed, early work reflected previous anthropological interests in the slums of Mexico, for example, and resulted in a host of pioneering ethnographic studies of life in the western industrial ghetto (see, for example, Thrasher 1927; Wirth 1928; Zorbaugh 1929).

The Chicago School gave rise to whole new branches of social science, developing *urban sociology* for example, which examines how major themes of sociology such as deviancy, power, class, status, race, gender and the like are played out in the city, and *human ecology*, which has now become an interdisciplinary concern focusing on the relationship between human behaviour and the built environment. Of particular relevance to our concerns in this book is the development of *symbolic interactionism*, a term coined by one of George Herbert Mead's PhD students, Herbert Blumer, in 1937 (Prus 1996) to reflect growing disciplinary interest in the social order as the ongoing accomplishment of human interaction (Blumer 1969). Spurred on by the pioneering efforts of Everrett C. Hughes, who saw the ordering of society as "very much a matter of man's (sic) relation to the world of work" and who fostered the study of "the orderly course of man's work life", symbolic interactionists built up a wide array of studies of a heterogeneous range of occupations (Hughes 1958). As Shaffir and Pawluch (2003) put it,

> Hughes sent his students into the city to study the janitor, the cab driver, the doctor, the union official, the factory worker, the musician, and others. Such studies helped lay the groundwork for the qualitative tradition in sociology and furthered our understanding of how workers organised their work and saw themselves.

Despite the achievements of the symbolic interactionists it is a startling feature of the sociology of work that the immense amount of empirical investigations they conducted seem to be largely ignored in reviews and introductions to the subject, let alone being an influence upon contemporary concerns in the sociological study of work. Only one of these studies, Donald Roy's *Banana Time* (1959) makes it into Grint's introduction, for example. Yet, despite the fact that their existence is mainly ignored in contemporary sociology, the Chicago School studies were the first serious attempt to engage in the *analysis of work itself* and to do so by investigating it 'from the inside', i.e., from point of view of the actors and the interaction actually involved in *doing* it. Donald Roy epitomises the point. He didn't just 'hang out' with workers in a garment factory in New York, conducting informal interviews and observations, he actually *did* the job in order to understand, as he puts it himself,

> … how one group of machine operators kept from 'going nuts' in a situation of monotonous work activity … (ibid.)

The monotonous activity in question took place in the 'clicking room' of a New York garment factory, where a handful of operators hammered out small pieces of material for garment assembly from sheets with dies in mechanical presses – simple, repetitive work as Roy describes it, conducted in isolation from the other employees in the factory. Roy's introduction to the job consisted of "an all-time minimum of training" – he was given a brief demonstration and told to keep his hands clear of the hammer and, after a similarly short period of practise, he was put to work.

So how did the machine operators stop themselves from going nuts in such a monotonous and isolated work situation? Roy first of all elaborates how he made clicking into a game to help pass the time – developing a "continuous sequence of short-range production goals with achievement rewards in the form of activity change" – but this is not how his colleagues coped with a nullifying situation of work day-in-and-day-out. Rather, Roy found that his co-workers, George, Ike and Sammy, had developed an "informal structure" of workplace interaction to make the monotonously long working day "liveable". This informal structure was manifest in what Roy called "times" and "themes", which shaped interaction. The notion of times refers to the *temporal punctuation* of clicking work, not only through the exchange of sheets and moving of boxes, or lavatory and lunch breaks, but through other brief interruptions as well. These interruptions occurred almost hourly. They included the consumption of food and drink outside of the official lunch break – which the workers referred to as coffee time, peach time, banana time, fish time, coke time, etc. – and other kinds of interruption that Roy called window time, pickup time, and quitting time. Sitting alongside and weaving through such distinct temporal punctuations were themes or *verbal interplays*, which became "standardised in their repetition" – serious themes, kidding themes, chatter themes, the poom poom theme, the professor theme, etc. Thus, through the daily round of times and themes the work of clicking was sustained and made into a "satisfying" job of work by the machine operators through an informal structure of social activity and horse-play that was "in constant flow".

That Roy's study is still mentioned in introductory texts to the sociology of work goes some way to mark the impact of his work. *Banana Time* raised a range of theo-retical considerations of relevance to sociological inquiry into the behaviour of small groups, particularly in factories. Roy's study suggests that, counter to rational theories of action, such groups are not generically 'instrumental' in nature but that their ecological situation drives local socio-cultural systems marked by 'consuma-tory' interaction – i.e., interaction done freely for the pleasure of it, rather than done to achieve some specific instrumental goal. Furthermore, in the course of working together the group's members produce distinctive sub-cultures having their own distinctive social structures that provide for the 'equilibrium' of the group. This does not increase productivity, but it does bring job satisfaction or "at least job endurance" to work situations that are largely bereft of creative experience.

Roy's studies are but an example of symbolic interactionist studies of work, which stand in stark contrast to those of the mainstream sociology of work in terms of their emphasis on the interactional context and situation, and in examining work not so much in terms of the social characteristics of those involved but in emphasis-ing an examination of the *interactional milieu*. In mainstream studies of work in sociology the actual work that is done seems to mysteriously *vanish*. It is taken for granted and so disappears from view. Take, for example, a very influential book from the 1950s *Coal is Our Life* (Dennis 1956), which provided a penetrating description of a way of life now passed of close-knit communities working together and supporting each other which were bound together by 'the pit'. Although evoca-tive of a mining culture, a culture dominated by the fact that men worked "down't pit", the actual doing of the hewing of coal, an actual description of the very well-spring of community life – the time spent underground with machinery extracting coal and bringing it to the surface, the actual interactional accomplishment of that job of work – is *assumed* and *in its place* is put an account of the ways in which economic forces structure social relations.

Similarly, the recognition by feminist sociology that 'housework' is unrecog-nised work but nonetheless work for that, unpaid and undervalued and constituted in a patriarchal social structure. However, again, the actual work of 'housework' is assumed and taken for granted. We might say that housework involves ironing, for example, but how is ironing done? How is a stack of clothes in a laundry basket ironed and moved into its storage spaces ready to wear? Are decisions made about what to iron and what not to iron, and if so how are they made? Is the first thing on the top of the pile ironed, or is the pile ordered into categories of ironing? How are judgements made about the temperature of the iron, are the temperature dials to be trusted, or are past experiences of ironing triumphs and mishaps taken into account? These and similar matters may appear to be trivial and of little interest to the sociologist who wants to talk about grand social structural matters, such as patriarchy or the economic drivers of social relationships, but to those who are doing the ironing as an everyday concern they are matters that enter into the very *doing* of the ironing which can, as the tradition of symbolic interactionism has demonstrated, be characterised in different ways for sociological purposes: in ways that seek to elaborate the *interactional ordering* of work.

However, it is with respect to the interactional ordering *of work* that interactionist studies are themselves problematic. While mainstream sociologists have simply ignored it, and continue to ignore it, symbolic interactionist studies, despite the promise they seem to hold, have not actually got to grips with it themselves. *Where*, for example, *is* the interactional order of work in Roy's study of clickers in the New York garment factory? We can read in Roy's account of the work that it involves the monotonous, repetitive, order 'click – move die', that new sheets to be clicked have to substituted for old ones that have been clicked by someone (who, and what their job is, we do not know) and that boxes of finished work have to be moved and empty ones put in their place, and we can read too that there is a clicker room lead-man who coordinates daily with the superintendent and communicates workloads to the clickermen, but how are any of these things actually ordered in interaction? How are the monotonous, repetitive actions 'click – move die' actually done: what do 'click' or 'move die' actually consist of *as* repetitive actions? What other actions are implicated in the achievement of clicking work? How do the sheets get into and out of position for 'click – move die' to take place? What happens when there are no sheets left to perform the actions on? How are sheets made available to the clickers to work in a timely fashion? How is the movement of boxes paced to ensure the smooth flow of work? How do the clickers manage and coordinate the day's workload? How do they know if they are on target, or if they need to slow down or speed up, etc.?

Roy provides a fascinating study of how people stop themselves going nuts in banal work situations, elaborating the social interactions that enable them to endure the working day, but he does *not* elaborate the interactional work and interactional order of *doing the job*. While symbolic interactionism has made interaction into a key analytic topic, it is the interaction 'going on around the work' that is of analytic interest, *and* what can be made of certain aspects of it for mainstream sociological consideration: the nature of small group formation in the workplace, the dynamics of group interaction, the development of sub-cultures and social structures, etc. – considerations that can, as Roy (1959) puts it, "be *abstracted* from the total existential flow of observable doings and sayings" (our emphasis).

Thus, and despite the turn to interaction, interest in the work of a setting and its accomplished order is subordinate to theoretical interests in the sociology of work. Little wonder, then, that interactionist studies are strangely mute about the actual interactional accomplishment *of the work* they are concerned with. In interactionist studies of work, although we are given descriptions of what people do when working, in the sense that we are given shallow characterisations of *what* machine operators do for example, we still do not know *how* those things are done, and in *missing* that order of detail much of the organisation of work itself remains untouched.

In place of the orderliness of work, we are offered the orderliness of social interactions surrounding the work and sociological abstractions on the nature of work and society. So although interactionist studies focus on the importance of interaction and the interactional milieu, Strauss's hoped for *analytic* emphasis is not realised. We are returned instead to scenic descriptions – to anything in the world *but* the actual doing of work as an interactionally ordered and accomplished achievement.

6.2   The Missing Interactional What

The issue of the 'missing interactional what' of interactionist studies was highlighted by Garfinkel in his consideration of a study of jazz musicians done by another of Hughes' protégés and a leading figure in the Chicago School, Howard Becker. Just as Roy's study of clicking work in the New York garment factory was conducted through participant observation, so too were Becker's studies of the playing of jazz music in Chicago dance halls.[1] Just as Roy's studies elaborated the interaction that surrounds the work of clicking, so too Becker's studies elaborated the interaction that surrounds the playing of jazz. Becker's studies showed that what was at the time considered to be a somewhat deviant culture, a view reinforced by jazz musician's express rejection of social norms, was nevertheless a highly organised occupation ordered through a distinctive set of occupational values embodied in the "colleague code". His studies elaborated how 'the code' shaped the career structure of the jazz musician, the fraternal organisation of work it gave rise to, the pressures of work and playing to the audience, the dilemma of commercialism versus prestige, and the impact of family on the musician's life and the conflict it generates (Becker 1951).

Becker's ground-breaking studies shed light on the hitherto unrecognised social *and* moral order of so-called 'deviant' cultures (Becker 1963). As illuminating as they are, they spurred Harold Garfinkel to make the following observations.

> Harvey Sacks speaks of a curiosity in the work and history of the social sciences: the 'missing interactional what' in lay and professional studies … For convenience we shall speak interchangeably of the 'missing what', 'missed what', or 'missed orderliness'. David Sudnow epitomises the issue as follows. On the basis of his studies of the gestural organisation of ensemble musical play (Sudnow 1978) he speaks of the 'Howard Becker phenomenon' in sociologists' studies of jazz. (Garfinkel unpublished manuscript)

The Howard Becker phenomenon is comprised of two parts. First, Sudnow observed of Becker's work that we come to understand where jazz musicians work, what they earn, who they work with and such like. However, and this is the second part, *how*, with the particular assembly of people to hand, within the particular circumstances in which they are playing, they pull off making music together is not available in Becker's account.

---

[1] Becker was a jazz musician, had been since the age of 15, and he complemented his own observations with informal interviews of other jazz musicians on the Chicago circuit.

> A curiosity of the reportage, Sudnow points out, is that Becker's articles speak of musicians' work and do so by omitting entirely and exactly the practices that for those engaged in them makes of what they are doing, makes up the recognisably just so, just what, just this going on: making music. Not music of a certain type, but this music; not music accomplished via behaviours in motivated compliance with valued and normative practices, (except perhaps in the work's own established terms) but music done as, and consisting of certain, local, witnessed, practically objective and practically observed materially particular musicians' practices. *That* is omitted from Becker's account, it cannot be recovered from the account … it is completely and essentially missing … Sudnow points out that even though it was written by a jazz musician, it is an *appreciation* of the work of jazz musicians. By an appreciation is meant that no reading that could be made of that published article will provide the *what* … … … … we wish to emphasize as a positive feature of the *missing what* the absence of a descriptive literature. The absence of such a literature is not restricted to the work of jazz musicians. A descriptive literature on occupational praxis is absent to the entire field of the sociology of occupations. It is nowhere to be found. (ibid.)

Today the situation has still not changed with respect to the sociology of jazz. In 2009, along with Robert Faulkner, another sociologist and jazz musician, Howard Becker published *Do You Know …? The Jazz Repertoire in Action*. On reading the table of contents it might be expected that the missing interactional what has been addressed: chapter one is called 'how musicians make music together', two 'repertoire as activity', three 'learning songs and building an individual repertoire', four 'the skills you need …', and so on. However, on actually reading the text it is clear that the interactional what of making music together is still *missing* (see Faulkner and Becker 2009).

The interactional what *of work* is still missing in ethnographic studies more generally. Not only in mainstream ethnographies of work, but also in symbolic interactionist studies and a great many ethnographic studies conducted for the purposes of systems design as well. The latter may well produce findings of interest, but like the studies of the symbolic interactionists they nevertheless treat interaction at the scenic level. The result is that an ethnographic study may at first glance appear to be taking on an examination *of work itself* in furnishing first-hand 'insider' accounts of interaction, but on closer inspection it transpires that the work is missing, supplanted by accounts of the interaction that surrounds work and what can be abstracted from it for the purposes of systems design. In sociology and design alike, Strauss et al.'s dismay at the lack of attention paid to work itself has largely gone unheeded. Nonetheless, if we view interactionist studies as an attempt to implement an interest in work itself, we still have to conclude that even when it seems to actually pay explicit attention to work it is more concerned to produce descriptions, as the sociologist Wes Sharrock puts it, of what people are unwittingly doing when they are wittingly working.

The failure to get to grips with the interactional what of work is reflected in recent calls for systems design to turn to the 'European field study tradition' (Bannon et al. 2011), as exemplified by studies of work undertaken in Germany and France. While the authors recognise the contribution ethnomethodology has made to design's understanding of work through its interactional studies of the what of work itself, they go on to say that design can learn so much more than is provided for by such studies, particularly about the ergonomics of work activity and the conditions of its undertaking. We find it ironic that this should be viewed as a step forward. Bannon, Schmidt and Wagner are returning us to traditional ways of apprehending work in sociology, for when the studies that we are exhorted to attend to are examined we find two very familiar sociological gambits at play. The first is that, again, the actual work as it is done by the parties to it is not available; like the symbolic interactionist studies before them, the what of work itself is missing. The second is that in place of the work itself we encounter, particularly in the arguments recommending these studies, not descriptions of work but *sociological definitions* of work. That is to say work becomes a matter not so much to be apprehended through the agency of its doing, but through the social scientist who first tells us what work is before we actually encounter it. These definitions do not so much provide a cultural lens, as we have seen in the context of ubiquitous computing in Chap. 4, rather they are prescriptions as to what work is and how it is 'shaped'. The return to the European traditions of field study, defined by Francophone ergonomics and German industrial sociology, is a return to the wastelands of sociological definitions and prescriptions, and leaves us with the traditional sociological business of at best producing scenic descriptions.

Scenic description orients us to anything in the world but the work that people do: the social attributes that frame it, the social interactions that surround it, the conditions that shape it, etc. At best, scenic descriptions of the kind symbolic interactionists provide put us onto *what* the work consists of, but leave the practices involved in actually pulling off the work untouched. Such studies are commonplace and fail, in Strauss's terms, to *analyse the ways in which work is done*. Now a response to this, from someone involved in design at least, might well be: "Who cares about work anyway? Systems design has moved on. We're into leisure, and play, and all kinds of new and interesting stuff. This is just old hat." Such a response would, however, fail to recognise a number of things. First, that the design of workplace systems does *still* occupy industrial design and research. Second, that the missing interactional what is relevant to ethnographic studies of all colours, shades and hues, even ethnographies in academic design and research, no matter the domain of inquiry or whatever new topics absorb the field. It was this very issue that we sought to convey in a CHI paper called *Ethnography Considered Harmful* (Crabtree et al. 2009). Our argument was, and is, that the turn to new domains and topics of interest does not mean that 'old' approaches to ethnography that focused on work should be so readily supplanted with 'new' ones as design continues to move out of the workplace or, at least, that systems designers should do so *with caution*, in cognisance of what it is they are buying into and casting off.

One of the key things we tried to get across in that paper was that the notion of 'work' in ethnomethodological studies is not restricted to what goes on in the workplace but is *generic* in that it draws attention to the fact that action and interaction, wherever it takes place, and whether it involves payment or not, is always an *achievement*. The idea of work in ethnomethodology recognises that people are involved in *doing* some activity, that they are involved in *making* it happen and *bringing* it about. The complaint about the missing interactional what is a complaint that the courses of action and interaction whereby clicking work, or making music together, or *any* other human activity is actually done are missing from ethnographic accounts, and indeed the accounts of social science as a whole. With it go the procedures, methods, or practices that members accountably employ to organise the activities they are engaged in (making music together, etc.). Two of us have made separate attempts to clarify this (Button 2000, 2012; Crabtree et al. 2005), however, the generic idea of work articulated in ethnomethodological studies continues to cause trouble and Schmidt (2010) goes some way to point this out:

> … to argue that just because we [can] use the word 'work' … for all sorts of phenomena, then all these phenomena are *of the same kind* and can be studied as more or less the same phenomenon … is the classical nominalist fallacy.

Taking his inspiration from Gilbert Ryle, Schmidt lays out an argument to demonstrate that the concept of work is a 'polymorphous' concept.

> If asked 'What does working consist of?' we should quickly object that there was no general answer … … … There is nothing which must be going on in one piece of work which need be going on in another. Nothing answers to the general description 'what work consists of'. (Ryle 1971)

Schmidt then proceeds, somewhat strangely given Ryle's comments, to make an argument about 'finite provinces of meaning' (Schutz 1962) – different kinds of social action (work, play, leisure, etc.) – to distinguish and justify a normative conception of work. His argument is that work as articulated in ethnomethodological studies in the way in which we have described it above is a derivative use, and that ordinarily speaking we mean by it the idea embodied in a 'job of work', which for Schmidt is its primary reference. However, it is important to appreciate the *irrelevance* of any 'primary sense' of work, in distinction to a generic technical conception of work, to ethnographic studies of social action. Nevertheless, Schmidt argues that the word 'work' *does* have a primary sense, providing a number of ordinary examples of its use to demonstrate this: how people complain that meetings get in the way of their work; or they are interrupted in their work by telephone calls; or enough talk, lets get to work. However, we can equally well offer examples of the ordinary and perfectly understandable use of the word outside of workplace contexts: it takes work to get out of bed in the morning; it's fun but hard work; I'm really having to work at not getting angry with him, etc. These are perfectly intelligible uses of the word 'work' and it is only by *fiat* that we would call some uses primary and other's derivative. It is the action done through the use of the word that counts, not a definition applied to it by a social scientist. But then Schmidt, as we have seen in his call for design to turn to the European field study tradition, sets much store by imposing particular meanings on words, however they are ordinarily understood and used.

Of course what Schmidt is really worried about is that the ubiquitous use of the term 'work' undermines the field of Computer Supported Cooperative Work, which for him is 'naturally' about what goes on in workplaces. However, there is really no concern here. In clarifying the way in which work has been used in ethnomethodology, an alternative conception of work is not being offered for CSCW or any other discipline: we are drawing on and making use of ordinary language not to specify what work is or what it consists of but to specify a *study policy* and to provide an *instruction* to fieldworkers and others involved in the design of interactive systems: attend to the missing interactional what of lay and professional studies, elaborate the interactional work that human activities consists of and get done through. Thus, we can as equally well elaborate the interactional work involved in doing and coordinating paid labour as we can elaborate the interactional work involved in doing and coordinating a host of unpaid activities. The annals of CSCW stand testimony to that, and CSCW has not disintegrated as a result of this.

Ironically, the problem that others have had with the ethnomethodological conception of work, and one that motivates calls for 'new' approaches to ethnography in systems design in particular, is the polar opposite of Schmidt's – champions of the 'new' think that we are *only* interested in, and only fit to study, what goes on in workplaces (see Crabtree et al. 2009). This is an unfortunate misunderstanding that is, perhaps, a consequence, as we mentioned in Chap. 1, of systems design's history and ethnomethodology's peculiar nomenclature. Historically, systems design's engagement with ethnography was motivated by a concern to develop technology for the workplace. This historical contingency gave rise to various phrases to describe ethnographic studies: studies of work, work practice studies and even workplace studies. It is easy to see how, on the face of it, ethnomethodologically-informed ethnography could be about understanding what goes on in workplaces, and that as design began to move out of the workplace 'new' or alternative approaches would obviously be required. Ethnomethodology's terminology does nothing to help matters here. The terms 'studies of work' and 'work practice studies' are of ethnomethodology's making. They were coined in a sociological context to reflect the disciplinary interests that ethnomethodology has in the production of social order.

In this context, the notions of studies of work and work practice position ethnomethodology's interests in the social order and how this contrasts with mainstream sociological treatments of the phenomenon. Thus, in contrast to practices of sociological theorising, which seek to provide interpretations and explanations of action with reference to the structural forces in society that play upon it and cause or at least shape it, the notion of studies of work and work practice posit an alternative viewpoint. Instead action and interaction is seen to be 'worked on' and 'worked up' by those involved in doing it; action and interaction is, as Garfinkel (1996) puts it, achieved. The invocation of studies of work and work practice orients us to the *achievement of social order* in and through action and interaction then, and thus defines a distinctive disciplinary interest in the production of social order. Concomitant to this is the disciplinary commitment to the idea that there is 'order at all points' (Sacks 1984), which is to say that anything and everything that people do – any and all courses of action and interaction – may be examined to find the ways in which they are socially ordered in their actual doing. Studies of work and work practice orient us as ethnomethodologists to the achieved character of action and interaction, then, and to the ways in which action and interaction is socially ordered *in the course of* its accomplishment (Button and Harper 1996; Crabtree et al. 2012).

Thus ethnomethodology has attempted to make visible the fact that people are not puppets animated by the omni-relevant socio-cultural structures and forces delineated in mainstream sociology's scenic descriptions of action, including those that Schmidt would orient us to. Rather, they are active participants in the construction of the action and interaction they find themselves engaged in, whatever it is and wherever they are, and that, consequently, action and interaction are always and entirely achieved, 'worked at' and 'worked up' matters, put together or assembled in orderly ways. Ethnomethodology has thus referred to the 'work' that people are engaged in, in the doing, indeed *in the design*, of their actions and interactions. This holds true whatever the action or interaction involved, whether it is work in workplaces, or the work involved in doing leisure pursuits, or domestic life, etc. The fact that Garfinkel fostered a program of studies of work that involved detailed examinations of different occupations has perhaps confused matters, making it seem that ethnomethodology only applies to the study of what goes on in workplaces. It does not.

It is a little ironic that ethnomethodology has been characterised as only interested in matters to do with occupations and the workplace, though perhaps indicative of the fact that those doing the characterisation have not properly engaged with that which they criticise. Ethnomethodological studies of work have spanned a broad range of settings and activities that its detractors might well be interested in, including so-called 'ludic pursuits' (Gaver 2001) such as playing the piano (Sudnow 1978), or video games (Sudnow 1983), or hop scotch (Goodwin and Goodwin 2000), even playing with a dog (Goode 2007), doing origami (Livingston 2008), or being drunk (MacAndrew and Edgerton 1969). Indeed two of the current authors, Tolmie and Rouncefield, recently edited a publication called *Ethnomethodology at Play*, which includes studies of cooking, bird identification, fishing, yachting, using music software as a hobby, having a day out in the country, rock-climbing, running, playing music together, line dancing and having a drink in the local pub (Tolmie and Rouncefield 2013). All appalling unworthy topics for mainstream social science with its eyes on the lofty theoretical and methodological issues of the day, such as globalisation and mobility in a massively networked world, which drive the call for 'new' ethnographies because ethnomethodology, with its distinctive focus on work, allegedly cannot handle them.

It is certainly the case that the bulk of ethnomethodological studies done in design to date have focused upon the workplace, but then that is because historically this has been where systems design's interest has lain. It should be appreciated by now, however, that ethnomethodology's interest in work is not restricted to what goes on in workplaces. Even a cursory look at Garfinkel's programmatic text *Ethnomethodological Studies of Work* (Garfinkel 1986) should suffice to make the point clear for here can be found, sitting alongside studies of occupations, studies of kung-fu and the occult, and the corpus of ethnomethodological studies of work further reinforces the point that studies of work are *not* restricted to the study of what goes on in the workplace.

In this respect, the call for 'new' types of ethnography in systems design misses the point about and significance of studies of work and work practice. Ethnomethodology is, no doubt, in part responsible for the fact that the point *can* be missed, but ethnography should not be tied to the object of study in the sense that one type of ethnography is suitable for some purposes, while another is suitable for others; this is quite a meaningless idea. Ethnography involves the study of social and cultural arrangements inside of their workings, *whatever* the social and cultural arrangements being studied may be. The question is, how is this study to be undertaken?

In asking this question we have throughout this book been raising problematic issues to do with 'new' approaches to ethnography imported from the social sciences in general and their problematic character for systems design. Thus we have questioned the very idea that studies of human action can proceed with any adequacy on the basis of sociological theorising and scenic description, as opposed to describing the organisation of action and interaction in terms of what is actually done and how that is actually achieved in an orderly way by the parties involved in doing it. To say that the kind of place in which an ethnography is done might make one type of ethnography more appropriate than another is, then, to say that the study of the workplace might be appropriately done ethnomethodologically, while the study of the home might be more appropriately understood in terms of an alternative approach to ethnography – e.g., by adopting a 'defamiliarisation' approach to understanding culture drawn from literary theory and appropriated by anthropology (Bell et al. 2005). Our point is that this strategy is essentially wanting because it fails to see that there are two very different understandings of what the social consists of and how in general social matters can be adequately described.

6.3   The Ongoing Relevance of the Missing What

If we examine some of the ethnographies of non-workplace settings and activities that have been done for the purposes of systems design in recent years then we discern some of the problems that we have raised with respect to our discussion of sociological ethnographies of work and occupations, which concerns their essentially scenic character. Such studies display a narrative character similar to the interactionist studies we examined earlier, which describe what is seen to be done in a setting; a description of human activity that has the character of "X did this, and Y did that", which proceeds to elaborate *what* is done without lifting the lid on *how* it is done as an organised interactional accomplishment. The 'interactional what' of the matter is set aside; missed. In the original CHI paper that gave rise to this book we referenced a paper that examined the use of large screen displays in some American 'mega-churches' to demonstrate the point (Wyche et al. 2007). We chose the study not to insult or slight the authors, as has been suggested (Grinter 2010), but simply because it provided a ready example of scenic description that anyone could take a look at and see what we meant by the term and the particular way in which it typically gets manifest in HCI – i.e., that the organised interactional accomplishment of human activity (prayer in this case) is missing, replaced instead by an analytically naïve narrative detailing *what anyone can see*.

Thus, on reading the paper we find that large screens are commonly placed "on both sides of a central stage", that the screens are used to display "words to hymns and bible verse", that people can be seen to be "looking at screens to know what verse to turn to" and to be engaged in "a flurry of paper turning", etc. However, while people may be seen to do these things, this type of description only touches what is going on in the lightest of ways. Certainly people may be seen to look at screens and to rapidly turn the pages of their hymn books but if asked upon leaving, "What have you been doing?", we think it highly unlikely that people would say, "Looking at screens" or "Turning the pages of a hymn book." They are more likely to say something along the lines of, "I've been to church", or "Worshiping God" or some other similar sort of description. The analytic question is not how members of the congregation might account for what they have been doing after the fact, however, but how is 'being at church' *done* as an interactionally organised matter? In attempting to address that question we might see one person announcing the hymn to be sung, we might see that displayed on a large screen, and we might see some people glancing at the display to find the hymn number and then turning the pages in their hymn books to find it, but in simply describing these *behaviours* are we describing how, in this case, a Christian act of worship is interactionally ordered?

If we describe what we hear in the first moments of a telephone call, for example – "Hello" "Hi, it's Ann" – are we describing how an exchange of greetings is ordered? No. Describing what we hear in terms of one person said hello, and then the other person said hi and recited their name is to *'merely observe'* – i.e., to render a scenic description of what anyone can see or hear. That anyone can see it and hear it is not in dispute. The issue is that to leave it at that is to just lightly touch and not even scratch at the *surface* of the socially organised character of human conduct. Instead of merely observing what anyone can see, we might instead treat the material at hand as something that might be interrogated to see *how* it is *ordered*.

Thus to describe the orderliness of greetings, for example, we might on examining the phenomena notice, as we described in Chap. 5, that they are situated in a rather obvious place in interaction: in an 'initial turn position' at the *beginning* of a conversation. Rather less obviously, it is available to observation that speakers clearly attach *priority* to greetings; it is not down to happenstance that greetings occur at the beginning of conversations then. It is apparent too, at least when we look at greetings being done, that speakers order greeting utterances *relative to one another*: with regards to doing greetings over the phone the relative order consists of the person who answers it offering the first part of the greeting, and the person who calls offering the second part of the greeting. In this respect it is visible that greetings are done in parts, and indeed in parts that are *adjacently paired* and which therefore involve *speaker change*. The change of speakers turns upon parties to the conversation being able to recognise *completion-transition points* – i.e., on recognising that the first greeting utterance has been completed and that it is appropriate for speaker transition to *now* take place; that it is now the caller's turn to speak and complete the second part of the greeting. Thus greetings can be seen to be ordered through the use of a *sequencing rule*: on the recognisable completion of the first part of greeting, the selected speaker does the return. The sequencing rule governing speaker change can also be seen to be *conditionally relevant*, which is to say that despite the priority attached to greetings in beginning conversations there is nothing in the world that says a greeting *must* be paired with a greeting. Rather, a greeting has to be *warranted*, which is why the caller not only says "hi" in return to the call answerer's greeting but also identifies herself as someone who has the *right* to call.

Greetings are much more complicated organisational things than we can do justice to here (see Sacks 1992; Schegloff 2007). However, the point of the example is not to elaborate greetings per se but, just as it was in our original CHI paper, to beg the question as to the *adequacy* of scenic descriptions that merely recount observed behaviour: to beg the question as to whether or not we can understand *how* people organise, in and over course of their interactions, doing 'greetings' or doing 'being at church' (etc.) from descriptions of surface behaviours?

Now designers interested in the use of large screen displays in American mega-churches and other settings may well say that they find such behavioural descriptions useful, but in making this point we are not, to emphasise again, trying to govern what designers may or may not pick up from fieldwork. We can quite well imagine how the behavioural description of hymn book thumbing might stimulate the design imagination: a design where the display of the hymn number on a large screen enables some in the congregation to turn to the correct page, while for others it automatically brings up the correct hymn on their portable device; or we can imagine the order of service being displayed on screen and highlighted as it proceeds; or upon reaching the collection point in the service a customised recommended donation figure is sent to each individual's portable device; etc. In critiquing scenic descriptions of surface behaviour we are not trying to legislate what designers may find useful, but are instead making the point that you *do not need ethnography or ethnographers* to describe what anyone can see. What, after all, is different here to a designer spending a day at church and seeing the behaviours for him or her self? Or watching a video someone has made of the congregation at the church? Or indeed sitting at their desk and imaginatively ruminating upon their own behaviours at church? Maybe such approaches are good enough for some design projects, maybe hanging around for a day would work for some design undertakings, but scenic description of surface behaviours will not furnish a social methodology for systems design. While such behavioural descriptions capture something of interaction they nevertheless fail to grasp how participants are involved in the *orderly production* of interaction and the distinctive *social occasions* it elaborates.

Scenic descriptions of the surface behaviours involved in 'being at church' miss how it is that just these people assembled here and now pull off just this assembly of people *as a congregation at worship together*. It is not just that they are meeting in a church – other kinds of assembly can and do occur in churches – and collective worship can occur in other places to churches; and it is not that it merely consists of such behaviours as looking at screens and turning pages, though doing that may be part of the orderly accomplishment of this particular social occasion, but (and this is the problem) how such behaviours are understood to be part and parcel of the orderly production *of the social occasion* is not provided for in the mere description of behaviour, for the behaviour in question (looking at screens and turning pages) may be part of other *orchestrated* interactions. In noticing this – i.e., that what is being observed is an orchestrated social occasion, consisting of a group of people being led through a series of pre-formulated or 'scripted' episodes, and in which one person performs particular actions which then provide for the rest of the assembly to perform en masse a series of actions made relevant by 'the conductor' – it may be possible to find that the activities observed in collective worship are ordered through *generally* operative social practices for producing orchestrated social events.

The interactions of people at worship, the interactions of people engaged in a musical recital, the interactions of people at a swearing-in ceremony, all share the characteristic of them being orchestrations. The problem, however, is how do we distinguish between them? How can we discern the orchestrated interactions that provide society's members with the mundane means of recognising that an assembly of people are situationally and collaboratively engaged in doing 'being at church', or doing 'being at a musical recital', or doing 'being at a swearing-in ceremony'? The answer, clearly, is not to be found in scenic descriptions of surface behaviours, but in the *specific* (and missing) 'interactional whats' that constitute each particular characterisable social occasion *as* the occasion that it accountably *is* for those involved in its orchestrated production. If design is turning to the social, and seeking to build the social into the design mix, then these situationally specific 'interactional whats' could be decisive for it, simply because they are decisive for those who are involved in the orderly production of the distinctive social occasions they are engaged in the first place.

However, if ethnography resides at the scenic level of description, detailing merely observed behaviour that anyone can see, as opposed to attempting to analyse the orderly production of the 'occasioned' character of social interaction (Zimmerman and Pollner 1970), it can and will *misdirect* designers' understanding of the foundational relationship between ethnography and systems design and what designers can hope to take away from ethnographic studies. A study by Blythe et al. (2010) illustrates this point and the ongoing relevance of the issue of the 'missing interactional what' to ethnographic studies done for the purposes of systems development. We pick up on this study for two reasons. First it positions itself with respect to studies of work designers have been used to (studies influenced by ethnomethodology) and argues that attending to the setting as a workplace fails to allow design to understand other possibilities for technology. Second, even though we have more space in a book than in the original paper, paying respect to the matters we criticise means touching them in some depth and this is not possible for each study we might find problematic. Thus we select this paper to illustrate our concerns because it is authored by a number of those who would argue that new settings for design require new ways of apprehending them.[2]

---

[2] One of the 'off-line' criticisms that we received of our original paper was that we were punching below the belt because we used examples that were written by 'junior' researchers. The paper by Blythe et al., however, is authored by robust, long in the tooth, senior researchers of professorial standing. Thus we hope that attention can be focused on the ideas, not the people offering them, which is what we were actually doing in the original paper.

Blythe et al. are interested in design possibilities with respect to a distinctive cohort they call 'the older old' – i.e., (on their definition) people over 80. They explored the possibilities of designing for this cohort in a residential care setting, suggesting that to treat this social setting in a 'conventional' way – as a workplace in which to gather requirements for the development of systems – would result in systems to support carers in their work of caring and managing those they care for, rather than for the residents. Developing an alternative cultural understanding of the setting and the cohort purportedly avoids this situation and subverts the conventional technological approach, which rests upon a 'techno-utopian vision' that seeks to delay and even avoid the placing of the 'older old' in residential homes through the development of 'smart' technology in single occupancy dwellings.

In an attempt to make living in residential care 'better' than living at home ethnographers worked alongside the residents, designers, artists, and school children to develop a range of 'ludic' technologies to enhance the 'lived experience' of being in a care home. The lesson for ethnography and systems design is humbling:

> … most … people … will not have experienced what is like to live in a residential home. There are large distances to be negotiated in order to try and understand the lived experience of our older old participants and to respond to that understanding through design … If we have succeeded at all in enhancing our participants' experience of aging through technological interventions, it is not by observing users, identifying needs, goals and activities, then specifying the requirements of design solutions. It is by spending time, living with them a little, and by letting our relationship grow to a point where we could respond empathically with something. (ibid.)

It is easy to be swayed by an appeal to our own lack of experience and the implicit emotional plea to respond empathically to the situation of others but this conclusion is, nonetheless, one that stands upon scenic descriptions that *mask* consequential aspects of the socially organised nature of life in a residential care home. Furthermore, in masking the orderliness of residential life, the alternative cultural account also masks opportunities that systems design may well have been able to capitalise upon to improve the lot of those who find themselves in such places; opportunities which could certainly involve understanding requirements for technologies but that might also involve just thinking about the *type* of technology and order of technological support, and even whether or not it might be better to try and improve the quality of life through non-technological means.

We can begin to appreciate these issues by considering the principle *scenic* observation: that the cohort, the participants or the people involved here are the 'older old'. This description of care home residents is cast in terms developed by ethnographers, it is a social identity constructed by them not by the residents, and one through which they can then impute certain attributes to those they study. However, the ethnographers are not really studying the 'older old' at all, as if this was an homogenous group of people who possess and display the social characteristics attributed to them by the ethnographers involved in the study. Merely reflecting on our own experiences substantiates the point. One of the authors of this book has an 89 year old mother who lives in her own flat. She does her own shopping; belongs to clubs; drives her car to visit friends and relatives, and to do her shopping;

she flies to foreign destinations; keeps in touch with her son using e-mail and video conferencing apps; she also uses her computer to create greetings cards, store and share photographs she has downloaded from her camera, and to shop online. The same author has also made friends with an 87 year old man whom he regularly meets for a 5 km walk through the French countryside, that is when the 87 year old is not driving to England to visit his relatives, or commuting between his flat in Marseilles and his house in the hills of the Var hinterland where he entertains his 60 year old girlfriend.[3]

The object of the study is not the 'older old' and what they do. They may be describable as very old, but to describe what they do *as* the actions of old people would require showing that, in how they did what they did, they oriented to what they were doing as very old people. The mother and friend cited above are doing things that people who are not 'older old' do. Older people may do just the sorts of things and in just the sorts of ways that people who are not old might do them, and they may also do things in ways that orient to their age; it depends on their personal situation. However, it seems to us that in the examples we are given of the actions of those studied by the ethnographers in Blythe et al.'s study that age and ability is not the primary point. That what really matters here is not that people might be described as 'the older old' but that they are 'residents', and importantly *residents in a care home* for the elderly, that matters. How is this fact consequential with respect to the question of what it is that members of the cohort do? Well, we can readily imagine that some of the things that they do are a result of being elderly and the afflictions that beset older people, whether they are in care homes or not. However, and importantly, as Blythe et al.'s study makes visible, many of the things that the residents do involves building into the design of their actions the fact that they are *residents in a care home*. Take the following observation, for example,

> Staff regularly coordinate group activities such as karaoke sing-a-longs, games of catch and quizzes … Quizzes often featured a flip chart to record answers to memory games. Occasionally these activities would be met with some resistance. A staff member would suggest, for example, a quiz to think of as many boys names beginning with 'B' as possible. Some residents would suggest names but others would mutter *'Bugger off'*.

This and other scenic observations offered in Blythe et al.'s study make it visible, but leave unexplicated, that many of the actions done in the care home are done in such a way that they display that they are being done by residents in *an institution*. As the 'bugger off' example illustrates, an oriented to feature of interaction in the care home is that it is partially regulated by 'staff'. It can also be seen, for example, that residents' actions display that they orient themselves to living in a care home in terms of turning up at meal times. That is they make visible that they reside in an environment that regulates their activities according to set routines and procedures,

---

[3] As we were writing this a very apposite news item appeared on one of the UK's television channels about a couple who were celebrating 80 years of marriage; she was 101 and he was 105 years old. They were interviewed in their home sitting on the settee, smartly dressed, quipping, holding hands, lucidly reminiscing about aspects of their life together and as 'on the ball' as the 30 odd year old interviewer.

at least by turning up or allowing themselves to be guided to known places at known times.

So, one way in which 'the older old' order their actions and interactions, at least on the basis of the scant data the paper presents, is as residents in an institution. In this respect residents' actions may display characteristics not of the 'older old' (whatever they might be), but of people living in institutions and the topic of the paper may be more about *institutional living* than being about what might otherwise be considered as 'being very old', for not everyone who is very old lives in an institution. In this respect, we might ask questions about institutional living, and institutional actions and interactions, rather than just questions about being old and in this regard a study by the interactionist Ervin Goffman has some distinct relevance (Goffman 1961).

Goffman's work on institutions attracted some notoriety by drawing together institutions that were traditionally considered to be very different from one another: the concentration camp, the prison, the hospital, and the monastery, for example. He noted that many institutions, and we can here include residential care homes for the elderly, have an organisational feature in common with one another, which is that they *encompass the entire daily round* of their 'residents' lives. He referred to these institutions as 'total institutions'. The rhythm of the daily life of those living within in them is provided for by the routines of the institution – through roll calls and meal times, for example. Thus the ways in which people within institutions act or interact with one another can build in and display an orientation to features of the institution itself. Now obviously there are differences between institutions within the category 'total institution'. Relatives do not visit inmates of concentration camps while they do visit inmates of prisons, for example, but under different conditions to those visiting residents of care homes for the elderly. Within these differences it is possible to find how the features of living within a total, all encompassing institution, are contextualised, and how it is possible to characterise one from another by attending to and explicating the 'missing interactional what' to make visible how they are differently and specifically 'occasioned' in action and interaction.

Blythe et al. set that very challenge aside, focusing instead upon a particular scenic feature – here we have some very old people – that sets the stage for how we might address their condition. Yet the very ways in which their condition is addressed – the use of simple ludic technologies alongside the interventions of artists and children – is less to do with old people per se and more to do with living in an institution, which regulates and organises their lives according to set rhythms and routines with little to punctuate or elevate the tedium and boredom of the intervals between them. Is it surprising then that in such an environment the residents responded well to novel technological interventions or the appearance of artists and children in an otherwise *predictable* life? No more so than one would be surprised by the rapturous response that the inmates of Folsom prison gave to Johnny Cash, whose performance punctuated their repetitive, monotonous, tedious and boring institutional lives as inmates in a secure facility.

By focusing on a particular scenic feature – the 'older old' – systems design is being encouraged to move away from the development of smart technologies to support the elderly in their own homes and from the development of better workplace systems to support the delivery of care, to instead focus upon making the lives of some old people 'better' by realising that they can have fun. We do not dispute the fact that new technology can be introduced that makes life in the care home more fun; but then so could more interesting board games or the introduction of imaginative entertainment programmes, some might even enjoy Johnny Cash if he was resurrected. But there are a number of questions here. Again, do we need ethnography to make this point, and an ethnography that seemed to take some time so that the ethnographers could build up empathy with the 'older old'? Do we even need ethnography to help us in the design of technologies to be used for fun? A scenic description may spark the imagination for a fun technology, but it may equally as well come about through a designer visiting an elderly relative in a care home.

However, if we move even a little from the scenic description – that here we have a group of people we will call the 'older old' – and take instruction from participants in the setting in how to *see the phenomena at hand*, the social 'thing' that *they* are actually engaged in, then we might find that there are issues that the design of fun technologies need to contend with. We might find, for example, that the parties to the setting's daily round are more than just the 'older old'. After all the setting of a residential care home for the elderly is a complex one. For some people it is their workplace, whereas for others it is their home, for others a place in which they are nursed, for others possibly the place in which they die, and for some it is a place they visit. How people build this complexity into the institutional order may be consequential for the design of technology to support life in the residential care home. The institutional rhythms and routines of the residential care home drive significant aspects of resident's lives. It may well be the case then that any attempt to alleviate the effects of institutional living would benefit from taking its rhythms and routines into account (Chevherst et al. 2003). It is not just having fun that is the issue, but having fun *in* a residential care home, and how this might impact upon the design of technologies when considered in the round. No matter how much fun a technology might be, if it clashes with the institutional order it might well turn out to be problematic. Understanding, then, how different members of the setting's cohort – residents, the healthy, the ill, the dying, staff, visitors, relatives, etc. – 'work' together to produce the daily round of life in the care home may be consequential to any technology's *actual embedding* within an institutionalised context. Simply taking a scenic feature of a setting – some of the people here are very old – and substituting that for another scenic feature – some of the people here are working or visiting – is really beside the point. The point is that saying fun can make the life of older people 'better' is just to touch the surface. The issue is how having fun can be done within an institutional context such that it is built in to the institutional circumstances of its conduct. Such issues cannot be answered through scenic characterisations, but are demonstrably *missed* by them.

References

Bannon, L., Schmidt, K., Wagner, I. (2011). Lest we forget: The European field study tradition and the issue of conditions of work in CSCW research. In *Proceedings of the 12th European conference on computer supported cooperative work* (pp. 213–232). Aarhus: Springer.

Becker, H. (1951). The professional dance musician and his audience. *American Journal of Sociology, 57*(2), 136–144.

Becker, H. (1963). The culture of a deviant group: The dance musician. In *Outsiders: Studies in the sociology of deviance* (pp. 79–100). New York: Free Press.

Bell, G., Blythe, M., & Sengers, P. (2005). Making by making strange: Defamiliarisation and the design of domestic technologies. *ACM Transactions on Computer-Human Interaction, 12*(2), 149–173.

Blumer, H. (1969). *Symbolic interactionism: Perspective and method*. Berkeley: University of California Press.

Blythe, M., Wright, P., Bowers, J., Boucher, A., Jarvis, N., Reynolds, P., & Gaver, W. (2010). Age and experience: Ludic experience in a residential care setting. In *Proceedings of the 8th conference on designing interactive systems* (pp. 161–170). Aarhus: ACM.

Braverman, H. (1974). *Labour and monopoly capital: The degradation of work in the twentieth century*. London: Monthly Review Press.

Button, G. (2000). The ethnographic tradition and design. *Design Studies, 21*, 319–332.

Button, G. (2012). What does 'work' mean in 'ethnomethodological studies of work'? *Design Studies, 33*(6), 673–684.

Button, G., & Harper, R. (1996). The relevance of 'work practice' for design. *Computer Supported Cooperative Work: The Journal of Collaborative Computing, 4*, 263–280.

Chevherst, K., Clarke, K., Dewsbury, G., Hughes, J., Rouncefield, M., Crabtree, A., Hemmings, T., Rodden, T. (2003). Designing with care: Adapting cultural probes to inform design in sensitive settings. In *Proceedings of OzCHI 2003* (pp. 4–13). Ergonomics Society of Australia.

Crabtree, A., Rodden, T., & Benford, S. (2005). Moving with the times: IT research and the boundaries of CSCW. *Computer Supported Cooperative Work: The Journal of Collaborative Computing, 14*(3), 217–251.

Crabtree, A., Rodden, T., Tolmie, P., Button, G. (2009). Ethnography considered harmful. In *Proceedings of the SIGCHI conference on human factors in computing systems* (pp. 879–888). Boston: ACM.

Crabtree, A., Rouncefield, M., Tolmie, P. (2012). Our kind of sociology. In *Doing design ethnography* (pp. 21–41). London: Springer.

Dennis, N. (1956). *Coal is our life: An analysis of a Yorkshire mining community*. London: Eyre & Spottiswoode.

Dourish, P. (2006) Implications for design. In *Proceedings of the conference on human factors in computing systems* (pp. 541–550). Quebec: ACM.

Faulkner, R., & Becker, H. (2009). *Do you know … ? The jazz repertoire in action*. Chicago: University of Chicago Press.

Firestone, S. (1970). *The dialectic of sex: The case for feminist revolution*. New York: William Morrow & Co.

Garfinkel, H. (1986). *Ethnomethodological studies of work*. London: Routledge and Kegan Paul.

Garfinkel, H. (1996). Ethnomethodology's program. *Social Psychology Quarterly, 59*(1), 5–21.

Garfinkel, H. (unpub. manu.). *About the missed orderliness of ordinary activities*.

Gaver, W. (2001). Designing for ludic aspects of everyday life. *ERCIM News: Online*, no. 47. www.ercim.org/publication/Ercim_News/enw47/gaver.html.

Goffman, E. (1961). On the characteristics of total institutions. In *Asylums: Essays on the social situation of mental patients and other inmates* (pp. 1–124). New York: Anchor Books.

Goode, D. (2007). *Playing with my dog Katie*. West Lafayette: Purdue University Press.

Goodwin, M., & Goodwin, C. (2000). Emotion within situated activity. In N. Budwig, I. Uzgris, & J. Wertsch (Eds.), *Communication: An arena of development* (pp. 33–54). Stamford: Ablex.

Grint, K. (1991). *The sociology of work: An introduction*. Cambridge: Polity Press.

Grinter, R. (2010). Scholarly debates: Revisiting ethnography considered harmful. http://beki70. wordpress.com/2010/01/19/scholarly- debates- revisiting-ethnography-considered-harmful/.

Hughes, E. C. (1958). *Men and their work*. Glencoe: Free Press.

Livingston, E. (2008). *Ethnographies of reason*. Farnham: Ashgate.

MacAndrew, C., & Edgerton, R. (1969). *Drunken comportment: A social explanation*. New York: Percheron Press.

Prus, R. (1996). *Symbolic interactionism and ethnographic research*. Albany: State University of New York Press.

Roy, D. (1959). 'Banana time' – Job satisfaction and informal interaction. *Human Organisation, 18*(4), 158–168.

Ryle, G. (1971). *Thinking and language* (Collected Papers, Vol. II, pp. 258–271). London: Hutchinson and Co.

Sacks, H. (1984). Notes on methodology. In J. M. Maxwell & J. Heritage (Eds.), *Structures of social action: Studies in conversation analysis* (pp. 21–27). Cambridge: Cambridge University Press.

Sacks, H. (1992). In G. Jefferson (Ed.), *Lectures on conversation*. Oxford: Basil Blackwell.

Schegloff, E. (2007). *Sequence organisation in interaction: A primer in conversation analysis*. Cambridge: Cambridge University Press.

Schmidt, K. (2010). 'Keep up the good work!' – the concept of 'work' in CSCW. In *Proceedings of the 10th international conference on designing cooperative systems* (pp. 265–286). Aix-en-Provence: Springer.

Schutz, A. (1962). On multiple realities. In M. Natason (Ed.), *Collected papers* (Vol. I, pp. 207–259). The Hague: Martinus Nijhoff.

Shaffir, & Pawluch. (2003). Occupations and professions. In L. Reynolds & N. Herman-Kinney (Eds.), *Handbook of symbolic interactionism* (pp. 893–913). Walnut Creek: AltaMira Press.

Strauss, A., Fagerhaugh, S., Suczek, B., & Weiner, C. (1985). *The social organisation of medical work*. Chicago: University Press of Chicago.

Sudnow, D. (1978). *Ways of the hand: The organisation of improvised conduct*. London: Routledge and Kegan Paul.

Sudnow, D. (1983). *Pilgrim in the microworld*. New York: Warner Books.

Thrasher, F. (1927). *The gang*. Chicago: University of Chicago Press.

Tolmie, P., & Rouncefield, M. (Eds.). (2013). *Ethnomethodology at play*. Farnham: Ashgate.

Wirth, L. (1928). *The ghetto*. Chicago: University of Chicago Press.

Wyche, S., Medynskiy, Y. & Grinter, R. (2007). Exploring the use of large displays in American megachurches. In *Proceedings of the SIGCHI conference on human factors in computing systems (extended abstracts)* (pp. 2771–2776). Atlanta: ACM.

Zimmerman, D., & Pollner, M. (1970). The everyday world as phenomenon. In J. Douglas (Ed.), *Everyday life: Towards the reconstruction of sociological knowledge* (pp. 80–103). Chicago: Aldine Publishing Co.

Zorbaugh, H. (1929). *Gold coast and slum: A sociological study of Chicago's near north side*. Chicago: University of Chicago Press.

Chapter 7
Ethnography, Ethnomethodology and Design

Abstract In this chapter we bring together different threads of our argument to consider the difference between ethnomethodology and traditional forms of social science that make use of ethnography. Ethnomethodology provides for a complete respecification of how the social should be apprehended through the *study* of the ways in which people achieve the orderliness of their actions and interactions through the methodical use of common-sense knowledge. Thus, in ethnomethodological studies of action and interaction can be found demonstrations of *members' methodologies* for doing and ordering social life. To understand this respecification we examine the ways in which social science is essentially a *natural language exercise* itself shot through with common-sense knowledge, common-sense understandings and common-sense reasoning. The social sciences feed off and, curiously, at the same time seek to rival common-sense thereby producing a *disjuncture* between the social world as known and understood by social scientists and the social world as it is known and understood by society's members. Ethnomethodology, by contrast, recognises that common-sense knowledge of social doings is the very *bedrock* of social life and makes it a topic of study in its own right. The suggestion here is that the study of "members' methods" provides a systematic means of *anchoring* systems design in the social.

7.1 Ethnography and Ethnomethodology

So far we have shown how calls for 'new' ethnography in systems design are not really new at all, but instead reflect the *traditional* concerns of anthropology and sociology. We have also attempted to make visible to systems designers the methodological arguments and assumptions that are built into traditional social science approaches to ethnography in a bid to make them aware of what they are buying into should they take up these calls. Concomitant to this we have attempted to show how these arguments and assumptions are problematic. We have not argued that systems design should not invest in these 'new' calls, but have suggested it might be useful for designers to understand the foundations they are based on in order to gauge the appropriate size of that investment and its possible value return. We have questioned the foundations of 'new' approaches to ethnography by drawing upon

© Springer International Publishing Switzerland 2015

G. Button et al., *Deconstructing Ethnography*, Human-Computer
Interaction Series, DOI 10.1007/978-3-319-21954-7_7

ethnomethodological critiques of the social sciences. We have warned, however, that although ethnomethodology has had an impact on systems design thinking (though not always in an explicit ethnomethodological guise), incorporating the social into the design mix through the ideas of 'work practice' and 'situated action', it nevertheless occupies a marginal position within the social sciences. While it once drew much attention, especially within sociology, ethnomethodology is now not well received within mainstream social science, which by and large continues much as it did before the publication of Harold Garfinkel's foundational book *Studies in Ethnomethodology* (Garfinkel 1967).

Our account of the ethnomethodological alternative to mainstream social science has thus far been piecemeal, with parts being surfaced for particular purposes. In this chapter we attempt to draw together the various ethnomethodological threads we have touched on by explicitly attending to its difference to traditional forms of social science, which include mainstream treatments of ethnography. We also look at why it has broken from tradition and the consequences this can have for systems design with respect to the development of a methodology for building the social into design. We are conscious, as we have been throughout, that designers are not social scientists and that they may not find it an important matter to follow the twists and turns of social science thinking with regard to how to study the social world. However, for those in design who do buy into the importance of understanding the social for design purposes then some understanding of ethnomethodology itself may support their understanding of how to differentiate between the accounts or descriptions of the social world they are presented with by social scientists.

Our underlying contention is a simple one: just as all designs are not equal, just as there are 'good' and 'bad' designs, judged on appropriate criteria that can be invoked to differentiate between the standard of a design, then so too in the social sciences it is possible to differentiate between the standard of a sociological undertaking. We want to provide some means, to put it very crudely, of appreciating that not all ethnography is 'appropriate' just because it involves interacting in some way with the people who may use a system or provides some kind of fieldwork resource to reason about systems and their design, whether it be in the details of some social undertaking or with respect to the cultural meaning that technology may have in people's lives. In this respect we wholeheartedly agree with Bell and Dourish when they lament that some in design think it possible to do ethnography in a day (though that does not mean that it must take years either; see Crabtree et al. 2013). More important, however, is to appreciate that undertaking ethnography – i.e., studying social life from within its midst – is not in itself sufficient to *anchor design in the social*. More is required, with the 'more' of the matter involving some means of analysing and understanding the social world. Again, we resonate with Bell and Dourish who are also interested in these matters, but as it should by now be clear, we locate that analysis and understanding in members' methodologies for doing social life rather than social science methodologies for interpreting, and imparting meaning to the social.

In this respect ethnomethodology provides a distinctive means of analysing and understanding the social. Rather than providing some methodological or theoretical apparatus constructed within the social sciences to analyse and understand the social, it makes visible how people in the social world go about analysing and displaying their understandings of the social in their everyday affairs. This stands in contrast to social science, which provides analyses and understandings on the basis of its disciplinary practices, as is plain to see when we look to see the ways in which ethnography works, which we have been detailing throughout this book. Consequently it is important to appreciate that ethnomethodology is *not* ethnography as this is understood in traditional social science. Ethnomethodological studies draw off ethnographic materials – i.e., materials that are gathered from within the ongoing midst of society's ordinary affairs – but the way in which it treats those materials is very different to ethnographic approaches in mainstream social science. While the way in which ethnomethodology treats these materials can, as history has proven, be an important resource for design as it seeks to build the social into the design mix it is, however, equally important to appreciate that ethnomethodology is not essentially about systems design, any more than ethnography is.

To appreciate the significance of what we are saying here it is important to understand ethnomethodology's marginalised status in contemporary social science. The reason for this marginalisation is not surprising: ethnomethodology provides for a complete *respecification* of sociology's problems and how the social should be addressed (Garfinkel 1991). We say sociology's problems because it is within professional sociology that ethnomethodology's arguments have primarily been played out, but the problems of sociology as a scientific discipline cut across the social sciences more generally.[1] Ethnomethodology's respecification rips those problems out of the hands of social scientists and returns them to the social world from which social scientists have themselves ripped them, to the effect, as Lynch (1993) puts it, of "dissolving any semblance of a foundation in the academic social sciences." Ethnomethodology would do away with social science as it stands then, dispersing the study of the social into "innumerable hybrids" (ibid.) or interdisciplinary endeavours, where studies of the social are built into other disciplines to shape their ongoing development, as for example building the social into systems design. Little wonder, then, that ethnomethodology has received short shrift within the professional halls of social science, just as it is no surprise to find that Wittgenstein philosophy similarly treated in its implied dissolution of philosophy (Hacker 1996). There have, of course, been attempts to tame ethnomethodology by drawing out common interests with social science, but such 'cosying up' misrepresents the radical overhaul Garfinkel proposed.

The turn towards 'innumerable hybrids' invests ethnomethodology with a keen disciplinary interest in developing interdisciplinary relationships (Button and Dourish 1996). However, and this might be the hard part for systems designers to appreciate where interdisciplinarity in design is concerned, ethnomethodology is

---

[1] See *Ethnomethodology and the Human Sciences* (Button 1991) for a detailed explication of this point. The text treats concepts common across the social sciences and psychology (hence the use of the term *human*), such as method, measurement, logic, and cognition, and examines ethnomethodology's respecification of them.

not primarily occupied with the problems of systems design, any more than anthropology or sociology are as disciplines in their own right. Rather, ethnomethodology's core concerns are to do with how the social is understood and with respecifying
what it considers to be erroneous formulations of what it is and how it can be studied. In this respect if design comes to ethnomethodology as a discipline in itself it
will find little of direct relevance to its own enterprise. Take, for example, Harold
Garfinkel's edited collection *Ethnomethodological Studies of Work* (Garfinkel
1986). At first glance this might seem relevant for design in its attempts to understand workplaces and the work that goes on in them in the effort to develop systems
supporting or automating that work. However, in Garfinkel's succinct two-page
introduction he makes it perfectly clear what *Ethnomethodological Studies of Work*
are about, and it is not about systems design's interest in work or the workplace:

> Ethnomethodological studies of work began in 1972 with Harvey Sacks' observation that
> the local production of social order existed as an orderliness of conversational practices
> upon whose existence all previous studies depended, but missed.

Garfinkel's remarks point to one of ethnomethodology's most important
respecifications of social science, which is the respecification of social order as a
local achievement: something brought about within actual social occasions, through
the practices of the parties to those occasions, rather than through theoretically
imputed social forces said by the social sciences to be operating across society at
large. Social order is thus a product of the mundane, situationally located, interactional work members inevitably find themselves engaged in as they go about conducting the business of daily life. Garfinkel's remarks here also point to the fact that
there is an orderliness of practices, conversational practices in this case, that people
use to bring off their talk and what they are doing through talking in an organised
way. He goes on to say,

> Soon after our … studies began it was evident from the availability of empirical specifics
> that there exists a locally produced order of work's things; that they make up a massive
> domain of organisational phenomena; that classic studies of work, without remedy or alter-
> native, depend upon the existence of these phenomena, make use of the domain and ignore
> it. (ibid.)

Garfinkel's point here is that, just as Sacks found with conversation, so too it can be
found for work: there exists an orderliness of practices that are used by people
locally to achieve it. And, of course, as was shown in Chap. 6, an orderliness of
practices can found in whatever people do. That whatever the action and interaction,
be it working in a factory, playing jazz, living in a care home, etc., it can be examined to find the locally achieved ways in which people bring it about as an orderly
enterprise, here and now.

Thus ethnomethodology's interest in 'studies of work' is not in what goes on in
workplaces, as the title of Garfinkel's book might suggest, but the interactional
work involved in doing any activity and bringing any social occasion about, and the
practices that participants use to order that work. These practices are otherwise be
referred to as "members' methods" for doing and ordering social life, and making
them visible, drawing them out from the camouflage of their ordinariness, is ethno-

methodology's business. This contrasts with sociology and the social sciences more generally, which rely upon members' methods and the social arrangements they produce to conduct their business, but do not treat them as topics for investigation in their own right. Rather, they exploit members' methods and their orderly products as resources for sociological theorising. Ethnomethodology respecifies the topics of social science inquiry. Rather than treat the orderly products of members' methodical practices – members' methodologies as it were – as resources for investigating the social order, ethnomethodology gives exclusive priority to the study of the methods or practices that people employ to assemble an orderly world. Thus in place of the grand topics of social science – power, patriarchy, postmodernity, etc. as variously defined by social scientists – stand studies of *the mundane production of social order*, elaborating the methodological ways in which the familiar settings and situations of everyday life are locally produced and ordered in members actions and interactions.

If design goes to ethnomethodology as a discipline in itself it will find little in its foundational texts of relevance then; it will find respecified sociological problems, worked out through particular studies of mundane order production in particular settings and situations. Studies of air traffic control (Hughes et al. 1992) or industrial print work (Button and Sharrock 1997), for example, which reveal the organisation of such undertakings in the particular interactional practices of those involved in doing them. However, it is in working through the problem of social order as a locally achieved phenomenon that those ethnomethodologists who have attempted to develop a relationship with systems design have come to gain purchase on design, for in the local ordering of action and interaction designers have found a *useful* design resource (Sommerville et al. 1992). What designers have got out of these studies has more recently been described, and we can but read the remarks as implying 'merely', as systems requirements (Dourish 2006), and this despite attempts as noted above to shape a more foundational interdisciplinary relationship (Button and Dourish 1996). Nevertheless, the contribution of studies of mundane order production to systems design is seen to be problematic, and such studies are charged with promoting 'empiricism' in ethnographic work and 'marginalising' social theory (Dourish 2006).

Our response to this charge, as we have elaborated in the preceding chapters, is threefold. First, do not denigrate this as many who design systems, particularly industrial systems, welcome contributions to requirements capture and scoping. Second, the call for sociological accounts that provide 'much more than requirements', as exampled in the kinds of theoretical ethnography that describe the cultural meaning of technology is a call to provide descriptions that are of exactly the same order that *anyone* can provide. This means that design does not especially need ethnography if it wants to explore such matters. There are plenty of other resources to tap into to find out about the meaning of technology in society, such as journalism or political parties and pressure groups, technology enthusiasts or conspiracy theorists or, indeed, the person standing next to you at the bar. Third, why studies to date should be thought of as just tied to requirements is baffling since they have obviously done much more: they have in part brought about a sensitivity to the social in design, and not just 'human factors', that design needs to be aware of; they have provided critiques of particular designs, and of some design practices; they have triggered new design ideas; and, importantly for one of the aims of this book, they provide the basis for thinking about how to move the social into design in a methodical as opposed to a piecemeal way.

Perhaps the charge is not so much that the studies to date have been aimed at requirements capture, perhaps what is behind this is the charge that they are *empirical*. That would be more apposite and it does resonate with other charges of realism we discussed previously. It might seem strange for anyone who is championing ethnography to level a charge of empiricism, though perhaps in this charge there is an inadvertent recognition of what the call for 'new' ethnography is really all about. Ethnomethodology *is* resolutely empirical. As we noted in Chap. 5 both Garfinkel and Sacks provided for a break with the traditional direction of travel in social science, which is to render the social and cultural character of action and interaction in theoretical terms, even when drawing off observations. The break involved abandoning theorising and turning to empirical *studies*. We have outlined the grounds for this break above, and note here that the charge that ethnomethodological studies done for design purposes are empirical is correct. In making that charge, however, the nature of 'new' calls are revealed as attempts to locate design's interest in the social in the old traditional ways of anthropology and sociology, in cultural theories and disciplinary interpretations. The 'new' thereby provides for design's future to be a thing of the past.

Ethnomethodology's *studies* contrast sharply with theoretical renderings of the social, even if they involve fieldwork and observation. Ethnomethodology's *studies* detail and draw out what Garfinkel describes as "work's things" – e.g., the *ongoing collaborative arrangement of flights strips* to order the safe flow of aircraft through the skies, or *forward loading and demand monitoring* to order the smooth flow of industrial print work, or any other interactional thing that people find themselves 'busied with' in the course of doing whatever it is they are doing. This distinctive interest in and *study of* the local, situated, ordering of work's things reconfigures the sociological project. It shifts attention from imputed structural accounts of social order that essentially construe order as the product of the operation of generic social factors *on* action and interaction (e.g., roles, rituals, rules, regulations, etc.), which are said to shape and thus order it, to instead elaborate the *incarnate* ordering of social structures *in* action and interaction. Such studies have proved to be of value to systems design's efforts, enabling designer's to appreciate the things that people actually do in some setting or domain and how they do them in practice, which in turn enables designer's to build systems around these understandings. In championing 'marginalised' social theory, Dourish ironically seeks to bring mainstream social science thinking into design, and put traditional specifications of social undertakings and the social sciences role in understanding them in place of *studies* of work's things.

Now it might seem that studying the particular things that people are busied with in particular settings and situations, and the particular ways in which they organise or order their business in action and interaction, is ethnography to some *but it is not*.

To appreciate the point it is important to remind ourselves, as discussed in Chap. 3, that ethnography is essentially a very simple idea: the study of the social world from 'within its midst' or from inside its own workings. This contrasts to studying the social world by looking in on it from the outside. Malinowski's portrayal of anthropology that we referred to in Chap. 3 exemplifies the point. A key part of his original exposition of ethnography was that anthropology was largely done 'on the veranda', conducted by people studying 'native enterprise' from afar, often on the basis of reports from colonial officials or selected representatives of the society in question, and in either case from outside the actual workings of the culture or society being studied itself. In marked contrast, Malinowski, as we have described, moved off the veranda and entered into the daily round of the people he was studying, witnessing the business of their social lives first-hand, and seeing their society and how it operated from their point of view (Kuper 2005).

On the face of it Malinowski's ethnography marked a radical departure from conventional social science, with its arsenal of research methods that seem to hold the very stuff of social life at bay. The very terms *culture* and *society*, for instance, become things in themselves that are seen to operate in orderly ways irrespective of people and the events they encompass. Indeed, as pointed out above, the social order is cast in terms of causal or quasi-causal *forces* operating on people, propelling their actions and interactions without any mediating thought, assessment or reasoning. Social theorising generalises, making actual instances of action and interaction annoying distractions. Conceptual schemas and typologies squeeze people and their actions into boxes designed in advance of naturally occurring events, selecting only those imputed characteristics that enable 'fitting' people and what they do into a given box. Statistics stand proxy for people, ignoring their own generation as a social process of institutional data collection and recording. Social science methods assure that actual courses of action and interaction can only be grasped and described in general ways. The tools the social sciences use to survey the social landscape thus assure that the social scientist, ensconced on the disciplinary veranda, sees only *abstract representational images* of the situationally embodied, socially organised business of everyday life.

Malinowski's contribution to social science was to step down from the veranda and enter *into* the social world. In doing so he became a witness to the actions and interactions of people in the societies he was studying. The things he witnessed became his data, not for example, statistical occurrences of something. In witnessing an exchange of gifts he could observe what exchange consisted of just here and now for these people doing it, rather than, for example, viewing it as a constituent element of an overall population of exchanges. Thus he recorded what he saw as he moved through the societies and cultures he was concerned with in notes of his observations, his impressions, speculations, and snippets of talk, of what those he was concerned with said either in response to his questions or as commentaries on what they were doing. Despite arguments such as the one we have discussed in Chap. 4 that call for multi-site ethnographies, little has changed with respect to *how* ethnography is done today. Thus ethnography in anthropology and sociology is still a matter of collecting observationally generated materials from inside society's workings, in the actual face of the doings of society's members, and within the local social contexts in which the things that people do are undertaken. It is also still a matter of holding onto what has been witnessed through notes and verbatim descriptions. Modern technology has become useful in this respect in as much as audio-visual technologies enable interactional scenes to be captured, re-examined, and shared with others.

In this respect, being witness to that which is being described and exploiting modern ways of holding onto those observations, ethnomethodology differs little from ethnographic undertakings. Ethnomethodological studies, like ethnographic studies done in anthropology, or interactionist studies in sociology, or the prolific constructivist studies of science and technology being undertaken across the social sciences today, or the scenic ethnographies done in design that we have criticised, are *rooted in* observationally-generated materials of witnessed occurrences. Ethnomethodologists, like all who gather their materials through ethnographic undertakings, spend time within the settings they are concerned with, observe and note what is seen, interact with the people in those settings, record what they do and how they see things, and gain an understanding of how society works by being a part of it. They use all of the tools used by others undertaking ethnography, such as interviews, recording raw observations in note form or electronically, holding things in mind, writing up notes at the end of the day, questioning people, trying to do what those they are with are doing, and the like.

The point of divergence with others who study ethnographically gathered materials turns, however, upon understanding how these materials are *described* or *accounted* for. Really this is a divergence from how social science in general describes and accounts for social matters through practices of sociological theorising to which ethnography, despite witnessing society from within, is *no exception*. In our examination of Malinowski's pioneering study of the Trobriand Islanders in Chap. 3 we described, for example, how despite the fact that his materials consisted of witnessed actions and interactions generated from within the occasions in which they were done, he nevertheless used the tools of conventional social science to describe and thus account for the orderliness of what he observed; in this case functionalist theory. Ethnomethodology, however, seriously departs from the mainstream of social science in that it suspends sociological theorising as a means of accounting for the social order and describes order instead in 'endogenous' terms (Garfinkel and Wieder 1992), i.e., in terms of work's things as they are manifest, made visible and recognised by the parties to their production.

It is important to appreciate that it is not the theory used by an ethnographer that ethnomethodology takes issue with – be it functionalist, Marxist, post-modernism, feminist, etc. – but theorising as *the* means of accounting for the orderliness of action and interaction. Theorising glosses the local production of order, selectively describing (as we have seen in Chap. 4) what is needed *to make itself work*, and thereby transforming work's things into abstractions stripped of their own orderly properties. Ethnomethodology's respecification is no mere quibble about the 'probativeness' or adequacy of description then, but a deep and significant divergence from conventional social science that redefines our understanding of the very topics of social order. The respecification relocates 'what anyone knows' about the social order, the man and woman in the street and the professional social scientist alike, in the taken for granted and ignored orderliness of work's things. It is in doing and elaborating work's things as orderly-things-in-themselves rather than as orderly-things-in-a-social-theory that ethnomethodology distinguishes itself from ethnography. Even though its studies make use of ethnographically generated materials, ethnomethodology and ethnography are not different words for the same thing.

7.2 Social Science and Common-Sense

The distinction we make between ethnography and ethnomethodology may be difficult for social scientists, let alone systems designers, to appreciate. As we discussed in Chap. 5, other professional social analysts have argued that conventional or 'classic' ethnographic approaches are just as well suited to unpacking the orderliness of work's things as ethnomethodology (see Blomberg and Karasti 2013). As Garfinkel and Wieder (1992) put it,

> Professional sociology and ethnomethodology [EM] agree that the animal they are hunting is the production and the accountability of order in and as immortal, ordinary society … It would look like classic studies and EM agree, and entirely … Nevertheless, they do not agree … classic studies of order … address the *lived* work of order production … They know of its existence. They depend upon its existence as grounds for their own demonstrable adequacy … But it is their point, too, in the material particulars of that preoccupation, in the craft of that preoccupation, they differ profoundly and without possibility of reconciliation … Thus they differ on the nature of 'immortal' society; on the work of its production and reproduction; on its objectivity and observability … its 'account-ability' … its intelligibility … its exhibitable analysability …

We appreciate that the profound difference between the two may not be easy to grasp on this reading. A first step towards apprehending it can be made in appreciating, as touched upon in Chap. 4, that social science is essentially a *natural language exercise*. This is to say that the tool that the social sciences use to describe the social world is no more, nor less, than *language* – how could it be otherwise? Language is also the tool that ordinary people use to describe the social world – again how could it be otherwise? Thus, social scientists and the rest of society's members use the *same tool* to describe the social world.

There are a number of consequences for social science of this fact. The first is that social science descriptions are predicated on common-sense understandings of social matters. Language, as Wittgenstein (1958) makes play of, is a public matter, it is shared in common. Natural language descriptions are thus replete with common-sense knowledge, common-sense understandings and common-sense reasoning. In appropriating natural language the social sciences create a problem for themselves for they have built into their descriptive apparatus common knowledge of the workings of the social world without understanding what those workings consist of. The problem here, as Harvey Sacks (1963) puts it,

... is *acceptance of common-sense categories as sociological resources* rather than as features of social life which sociology must treat as subject matter.

This is another way of putting ethnomethodology's respecification of the social sciences, for instead of building descriptions of the social world based upon unacknowledged common-sense understanding and reasoning, ethnomethodology makes the task of social science the examination of that reasoning and understanding. Not in terms of providing a social science account of it but in terms of making visible what it consists of in its own right, of making visible its ordered properties and how people use those ordered properties in their actions and interactions. Given that the only tool we have to produce descriptions of the social world is language, and given that language is shared in common with everyday language users, then it would be to fall into the same trap as social science in general if addressing language use was done as a description of what it is. This is not the point. The point is that everyday language use is *orderly*. Our use throughout this book of greetings as examples has, we hope by now, made that point, and that this orderliness is visible to people and used by them. Ethnomethodology's respecification of social science is thus directed not to offering a sociological description of natural language use, a theory of natural language as it were, but is rather concerned to make the orderliness of language use explicitly visible (see Sacks 1992).

The use of natural language by social scientists to describe society does not mean that their descriptions *correspond* with common-sense accounts. This is because the social sciences take common-sense categories and provide them with specialist definitions. This takes us to a second consequence of using natural language to describe the social, which is that social science descriptions *contend* with common-sense descriptions. For example, as we have previously mentioned, sociological accounts of software engineering may well result in the software engineer being described as someone who contributes to 'world hegemony' in the doing of their engineering work. Whereas the engineer may describe what they are doing in the terms of its own undertaking; for instance "I'm figuring out the relationship between these two modules." Another ready example is Malinowski's description of the Kula Ring, which we examined in Chap. 3. Malinowski's description is that the Kula Ring performs a social function in society, bonding social groups together, a description that is unlikely to be offered as an account of what they are doing by participants themselves. Thus social science accounts can and do *diverge* from the ordinary descriptions that people in society may provide of their activities. Importing common-sense categories and the knowledge of society that attaches to them does not mean that sociological descriptions reflect their ordinary use.

A more detailed example might be helpful here to aid understanding of the impact of ordinary language use on sociological description, and how this ramifies for systems design. In recent years *expertise* has become an important topic in the area of science and technology studies. These studies revolve around issues of what expertise is, who can be called an expert and the role of the expert in society. Some of this work has been used in thinking about how to develop expert systems. The categories 'expert' and 'expertise' are, inevitably, everyday matters, common-sensically understood. The everyday grounds for calling someone an expert resides in the recognition of what and how they do something. So a civil engineer may be called upon to advise in the design of a bridge spanning a river, rather than just anyone off the street, because he or she is an expert. However, we know that it is not *just* because the engineer is an *expert* that he/she is called upon. A linguist, for example, may also be an expert, but they might not be called upon to be an advisor to the bridge building project. Therefore it is not that somebody is an expert that is relevant, but that they possess expertise in *doing some particular thing*, and the doing of that is occasioned as a relevant matter in some way. Thus the civil engineer is not called in because he/she is an expert per se, but because he/she is an expert *in* civil engineering, and is capable of undertaking the engineering of the bridge in recognisably expert ways.

Of course, someone may claim expertise, or we may think of them as experts, because of their organisational position or because of their qualifications and we may treat them, accordingly, as experts without ever witnessing them doing what they are expert in. However, in the end such positions and qualifications are recognisably grounded in practice. The warrant for ordinarily describing someone as an expert resides in the recognisability of what it is they can *do* and how they *display* expertise in the course of some practical undertaking. The terms expert and expertise, the demonstration of those matters, how they can be challenged and substantiated are, then, perfectly well understood in everyday life. What the terms expertise and expert refer to is not a puzzle, any more than how in any particular case confusion as to their appropriate designation can be cleared up. The warrant for the common-sense use of these terms resides in how experts and expertise are *accounted for*, which is provided by the *practices* that display their commonly understood characteristics.

The social sciences are in accord with the layman operating under the auspices of common-sense reasoning and thus recognise that there are such things in the world as experts and expertise. However, the ways in which social scientists construe of and understand these phenomena is quite different. Collins and Evan's (2007) have argued, for example, that some of their number in the field of social studies of science and technology are trying to level the playing field between scientists and non-scientists in arguing that people other than scientific experts have an equal claim to representation in policy determining forums. Part of Collins and Evans' argument is that the constructivist agenda in this area of social science has gone too far. This agenda, in describing the way in which science is constructed through social practices, has attempted to show, in Collins and Evans' terms, that science is not what it was popularly thought to be, but is rather driven by political and institutional matters just as much as any other domain of life. They cite a study by Wynne (1996) who examined the arguments that arose between Cumbrian sheep farmers and scientific experts of the Department of Agriculture in the UK with respect to the consequences of the Chernobyl nuclear reactor explosion for sheep farming in the UK.

Collins and Evans argue that Wynne is saying that the sheep farmers had *lay* expertise and that this is on a par with scientific expertise. Though we would dispute the accuracy of Collins and Evans' interpretation of Wynne here, they are neverthe-less concerned to disabuse us of the idea that lay expertise can be equated to scien-tific expertise, and that the scientific expert has no privileged hold on the matter. It is, however, the manner in which Collins and Evan's go about their critique of Wynne that concerns us here, for they argue that the sheep farmers did not posses *lay* expertise, but *specialist* expertise, and thus the contrast is not between the lay and scientific expertise, but two specialist domains of expertise. To substantiate this and to help us understand what expertise is Collins and Evans construct a taxonomy that maps out different kinds of expertise: 'contributory expertise', 'local discrimi-nation', 'beer-mat knowledge', 'popular understanding', 'primary source knowl-edge', 'interactional expertise', etc. We will not go into each of these categories here, but note that we emerge from Collins and Evans' exercise with a very different understanding of the words 'expert' and 'expertise' from the understanding that we might ordinarily have of them. In either case, we now have a sociologically defined understanding of experts and expertise that stands alongside our everyday use and understanding of these terms.

Except the social scientist does not actually stand their understandings alongside ordinary understandings. Rather the sociologically defined understanding is used to *replace* the understanding at work in the everyday world from which the terms expert and expertise were taken. Sociological *re*-descriptions of the common-sense world are, however, themselves contended. The source of contention being the other definitions that other social sciences have produced, and the arguments that ensue over whose definition is 'better'. Thus, and for example, there was a strong backlash in the social science community to Collins and Evans taxonomy and definition of expertise. There is nothing out of the ordinary in this, it is business as usual in the social sciences, a perennial affair that prompted Harold Garfinkel to suggest that the social sciences are "talking sciences" essentially occupied with the business of "shoving words around" (Garfinkel et al. 1981).

The production of contending accounts of social phenomena leads to a third key problem with the appropriation of natural language as a descriptive resource. The problem is this: there is an inevitable *disjuncture* between the social world as under-stood and known about by social scientists in their descriptions and the world as it common-sensically understood and known about by society's members in their descriptions. The disjuncture is licensed and legitimated by scientific practice: social science descriptions are warranted by long-established disciplinary practices of abstraction and generalisation (Sacks 1963), whereas everyday descriptions are warranted by what anyone knows, by common-sense knowledge of the social world. On the face of it there would appear to be no contest. Common-sense understand-ings would seem to come in a poor second to the understandings of social phenom-ena developed by professional social scientists.

Social science descriptions are not only in competition with one another then, they are in competition with members' accounts of social life and its organisation. The competition is serious. Social science accounts do not simply seek to develop more detailed, thorough, systematic and comprehensive accounts of social phenom-ena as befits a science. Those accounts are intended to *replace* common-sense understandings. The notions of experts and expertise common-sensically under-stood and articulated in practice are to be replaced then, as any other common-sense categories treated by the social sciences, by an understanding of the phenomena as articulated in the disciplined studies, writings and attendant conceptual and theo-retical schema of the social scientist. That the very terms they use to re-describe the social world live and work in the world itself independently of the social sciences does not seem to be a matter of scientific concern. So what?

> The 'so what' argument assumes sociology to be a disciplined investigation that is fully *competitive* with members' relaxed investigation … Such an assumption leaves unexpli-cated members' methods for analysing, accounting, fact-finding, and so on, which *produce* for sociology its field of data. (Zimmerman and Pollner 1970)

Despite the lofty ambitions of the social sciences to replace common-sense knowledge of social matters with disciplinary knowledge, common-sense does not just disappear, it remains intact. It is, ironically, the perennial sociological resource, continuously furnishing social scientists with words to appropriate, shove around, and re-impose upon the world. Nonetheless, it is on the basis of ordinary, common-sense ways of understanding the world, embedded in natural language descriptions, that social life proceeds. The very issue of, for example, expertise as articulated, used, known about, and demonstrated, in peoples' actions and interactions is what turns the social world, irrespective of social science re-descriptions. In this respect what makes the everyday world work is *lost* to the social scientist. The point then for those designers who would turn to 'new' approaches to ethnography, is that in turning to conventional means of describing and accounting for the social they are turning to approaches that draw on common-sense knowledge, common-sense understandings and common-sense reasoning but leaving the very grounds on which the social world stands and operates *untouched*. What you get with mainstream social science is common-sense remastered, rather than an empirical elaboration of common-sense's workings: workings which are constitutive of the social settings and situations in which systems will actually be placed.

7.3   Common-Sense in Its Own Right

So, on the basis of the arguments above, ethnomethodology is turning attention away from social science knowledge of society and towards common-sense knowl-edge instead. We can imagine that those designers who have worked with ethno-methodologists might begin to feel a little uneasy to have it explicitly spelled out that ethnomethodology turns out to be founded on studies of common-sense reason-ing about social matters. Common-sense is a much maligned term in academic dis-ciplines as it is associated with the lumpen opinions of the masses, so let us be clear that in making common-sense a topic of study in its own right we are not referring to matters such as people's opinions on social matters. We are referring to the very *bedrock* of social life: the fact that people *know* by virtue of them being competent members of society how to *do* social life, and that they know how to do it because they share in common a stock of knowledge of social life and its conduct (Schutz 1932). A Martian or, perhaps more plausibly, a member of a rainforest tribe who has no cognisance of, for example, a 'Western' way of life would not know by observing the arrangement of bodies at a supermarket checkout that they are involved in paying for the goods they have taken off the shelves. But any competent member of 'our' society knows that they are doing this. To describe what people are doing at the supermarket checkout as "purchasing goods" displays the ordinary knowledge that people have by virtue of being competent members of society, and the knowledge members posses even in such simple cases is manifold in nature, displaying in its use understandings of, for example, monetary systems, the nature of financial transactions, banking systems, occupations and entitlements, appropriate behaviour, and on and on.

People's *opinions* about these sorts of things are, however, *another matter*. One might believe that the supermarket giants are destroying small shops and restricting peoples' choices. Others might argue that they are convenient and better suit modern living. However, *whatever* the opinion, it is based upon a shared common-sense understanding of what a supermarket *is*. We could not hold different opinions about supermarkets unless we *agreed* about what the thing we might disagree about was. That the thing we hold different opinions about *is* a supermarket, for example, shared and agreed knowledge of which we express when we use the word. Thus common-sense knowledge refers to the stock of cultural knowledge that people hold in common of their social world, not to matters of personal preference, bias, opinions, etc.[2]

In simply moving around the social world people display that they have in common with one another knowledge of how social matters, including language, work. They display this fact in recognising actions and the things being done in action as the things that they are, and in responding appropriately to them. Not only do people display that they have and use common-sense knowledge of social matters in moving through the social world, they also display in its use that common-sense knowledge is ordered. Certain things follow other things, for example. You walk up to the ticket kiosk in any cinema, offer your money or your card and you *will* receive a ticket or some proof of purchase that allows you access to the screen. And if you do not, then the fact that this is not happening is accountable, it requires an explanation; your card has been declined, for example. If you doubt this try disrupting the commonly understood order of things. Try walking out of the supermarket or entering the cinema without paying and see what happens.

---

[2] One of us was involved in a ludicrous argument at a conference held at Loughborough University in the UK where the word 'fork' as a description of something was disputed and were told that it was not a fork, it was a *weapon*. Thus what a fork is, the meaning it has was seen as being dependent on how we describe it. The ludicrousness of shoving the word fork around in this way, indeed the ludicrousness of 'anti-realist' positions encountered in Chap. 5, resides in the mis-use of ordinary words. Describing a fork as a weapon turns upon first knowing what a fork is, and then appropriately saying that the fork was used *as* a weapon.

It is a primordial feature of social life that society's members have and hold a stock of knowledge in common, a stock of cultural knowledge that is ordered and used to order social action. Of course when someone goes to another country or society there will be local ways of doing things that at first you might be baffled by. But these are easily rectifiable matters and you can learn that 'this is how we do *this* here'. When catching a local train from Cairo to Luxor you only need to do it once to know that you do not obtain a seat on a train in the way in which you do in the UK in queuing by the doors, but that if you want a seat you push, jostle or use the windows to get in first. First in the queue by the door, is quickly replaced by first in, first served.

Possessing and using common-sense knowledge of the social world means that people are perfectly capable of describing and understanding the orderliness of social phenomena. Indeed, you might say that it is their business to know and understand the social order, and that they are masters in its production, even though they would be hard pressed to spell it out for you, as mundane order production is utterly taken for granted, an unremarkable feature of everyday life. However, it is with respect to common-sense knowledge of the social world that traditional social science, including ethnography, and ethnomethodological studies diverge in the ways we have outlined above; that is, in repurposing natural language and the common-sense knowledge built into it to re-describe the orderliness of social life. Ethnomethodology provides for social science an alternative trajectory of investigation, for instead of attempting to replace common-sense knowledge of the social with disciplinary knowledge, it wants to address how common-sense knowledge is organised and used by society's members, locally, to order their actions and interactions and to thereby produce the recognisable scenes of social life. It wants to make the locally ordered properties of common-sense knowledge, which are taken for granted by any competent member of society into a topic of investigation in its own right. Thus, instead of attempting to replace common-sense knowledge of the social world, ethnomethodology respecifies the task of social science as one of making visible that which everyone knows and takes for granted, and how that knowledge is used in the doing of social life.

We can concretise this through an example, *conversation analysis* (CA). This is the branch of ethnomethodology acknowledged by Garfinkel in his introduction to *Ethnomethodological Studies of Work*, and is the study of the local ordering of talk-in-interaction. It is about what everyone knows in being able to talk to one another, about making visible the methods through which people order turns at talk. Systems designers may be familiar with CA through Lucy Suchman's seminal work (Suchman 1987), where she drew on Sacks' work to drive the social into the design mix in elaborating how human interaction with a computer (an expert help system embedded in a photocopier) was ordered through common-sense methods of communication. Systems designers may also be familiar with the approach through the work of Christian Heath, Paul Luff and John Hindmarsh. Their studies of interaction in London Underground control rooms (Heath and Luff 1991), collaborative virtual environments (Hindmarsh et al. 2000), museums (Hindmarsh et al. 2002), and video-mediated environments (Luff et al. 2003), for example, have been used to address and elaborate a variety of design challenges.

CA makes use of audio and audio-visual recordings of naturally occurring inter-action, which are transcribed to support subsequent analysis. Naturally occurring interaction refers to occasions of interaction 'as it happens' in the ordinary course of everyday life; 'in the wild' as it were rather than in occasions that have been experimentally designed, or occasions that have otherwise been orchestrated for the purposes of study. In his early work Sacks used telephone recordings made of calls to a Los Angeles suicide prevention centre, and calls made to and from his neigh-bour's phone, which he was able to overhear because they were made on a party line (at that time some phone lines were shared by multiple users). A broad range of social settings have been subsequently used to generate material for analysis.

CA is unique in the social sciences in as much as what it makes available for analysis is the *very material of social interaction*, presented in terms of transcripts of audio recordings and descriptions of the action and interaction embedded in audio-visual recordings. Using such material does away with the problem of having to remember what was said or done in a setting. It documents actual occurrences of interaction involved in the conduct of actual social events, and provides empirical data for sociological analysis that can be revisited again and again and be repeatedly inspected. Conversation analysis thus roots the study of society in society's 'lived' materials – what is recorded is not a matter of speculation but something that actu-ally occurred, something that made sense to the parties involved, and something that makes sense to others who listen to and watch the recordings and read the accom-panying transcriptions and descriptions of interaction. It may well be that we do not know much about the interactional occurrences in terms of the people involved, when they were talking, where they were when they were talking, etc., but the mate-rial makes visible and available to analysis what is going on and being done by the participants because what is being done is not gibberish, it is quite understandable. That understandability – the intelligibility of action and interaction – is provided by common-sense knowledge of interactional conduct; taken for granted knowledge that we all develop through our participation in a culture, and it is for this reason that Sacks referred to the recordings he made as capturing 'slices' of culture.

CA has had more of an impact in linguistics where the study of discourse is well established, in education where the observation of interaction in a limited domain (the classroom) is well established, and in communication studies, than it has in sociology where the study of mundane conversation is often deemed to be *too trivial* for disciplines concerned with such weighty matters as class conflict, gender inequality, globalisation, the meaning and impact of technology in society, etc. Sacks challenges the view that the social order can only be addressed through the study of such 'big issues', arguing to the contrary that there is 'order at all points' – i.e., that order is to be found in *anything* that human beings do regardless of its status in sociological theorising. Concomitant to this, Sacks also argues that we may well find that 'enormous generalisability' is built into mundane order (Sacks 1984). Turn taking in conversation exemplifies both points.

In a seminal text *A Simplest Systematics for the Organisation of Turn-Taking for Conversation*, Sacks et al. (1974) elaborated 'a locally ordered, party-administered, interactionally controlled systematics of turn-taking in conversation', which is fundamental to conversation of all kinds whether it be about big issues, mundane ones, the downright trivial, foolish or banal. More prosaically they found in their studies,

> ... the existence of organised turn-taking ... that, overwhelmingly, one party talks at a time, though speakers change and though the size of turns and ordering of turns vary, that transitions are finely coordinated; that techniques are used for allocating turns ... and that there are techniques for the construction of utterances relevant to their turn status, which bear on the coordination of transfer and the allocation of speakership. (ibid.)

The 'techniques' they talk about, which are elaborated in detail in their paper, elaborate an interactional 'machinery' known and used in common by society's members to order conversation. A machinery whose methodical operation applies generally, *anywhere* where people can be found in conversation together.

Sacks et al.'s work provides a canonical example of the fact that even the most mundane of human interactions are *orderly* matters. Furthermore, that mundane order, which encapsulates any and every topic of common-sense reasoning drawn on as a resource by sociological theorising, is accomplished in *methodical ways* that make interaction accountable and thus mutually intelligible to those involved in it and to those who witness it. Sacks and his colleague's achievement cannot be overstated. His work provides the most extensive demonstration available of the ways that people actively organise their interactions locally in the unfolding course of their conduct through the use of common-sense methods; methods through which social life is routinely conducted time and time again across people and across settings within a culture; methods that bring about in their taken for granted and unremarkable use the orderliness of a social world that professional social science is predicated and parasitic upon but refuses to acknowledge.

Thus, like Garfinkel, Sacks' work orients us to a practically indispensible *yet ignored* domain of study: members' methods for doing and ordering social life. His studies not only elaborate members' methods, their description provides for the reproducibility of the commonplace activities they are part and parcel of, for their orderly conduct next time through. Have a chat with someone and see for yourself how you can do no other than engage in the orderly business of turn allocation if the conversation is to proceed; try to hold the floor and see what happens. That you will see common-sense methods 'at work', that you do not need to be mastered in the arts and craft of abstract sociological reasoning to see them, is a non-trivial point. As Sacks put it,

> I take it ... that lots of the results I offer, people can go and see for themselves. And they needn't be afraid to. And they needn't figure the results are wrong because they can see them. Since beforehand they didn't know it, and now they can see something they didn't even know existed. As if we found a new plant. It may have been a plant in your garden, but now you see it's different than something else. And you can look and see how it's different, and whether it's different in the way that somebody said. (Sacks 1992)

Sacks' explication of members' methods through theoretically unmotivated socio-logical analysis of empirical materials moves us beyond the perennial business of contestable storytelling in the social sciences and shoving words around. His studies focus analytic attention on matters that incontestably occur, and make visible the methodical ways in which a significant part of social life – talk – is ordered by people in their actions and interactions as an intelligible cultural matter. In doing so, Sacks elaborated a rigorous analytic base for whatever might pass as ethnography in the social sciences or systems design.

Sacks' conversation analysis inspired ethnomethodology's *studies of work* pro-gram. Ethnomethodological studies of work extend beyond the analysis of conver-sation's orderly ways to address the orderly character of other modalities of action and interaction and domains of human activity. There has been much debate between conversation analysts and ethnomethodologists about the relationship between the two (see Maynard and Clayman 2003). However, insofar as ethnomethodological studies of work are directed at the respecification of the sociological problem of order as a local production and accomplishment then they resemble conversation analytic studies in one very important respect. They seek to elaborate, through empirical investigations and analysis of society's 'lived' materials, the common-sense methods that society's members employ to assemble their actions and interac-tions as intelligible, understandable, accountably ordered matters. This issue of members methods is captured in the term 'ethnomethodology', which refers to the study of *ethno* (folk) *methodology*, as in ethnobotany or ethnomedicine, but focus-ing on the knowledge and methodical ways in which it is used (the methodologies) that society's members employ to produce the organised scenes of everyday life.

Garfinkel described his coining of the term at the Purdue Symposium on Ethnomethodology (Hill and Crittenden 1968) as follows.

> Back in 1954 ... Fred ... Strodtbeck ... had 'bugged' the jury room in Wichita. He asked me to ... listen to the tapes of the jurors ... the notion occurred to me of analysing the delib-erations of the jurors ... these magnificent methodological things ... like 'fact' and 'fancy' and 'opinion' and 'my opinion' and 'your opinion' and 'what we're entitled to say' and 'what the evidence shows' and 'what can be demonstrated' and 'what actually he said' as compared with 'what only you think he said' or 'what he seemed to have said' ... Here I am faced with jurors who are doing methodology ... Its not a methodology my colleagues would honour if they were attempting to staff the sociology department ... Nevertheless, the jurors' concerns for such issues seemed to be undeniable ... That is what ethnomethod-ology is concerned with. It is an organisational study of a member's knowledge of his ordinary affairs, of his own organised enterprises, where that knowledge is treated by us as part of the same setting that it also makes orderable.

In treating members' knowledge of ordinary affairs – common-sense knowledge – as a topic to be investigated, ethnomethodological studies uncover *how* the mun-dane world of 'social facts' – the world of 'organised enterprises' or social arrangements known in common by the man or woman in the street and social sci-entist alike – are given *as* facts to society's members and thus become available as a resource for sociological theorising (Garfinkel 2002). In making common-sense a topic of investigation in its own right, ethnomethodology's studies do not rival common-sense knowledge, common-sense understandings and common-sense reasoning. Ethnomethodology is not in competition with common-sense, it does not seek to replace it, but neither does it valorise it. Rather it recognises that *any* understanding of the social world is rooted in, built upon and exploits folk methodologies, including (as elaborated in Chap. 4) mainstream social science understandings.

Consequently, just as Gilbert Ryle (1949) pointed out that there was an alternative path for psychology provided for by phenomenology, ethnomethodology creates an alternate path for the study of the social in making common-sense a problem to be investigated rather than a taken for granted resource for sociological theorising. The two paths cannot, as Garfinkel and Wieder (1992) tell us, be reconciled. On the one hand, we have the traditional study of social life rooted in common-sense knowledge of society and making use of it as a resource for its disciplinary descriptions of social order, and on the other, the study of social life through descriptions of the socio-cultural methods society's members use to assemble their actions and interactions as orderly features of ordinary society. In elaborating ethnomethodology's distinctive orientation to the study of the social, we have attempted to make a little more explicit why it is that ethnomethodology has sought to respecify the topics and the practices of social science: that the conventional preoccupation with repurposing ordinary language and re-describing what everyone knows through generic sociological theorising creates a disjuncture between common-sense and social science understandings, and sets up an absurd rivalry between them. In turn, conventional sociological accounts of the orderliness of everyday life come, quite curiously, to *hover above* and at some *remove* from its mundane methodological production, which is ignored and left untouched.

7.4 Anchoring Systems Design in the Social

We return, in conclusion, to the question of what possible concern this can have for systems design? If a designer finds that a story brought back from the field sparks their imagination, what does it matter if it is a story that anyone could have come up with? If a designer finds that a particular analytic orientation or 'world view' suggests a design path to follow, what does it matter if that world view is generated through the methodological apparatus of conventional social science? If a designer is puzzling over the requirements for a system and finds that a standard social science questionnaire or interview sheds light on what they should be designing for, what does it matter? To answer these questions we need to reflect upon another: how successful has the design of interactive software systems actually been? For sure it is possible to point to a great many success stories, but then, if we are honest, there have been a great many failures too. IEEE tells us that "we waste billions of dollars every year on entirely preventable mistakes", citing a host of industry and government projects in its "hall of shame" (Charette 2005). Industry analysts have documented a costly "catalogue of catastrophe" that plagues governments and industry around the world (Calleam Consulting 2014a). While the exact figures are debatable, industry analysts estimate that the global cost of IT project failure runs between

3 and 6 *trillion* dollars annually (Krigsman 2012). Despite the hype, the information revolution would appear to be a deeply troubled enterprise. Indeed, as one industry insider puts it,

> If building engineers built buildings with the same care as software engineers build systems, the first woodpecker to come along would be the end of civilization as we know it. (Dorsey 2005)

High profile failures of the kind we often hear about in the news, such as the troubled healthcare platforms in the US and UK, are but the tip of the iceberg. The Standish Group's periodic CHAOS reports make it clear that the success rate of software development across industry is alarmingly *low*. The 1995 survey reported that only 16 % of software development projects were completed successfully, where success means that they were completed on time, on budget and delivered expected functionality or services; 31 % of projects were cancelled before completion, and 53 % of projects had major cost overruns (Standish Group 1995). Nearly two decades later the 2013 survey reported that the success rate had improved to 39 %; cancellations had dropped to 18 % and the rate of 'challenged' projects (running late, over budget and/or delivering less functioning features than required) was running at 43 % (Standish Group 2013). The situation is improving then, but it is far from satisfactory.

Given the poor picture painted of the systems design industry it is unsurprising that the CHAOS figures have been challenged, though not especially by industry itself. Members of the academic design community have taken the CHAOS reports to task and query the underlying methodology and findings, both of which are found wanting: biased, inflated, misleading are words that pepper these works and lead to the view that the results of the CHAOS surveys are 'meaningless' (see, for example, Glass 2006; Jørgensen and Moløkken 2006; Eveleens and Verhoef 2010). There are, of course, other surveys of software success rates but none of them paint a particularly rosy picture (see Calleam Consulting 2014b, by way of example). However, whichever view you ascribe to regarding the scale of failure, there is broad consensus about its causes. Amongst a litany of technical problems, report after report places 'people issues' high on the list: 'lack of user involvement', 'poor user input', 'vague requirements' and other variations on these themes are longstanding issues frequently cited even today as *major* causes of project failure (see, for example, May 1998; Keil et al. 1998; Kessler 2001; Yardley 2002; Standish Group 2013 CHAOS report).

This is industry though, and systems design is also practiced in universities, where the criteria of success are rather different, being concerned, for example, with the conduct of novel research and the development of PhD theses. While the development of talent and expertise, and innovation and new ways of thinking about systems, rather than building and delivering working systems to meet end-user needs, may be the principle success criteria of design in this context, it nevertheless seeks to engage with the real world and real people to understand and shape new technological possibilities. It is curious, then, that despite the vast wealth of weird and wonderful designs presented at international conferences every year, so few ever see the light of day and find their way into mundane use. Very rarely, despite the billions invested in academic research, does a university-based project result in a widespread usable system. It might be argued that this is not the object of university research but this argument would, of course, be disingenuous. Labouring under and championing the latest computational trends – ubiquitous computing, cloud computing, the internet of things, etc. – academic developers are just as interested in creating the game changer, the small project that goes virile, and these can occasionally be pointed to, but how many go by the wayside? It is perhaps unsurprising then, in the UK at least, that the research councils increasingly demand more tangible 'impact' as a return on their investment.

There is a sense in which systems design in both industrial and academic contexts is much like traditional social science with respect to its *connection* with the social world. There is a visible disjuncture between systems design, and design ideas, and the social world those ideas and artefacts are intended to engage with. All too often it would seem that systems design, like social science, hovers over and above the social, not connecting, not engaging, not bringing the promised impact about whether it will be supporting, automating or offering new ways of doing things. In turning to ethnography some designers see a way of bridging the gap and anchoring systems development to the social; certainly those who do ethnography for design purposes hold out that promise. However, a social science that hovers over and above the very world it describes may not provide a sufficient methodology for systems design to get a hold on the social. In respecifying social science problems ethnomethodology offers an alternative methodology. It is *not* a social science methodology – not a methodology, as Garfinkel puts it, that would be honoured by the social sciences – but a *members' methodology* for assembling the organised settings and scenes of everyday life, settings and scenes in which computing systems, applications and services have to gear into if they are to survive. While ethnomethodology has nothing to do with systems design as a discipline in itself, its empirical studies of the mundane methodologies that people use to organise their everyday activities can be purposed by those who wish to anchor design in the social. The methodology we refer to in the title of this book is not a methodology we as sociologists who employ ethnographically-gathered materials are offering then. It is, rather, to put forward the idea to systems design that *members' methods* for the local production and achievement of social order can be a means of anchoring design in the social. What we want to do in the next chapter is demonstrate this proposition.

References

Blomberg, J., & Karasti, H. (2013). Reflections on 25 years of ethnography in CSCW. *Computer Supported Cooperative Work: The Journal of Collaborative Computing, 22*, 373–423.

Button, G. (Ed.). (1991). *Ethnomethodology and the human sciences*. Cambridge: Cambridge University Press.

Button, G., & Dourish, P. (1996). Technomethodology. In *Proceedings of the 1996 SIGCHI confer-ence on human factors in computing systems* (pp. 19–26). Vancouver: ACM.

Button, G., & Sharrock, W. (1997). The production of order and the order of production. In *Proceedings of the 5th European conference on computer supported cooperative work* (pp. 116). Lancaster: Kluwer.

Calleam Consulting. (2014a). Why projects fail: Catalogue of catastrophe. http://calleam.com/WTPF/?page_id=3.

Calleam Consulting. (2014b). Facts and figures. http://calleam.com/WTPF/?page_id=1445.

Charette, N. (2005). Why software fails. IEEE Spectrum. Sept 2005. http://spectrum.ieee.org/com-puting/software/why-software-fails.

Collins, H., & Evans, R. (2007). *Rethinking expertise*. Chicago: University of Chicago Press.

Crabtree, A., Tolmie, P., Rouncefield, M. (2013) 'How many bloody examples do you want?' – fieldwork and generalisation. In *Proceedings of the 13th European conference on computer supported cooperative work* (pp. 1–20). Paphos: Springer.

Dorsey, P. (2005). *Top 10 reasons why systems projects fail*. Woodbridge: Dulcian.

Dourish, P. (2006). Implications for design. In *Proceedings of the conference on human factors in computing systems* (pp. 541–550). Quebec: ACM.

Eveleens, J. L., & Verhoef, C. (2010). The rise and fall of the CHAOS report figures. *IEEE Software, 27*(1), 30–36.

Garfinkel, H. (1967). *Studies in ethnomethodology*. Englewood Cliffs: Prentice-Hall.

Garfinkel, H. (Ed.). (1986). *Ethnomethodological studies of work*. London: Routledge and Kegan Paul.

Garfinkel, H. (1991). Respecification: evidence for locally produced, naturally accountable phe-nomena of order. In G. Button (Ed.), *Ethnomethodology and the human sciences* (pp. 10–19). Cambridge: Cambridge University Press.

Garfinkel, H. (2002). *Ethnomethodology's program: Working out Durkheim's aphorism*. Lanham: Rowman and Littlefield.

Garfinkel, H., & Wieder, D. L. (1992). Two incommensurable, asymmetrically alternate technolo-gies of social analysis. In G. Watson & S. M. Seiler (Eds.), *Text in context: Contributions to ethnomethodology* (pp. 175–206). New York: Sage.

Garfinkel, H., Lynch, M., & Livingston, E. (1981). The work of a discovering science construed with materials from the optically discovered pulsar. *Philosophy of Social Science, 11*, 131–158.

Glass, R. (2006). The Standish report: Does it really describe a software crisis? *Communications of the ACM, 49*(8), 15–16.

Hacker, P. M. S. (1996). *Wittgenstein's place in twentieth-century analytic philosophy*. Oxford: Blackwell.

Heath, C., & Luff, P. (1991). Collaborative activity and technology design: Task coordination in London underground control rooms. In *Proceedings of the European conference on computer supported cooperative work* (pp. 65–80). Amsterdam: Kluwer Academic Publishers.

Hill, R., & Crittenden, K. (1968). Proceedings of the Purdue symposium on ethnomethodology. West Lafayette, Purdue Research Foundation. http://aiemcanet.files.wordpress.com/2010/07/purdue.pdf.

Hindmarsh, J., Fraser, M., Heath, C., Benford, S., & Greenhalgh, C. (2000). Object-focused inter-action in collaborative virtual environments. *ACM Transactions on Computer-Human Interaction, 7*(4), 477–509.

Hindmarsh, J., Heath, C., vom Lehm, D., Cleverly, J. (2002). Creating assemblies: Aboard the Ghost Ship. In *Proceedings of the conference on computer supported cooperative work* (pp. 156–165). New Orleans: ACM.

Hughes, J., Randall, D., Shapiro, D. (1992). Faltering from ethnography to design. In *Proceedings of the 1992 ACM conference on computer supported cooperative work* (pp. 115–122). Toronto: ACM.

Jørgensen, M., & Moløkken, K. (2006). How large are software cost overruns? A review of the 1994 CHAOS report. *Information and Software Technology, 48*(8), 297–301.

Keil, M., Cule, P., Lyytinen, K., & Schmidt, R. (1998). A framework for identifying software project risks. *Communications of the ACM, 41*(11), 76–83.

Kessler, G. (2001). Why technical projects fail: Avoiding disaster. *Inside Project Management, 1*(2), 1–6.

Krigsman, M. (2012). Worldwide cost of IT failure (revisited): $3 trillion. ZDNet. Apr 2012. www.zdnet.com/blog/projectfailures/worldwide-cost-of-it-failure-revisited-3-trillion/15424.

Kuper, A. (2005). Alternate histories of British social anthropology. *Social Anthropology, 13*(1), 47–64.

Luff, P., Heath, C., Kuzuoka, H., Hindmarsh, J., Yamazaki, K., & Oyama, S. (2003). Fractured ecologies: Creating environments for collaboration. *Human Computer Interaction, 18*, 51–84.

Lynch, M. (1993). *Scientific practice and ordinary action: Ethnomethodology and social studies of science*. Cambridge: Cambridge University Press.

May, L. (1998). Major causes of software project failure. *Crosstalk: The Journal of Defense Software Engineering*, July edition, pp. 9–12.

Maynard, D., & Clayman, S. (2003). Ethnomethodology and conversation analysis. In L. Reynolds & N. Herman-Kinney (Eds.), *The handbook of symbolic interactionism* (pp. 173–202). Walnut Creek: Altamira Press.

Ryle, G. (1949). *The concept of mind*. London: Hutchinson.

Sacks, H. (1963). Sociological description. *Berkeley Journal of Sociology, 8*, 1–16.

Sacks, H. (1984). Notes on methodology. In J. M. Maxwell & J. Heritage (Eds.), *Structures of social action: Studies in conversation analysis* (pp. 21–27). Cambridge: Cambridge University Press.

Sacks, H. (1992). In G. Jefferson (Ed.), *Lectures on conversation Volumes I & II*. Oxford: Blackwell.

Sacks, H., Schegloff, E., & Jefferson, G. (1974). A simplest systematics for the organisation of turn-taking for conversation. *Language, 50*(4), 696–735.

Schutz, A. (1932). *The phenomenology of the social world*. Vienna: Julius Springer.

Sommerville, I., Rodden, T., Sawyer, P., Bentley, R. (1992). Sociologists can be surprisingly useful in interactive systems design. In *Proceedings of the 7th conference of the British Computer Society Human Computer Interaction Specialist Group* (pp. 341–341). York: BCS.

Standish Group. (1995). *CHAOS report*. www.projectsmart.co.uk/docs/chaos-report.pdf.

Standish Group. (2013). *CHAOS report*. www.versionone.com/assets/img/files/CHAOSManifesto2013.pdf.

Suchman, L. (1987). *Plans and situated actions: The problem of human-machine communication*. Cambridge: Cambridge University Press.

Wittgenstein, L. (1958). *Philosophical investigations*. Oxford: Basil Blackwell.

Wynne, B. (1996). May the sheep safely graze? In S. Lash, B. Szerszynski, & B. Wynne (Eds.), *Risk, environment and modernity: Towards a new ecology* (pp. 44–83). London: Sage.

Yardley, D. (2002). *Successful IT project delivery: Learning the lessons of project failure*. New York: Addison-Wesley.

Zimmerman, D. and Pollner, M. (1970). The everyday world as a phenomenon. *Understanding everyday life* (ed. Douglas, J.), pp. 80–103, Chicago, Aldine Publishing Company.

Chapter 8
Members' *Not* Ethnographers' Methods

Abstract In this final chapter we offer a demonstration of the proposition that design *can* be systematically anchored in the social through the study of members' methodologies. We start by reviewing Suchman's foundational studies of human-machine communication before moving on to consider Dourish and Button's reflections on accountability as a resource for design. To elaborate this more fully we look at Xerox's Virtual Help Desk and how studies of the methodical ways in which action and interaction is account-ably conducted and ordered shaped the design of this award-winning piece of software. Finally we consider ethnomethodological studies undertaken outside of the workplace to inform other kinds of interactive and ubiquitous computing systems. The demonstration makes it plain to see that that the methodological apparatus of the social sciences is not required to understand the social and build it into systems design. There is a viable alternative. One which has already contributed enormously to the work of design over the last 30 years and produced a diverse body of work demonstrating that design efforts to change the world through the development of computational artefacts may be *constructively* informed and *shaped* around the social through the explication of the methods that members employ to order action and interaction.

8.1 Ethnomethodology and Design

This book has been prompted by arguments made in recent years concerning the use of ethnography in the design of interactive and ubiquitous computing systems. The arguments juxtapose 'old' and 'new' forms of ethnography, and turn on the following points.

1. Ethnography as articulated for systems design has largely been associated with the design of workplace (mainly office) environments and with work related activities, but with the advent of design interests in ubiquitous computing a 'new' (sic) type of ethnography is called for, ethnography tailored for non-workplace settings and non-work activities.

2. 'Old' ethnographies of the workplace, and of work related activities, have mainly resulted in either 'implications for design', in requirements for particular design undertakings, or a concern to understand technology-in-use, but ethnography

© Springer International Publishing Switzerland 2015

G. Button et al., *Deconstructing Ethnography*, Human-Computer
Interaction Series, DOI 10.1007/978-3-319-21954-7_8

offers much more to design, including the opportunity to reflect upon cultural matters that impact design in general, such as the role of computing in social life, or the meanings that people attach to it.

3. If the ethnographer enters a setting with a work activity or workplace mentality then they will only see work activity and workplace design relevancies and miss the opportunity to see relevancies for other types of activities and systems.

4. The ethnographic studies of work and the workplace that design is familiar with have mainly focused upon action, interaction and technology-in-use, but there is a rich tradition of ethnographic studies in the social and human sciences that is relevant for design and can enable designers to encounter and address broader 'structural' issues that shape computing.

5. Systems are not just confined to particular settings, many transcend social and cultural boundaries and, in as much as cultures may differ, an appropriate understanding of the diverse social and cultural character of computing requires 'multi-site' ethnographies.

6. 'Old' ethnographies oriented to design have been empirical in nature offering up observations of 'social facts'. However, because all social matters, including the doing of ethnography are driven by theoretical perspectives, the theoretical lens through which the ethnographer is viewing the social must also be considered; consequently design needs to grapple with social and cultural theory and its constitutive role in the production of 'social facts'.

7. The empirical naivety of ethnography in design with respect to the constitution of social facts is matched by a naivety regarding the constitutive role of the ethnographer in a social setting, and reflecting upon how ethnography is conducted is, consequently, as important if not more important than the 'story' the ethnographer produces.

In the preceding chapters we have attempted to critically address these points. Although we have articulated these arguments *for* design, a number of them arise outside of the context *of* design. Our arguments transcend design in some respects insofar as it becomes a platform from which to view the various arguments that generally surround ethnography in the social sciences. However, whether seen from the point of view of social science or systems design our arguments regarding ethnography boil down to one essential observation: *ethnography is not the point.*

We have attempted to emphasise two matters in this respect. First, that the traditional methodological apparatus of social science which, as we have attempted to make visible can still be found at work in so-called 'new' approaches to ethnography, cannot and does not provide any more insight into the orderliness of society and social situations than can be found in non-social science accounts: e.g., in the accounts of journalists, writers, story-tellers, tourists, in political and moral rhetoric or, in short, in *common-sense reasoning* about the social world. While we may, at an individual level, be swayed by one or another social science description because, for example, it reinforces some ideology or world view that we are enamoured with, or because of the fact that the anthropologist must, by virtue at least of their immersion in a particular culture, be more informed than the 2 week vacationer, there is no inherent '*in principal*' privilege built-in to a social science account or the methods of its production that makes it 'stand over and above' any other account of the social world.

Simply put, social science accounts are not a *different kind* of account to those that anyone else offers. This is not to say that systems designers cannot find anything of value in social science descriptions or the methods of their production. Designers may well find that some cultural theory stimulates their imagination or supports them in thinking about the role of computer systems in social life and how they may address or change that. We have, to reiterate, emphasised throughout this book that we have no interest in legislating as to where designers might turn for inspiration. We have, however, been concerned to make visible just what is being bought into in the turn to the descriptive methods and accounts of ethnography and social science more generally so that there is no confusion over the matter: social science qua social science has *no special authority* with respect to the social. You might just as well talk to a journalist, a writer, a tourist, a politician, or the 'man-in-the-street' if you want inspiration or if you want to reflect upon computing in the modern world. In saying this, we do not mean the account offered by a social scientist, who may have thought long and hard about the nature and role of computing in contemporary society, can be of no more interest to a designer than an account offered by a tourist flushed with the excitement of a recent trip abroad. What we mean, and we would emphasis this, is that the social scientist *cannot* and *does not* bring a *different order* of reasoning to the table. What is offered is just another 'mundane version' of common-sense reasoning (Pollner 1978).

The second matter we have attempted to emphasise is that if design wants to build-in the social in a *systematic* rather than piecemeal way it is to the methods that society's members employ to order and reason about action and interaction, and not the methods that ethnographers employ to reason about and describe order, that it should turn. It is in members' methodological doings that the social settings, scenes and events that make up society at large are brought about, and it is in *within* these methodological doings that technology is located, purposed and used. Ethnomethodological studies aim to make these methodological doings visible and thus surface the methods that members use to locally assemble and achieve the orderliness of the everyday world.

This was first brought to the attention of *systems design* in Lucy Suchman's seminal work on human-machine communication (Suchman 1987). While other traditions may now wish to lay claim to her studies, and irrespective of whether or not Suchman is currently pursuing such studies, it is as plain as it could possibly be that her seminal work is explicitly rooted in ethnomethodology's concerns with members' methods.

> The methodology of interest to ethnomethodologists … is not their own but that deployed by members of the society in coming to know, and making sense out of, the everyday world of talk and action.
>
> To designate the alternative that ethnomethodology suggests … I have introduced the term *situated action*. (ibid.)[1]

---

[1] Note that Suchman is invoking a ubiquitous idea of 'situated action' not a restricted idea that confines interest to the workplace or to jobs of work, although she was conducting her studies in a workplace and observing people doing office work.

'Situated action' is Suchman's gloss on ethnomethodology's concern with the local methodological production of order, and that it is so becomes transparent when we consider her seminal study of human-machine communication at Xerox PARC.

The study focused on an expert help system attached to a photocopier. The system presented a set of procedures to novice users via visual displays instructing them how to use the photocopier and providing feedback on the photocopier's operational status; an interactional scene that many of us are familiar with today. Familiar too is the way in which such a system presents instructions, not as a manual to be consulted and applied but as a 'stepwise order' of interaction, within which each next instruction is presented on the user's completion of the last. The sequencing of instructions turns upon the system recognising the actions a user has performed *and* on the user recognising the orderliness of the instructions provided. The system does this by prescribing actions whose effects are detectable by the machine. Thus, and as Suchman puts it,

> ... the design relies on a partial enforcement of the order of user actions within the procedural sequence. This strategy works fairly well insofar as a particular effect produced by the user (such as closing a cover on the copier) can be taken to imply that a certain condition obtains (a document has been placed in the machine for copying), which, in turn, implies a machine response (the initiation of the printing process). In this sense, the order of user and machine 'turns', and what is to be accomplished in each, are predetermined. The system's 'recognition' of turn-transition places is essentially reactive; that is, there is a determinate relationship between certain actions by the user, read as changes to the state of the machine, and the machine's transition to a next display. By establishing a determinate relationship between detectable user actions and machine responses, the design unilaterally administers control over the interaction, but in a way that is conditional on the actions of the user.

This extract makes it clear that Suchman locates such human-machine communication within the mundane methods of 'turn-taking' in conversation identified by Sacks et al. (1974), which we discussed in Chap. 7. These are elaborated at length by Suchman, both as a preface to her study of photocopier interaction and as a feature of it, and her work makes it clear that there is strong sense in which the actions and interactions implicated in 'communicating' with the machine are predicated on the methods that members routinely employ to order talk. Indeed, as Suchman puts it,

> In the interest of conveying the intent of the design to the user, and in doing so interactively, the designer tacitly relies on certain conventions of human conversation. Most generally, designer and user share the expectation that the relevance of each utterance is conditional on the last; that given an action by one party that calls for a response, for example, the other's next action *will be* a response.

Turns, turn transition places, the conditional relevance of utterances (i.e., instructions in this case), are all mundane methodological features of ordinary human conversation and Suchman goes on to elaborate in 'situated' detail that it is not only designers that trade on the 'conventions of human conversation', but that the methods people use to locally order talk also underpin users interaction with the machine, and give rise to a host of interactional 'troubles' that can be 'fatal' for human-machine communication.

The troubles that Suchman speaks of and elaborates in her seminal work are occasioned by 'breaching' the methodological ways in which conversation works. The breach becomes visible in the gap between issuing an instruction and accomplishing the actions that bring it about. Suchman likens the situation to someone doing shopping with a list to convey the significance of the point. The list has items written on it and the shopper goes around the supermarket picking up items off the shelf and placing them in her shopping basket.

> The subject of the present analysis, the user of the expert help system, is in the position of the shopper with respect to the instructions that the system provides; that is, she must make her actions match the words. But in what sense? Like the instructions, a shopping list may be consulted to decide what to do next or to know when the shopping is done, may be cited after the fact to explain why things were done the way they were, and so forth. But also like the instructions, the list does not actually describe the practical activity of shopping (how to find things, which aisles to go down in what order, how to decide between competing brands, etc.); it simply says how that activity is to turn out.

The instructions issued by the machine are of this order: they do not 'tell' the user how to follow them, only how that activity is to turn out. The machine does not recognise the actions and interactions involved in 'following an instruction' then, it only recognises detectable machine states, and they may be wrong (it does not follow, for example, that just because the cover has been closed on the copier that copying can be initiated). However, in issuing a next instruction the user assumes that they have done the right thing because a next instruction has been issued. Thus, the gap between action and outcome reveals 'misunderstandings', which result in users being led up the 'garden path' and inevitably so because there is no possibility of *repairing* the situation as there is in ordinary conversation.

The possibility of communicative repair is excluded because the machine only trades in detectable outcomes, not the actions and interactions involved in realising an instruction and the methodical ways in which these are accomplished in the course of 'communicating' with the machine. Thus, as Suchman puts it, the relationship between the 'ordering device' (the machine instructions) and the 'contingent labours' (the user's methodical actions and interactions) in and through which that order is 'made accountable to ongoing activity' (photocopying) 'breaks down'. In drawing out the communicative asymmetry of computational machines, Suchman introduced systems design to the idea that members' methods are critical to understanding action and interaction and making machines *accountable to users*. Her early work underscores the point that designers do not need to turn to social or cultural theories to get a fix on the social character of action and interaction. That they can instead turn to what people *do*, rather than what the social sciences say about what they do. Turning to what people do does not have to involve the disciplinary methods of social science, as the things that people do are replete with their own methods. The professional methodological apparatus of mainstream social science was refreshingly absent in Suchman's study, instead it was the methods in and through which action and interaction is methodically assembled and accountably organised in real time that she made available to design.

In reviewing the different ways in which ethnomethodology had been configured within systems design subsequent to Suchman's initial study, Dourish and Button (1998) attempted to demonstrate how turning to the methods that members use to order and reason about action could *generally* impact the design of interactive systems. Up until this point, ethnomethodology had, following Suchman's initial work, been used to critique particular designs and sensitise design to the socially organised character of interaction, or to generate requirements for particular design undertakings. Dourish and Button, however, wanted to emphasise how the turn to members' methods could provide design with a generic resource for building the social into systems design. Of particular issue here was Harold Garfinkel's foundational observation about how social action is done so as to be *account-able* (Garfinkel 1967), and how this could be leveraged for design purposes.

In elaborating the salience of this particular insight to systems design, Dourish and Button spoke (as many ethnomethodologists do) about the 'accountability' of action and interaction, but the hyphen is important to Garfinkel's original usage of the term. Account-able is not actually the same as accountable. It does not mean that persons justify their actions but rather that they make their actions 'observable and reportable' as they unfold. Thus, we can *see* and *say* of someone *in the course of action* that they are waiting to cross the road, waiting for a bus, buying a cup of coffee, etc. The broad point, of course, is that action is generally done in this way: i.e., done so as to be observable and reportable or account-able. If action was not made account-able in the very course of its conduct it would be difficult for social life to proceed, for it would be difficult for an interactant to know what it is they should do next (slow to let them cross the road, stop the bus, ask them what coffee they want, etc.). Action often provides for a next action, and interaction thus proceeds with respect to action's account-able character. If action is not done so that it is observable and reportable, and thus made recognisable to others, then there is no resource for an interactant to draw on and respond to and so, as with Suchman's photocopier users, interaction breaks down.

We have throughout this text used the simple example of a greeting to convey many of the analytic points we make. A greeting is an account-able action. It provides for an appropriate next action to be undertaken by an interactant: a return greeting. We all do this all the time and we know, in our capacity as members, that issuing a greeting in return turns upon our first recognising that we have been greeted. We know too that greetings are done in such ways as to make them recognisable as the things that they are, by doing a greeting in an initial turn position in interaction, for example, and by employing recognisable greeting terms and/or gestures. This is a simple, and obvious example, but hopefully it makes the point that interaction turns upon the account-able character of action and interaction.

Dourish and Button (1998) explored how this observation could provide a foundation for building the social into systems design. The observation was put to work with respect to the 'most fundamental tool of system design' (ibid.), *abstraction*.

Abstractions help us manage complexity by allowing us to selectively hide it. In systems design, abstractions typically function as 'black boxes'. They are defined by the nature of their interactions with the outside world (human users or other pieces of code – the 'clients' of the abstraction), which are typically defined in terms of the available functionality, procedure call conventions and return values – what we typically refer to as the 'interfaces' to the abstraction. The system's internal mechanisms, which describe and control how it goes about doing the work it does, are intentionally not available to inspection … In user interface design, the same models of abstraction show through. Human users interact with abstract interfaces to the system's functionality (such as a print dialogue, or a direct manipulation view of a file system) which provide simple, consistent interaction by hiding the complex realities of the system mechanisms (creating a Postscript file and sending it to the printer, or copying files from a local disk to a server across a long-distance network connection).

As a preface to exploring how the account-able character of action might impact abstraction in design, Dourish and Button set about drawing out and emphasising key similarities and differences between abstractions in human interaction and computational abstractions. Thus, what computational abstractions share with abstractions in naturally occurring interaction (e.g., direction maps) is that they are organised to reveal certain things and hide others for certain purposes. However, what is not common to both, what computational abstractions do *not* share with abstractions in everyday life, is account-ability. In short, you cannot, in the course of interaction with a computational machine, inspect a computational abstraction to 'see' what it could be 'speaking' of or 'telling' you about, as you can a direction map (Psathas 1979), because it is 'black boxed'. Computational abstractions are 'intentionally *not* available to inspection', they are *not* observable and reportable, and are therefore *not* account-able to interaction. Little wonder then that human-computer 'communication' becomes problematic and even breaks down in the course of interaction.

Now one inference that might be drawn here about account-ability is that computational machines should be designed so that people can understand them but, as the authors point out, that would hardly be news.

Making systems understandable, less inscrutable and more open to examination has after all been the primary focus of HCI for all these years. But, of course, we are saying more than this. What ethnomethodology tells us is that the production of an account of action is an indexical (or situated) phenomenon. In other words, a user will encounter a system in myriad settings and circumstances, and will attempt to find the system's behaviour rational and sensible with respect to whatever those infinitely variable circumstances might be, day to day and moment to moment. What this implies, then, is that the creation of an account for a system's behaviour is not a 'one-off' business. It cannot be handled once-and-for-all during a design phase conducted in the isolation of a software development organisation in Silicon Valley. The creation of the account happens, instead, in every circumstance in which the system is used, because the account and the circumstance of the use are intimately co-related. In technical terms, an account is a run-time phenomenon, not a design-time one.

The 'run time' nature of the phenomenon is key, and makes perspicuous that account-ability involves making the underlying behaviour of the system, hidden by computational abstractions, visible and available to interaction *in the course of* the machine's operation. Thus, the aim is to provide 'translucent interfaces' that 'show and tell' what the machine has done, is doing, or will do next *within* the immediate circumstances of interaction.

Dourish and Button presented a file copying scenario to convey the point, a scenario which is familiar to most computer users. The scenario involves dragging and dropping files into a folder over a network, the progress of which is reflected in a file transfer percentage bar. At 40 % the copy operation fails. The authors ask, what resources are available to the user to understand what has happened, and to understand what options are now available? Have 40 % of the files been read from the local drive or been written onto the network drive, or have 40 % of all the files been read or written? There is no way of telling. The computational abstraction ordering file copying hides the details upon which such understandings could be based. The alternative is to make the underlying file copying mechanism translucent. This would involve surfacing the 'structural properties' of the system's behaviour hidden by the file copying abstraction. For example,

> Between the file source and destination are arrayed a number of staging posts (data buckets). File data flows from the start-point to the end-point by moving from one bucket to another along a data path. As data flows from one bucket to the next, the buckets are related to each other by flow strategies, by which the movement of data from one to the next is regulated ... The flow of data through these, and the activation of the flow strategies, provides a framework for the relationship between the action in which the system engages and the reading and writing of data files.

Surfacing the hidden structure of file copying by making data buckets and data flow translucent provides resources that can be drawn on to answer the sorts of questions raised above: to monitor the flow of data and determine just where within it copying has reached when it stalls, for example, thereby allowing the user to make some sense of what the percentage-done bar is actually reporting.

Making computational abstractions account-able to users by providing representations that surface the system's underlying behaviour provides resources to understand the machine's conduct. The account – the representation – is not a justification or explanation of the system's behaviour, however. The account arises reflexively in the course of action, rather than as a *commentary upon it*, and elaborates the way in which the machine's actions are organised so that they can be made reasonable within the unfolding 'in vivo' circumstances of interaction. The distinction between external explanation (as one might find in a manual, for example) and in vivo elaboration of machine actions and their organisation is critical. As Dourish and Button put it,

> ... it is important to notice that, by being offered *within* the action rather than from outside it, these sorts of interface accounts provide not just for recovery from failure, but also for more detailed ongoing monitoring of action ... In the case of file copying, an explanatory system organised around failure would be useless in order to make decisions like, "why is this taking so long?" or "will this finish before my ride home arrives?" – the sorts of questions which potentially lie at the heart of decisions to stop the copy, to do it in another way, to copy a subset of the files, and so on. In other words, an explicit failure model sets limits not only on the sorts of questions which might be asked, but also, in organising them around specific breakdowns, on the *reasons* that those questions might arise.

The in vivo account-ability of machine actions and their organisation extends beyond failure cases to provide information without making a prior commitment to the reason that information might be useful. Making computational abstractions account-able is not about error reporting then, but about making accounts of underlying system behaviour part and parcel of ordinary interaction with a computing system. This orientation to design is rooted in and reflects the ethnomethodological perspective on interaction, where account-ability arises not out of specific requests for information, but as a naturally occurring part of interaction that enables *concerted* interaction to arise.

In elaborating the 'accounts model' of design, Dourish and Button were attempting to make explicit for design that a concern with the *methodical* ways in which social action is done could provide design itself with a methodology for building the social into the design mix. The method of the matter is not just that action is always account-able but that it is made so in *particular* methodical ways: through the methods of turn-taking implicated in using an expert help system, for example, or the design of translucent interfaces that make file copying accountable to users. Account-ability is something, as Suchman demonstrated, that interaction with computational machines trades on and something, as Dourish and Button demonstrated, that can be built into computational machines to enable effective interaction. Thus Dourish and Button argued that a 'deep foundational relationship' could be forged between ethnomethodology and design, predicated on understanding the particular ways in which action is made account-able in different design domains and application areas and using that understanding as a resource for systematically building the social into design. This was a *general* point, it was not a point aimed at the design of a better interface for file copying or with respect to the operation of a particular machine. It was concerned to demonstrate how one of ethnomethodology's key observations of how action is ordered in the real world could be used to think about how design might proceed in, for example, its necessary use of abstractions, and it was an elaboration of the point made by Suchman that members' methods can provide design with a way of building the social into the design mix that supports the placement of systems in the social world; a world that is itself constituted through common-sense methods for ordering and understanding interaction.

8.2 Members' Methods as a Design Resource

The turn to account-ability and members' common-sense methods of locally ordering, reasoning about and understanding action provides a concrete resource for developing systems that build-in and support the social character of interaction. The point is exemplified by the Virtual Help Desk developed at Xerox Research Centre Europe. Recipient of the Wall Street Journal's 2011 Innovation Award for Software (Wall Street Journal 2011), development of the Virtual Help Desk was motivated by Xerox's 'Total Satisfaction' policy. The policy sought to guarantee customer satisfaction with the machines the company sells. Delivering on its promise involved deploying engineers to customer sites to solve problems, but this was a costly undertaking and in many cases the problems were simple and could have been resolved by the users themselves if they had known some simple things about the machines they were using. Thus the company developed a 'knowledge base' for its major products that customers could use to solve problems. It also put a trouble-shooting hotline in place, with the trouble-shooters using the same knowledge base that was available to customers. The company found that customers preferred to use the trouble-shooters rather than the knowledge base, which although not as costly as on-site visits by engineers, nevertheless involved a cost to the company that it was keen to reduce. The company's goal was to migrate the majority of problem-solving activity to customers themselves through use of the knowledge base. This occasioned observational studies of customers trying to solve machine problems through the use of the knowledge base, and of trouble-shooters trying to solve customer problems, in a bid to understand what was preventing the sought after migration. The studies revealed a number of pertinent issues for the design and deployment of the knowledge base made apparent in the common-sense ways that customers and trouble-shooters went about describing and solving problems.

The studies revealed that in their mundane interactions with the knowledge base, machine users reasoned about and described the problems they had by drawing upon everyday vocabulary. Thus they might describe unwanted lines on the paper as 'squiggles', or deposits of ink as 'blotches'. When these common-sense descriptions were entered into the query system, the knowledge base would routinely return a 'not found' reply, which occasioned users turning to the trouble-shooting hotline. However, observations of the trouble-shooters receiving such calls revealed that the solution to problems vernacularly described was often contained within the knowledge base. Thus, for example, what might vernacularly be reasoned about as a 'squiggle' was caused by a 'misalignment of the paper feeders', and if the user had typed this in then the knowledge base would have returned a description of how to achieve a re-alignment, which is a simple matter.

Thus users reasoned about and described the problems they encountered in common-sense ways. The designers of the knowledge base were, however, engineers, and the design of the knowledge base was based upon their ways of reasoning about and describing problems in the *technical* terms of engineering. Thus everything on the knowledge base was described and arranged in technical terms of possible *faults* and associated *solutions*. For example a typical entry might be: Noise from the high capacity feeder. Clicking on this took the user to the following solutions: (1) Remove misfed paper from the lower paper path area and the paper tray being used/(2) Clear jams in the high capacity feeder. Clicking on either of these then took the user to step-by-step instructions on how to solve those problems. However, a problem here is that 'Noise from the high capacity feeder' does not really tell a user what sort of a noise they might be listening out for. Furthermore, telling a user about a noise coming from a high capacity feeder is only useful if they know what the high capacity feeder is and where it is located on the machine. These kinds of organisational features made it clear that the knowledge base had been designed in terms of how an engineer might reason about and describe a device, not someone possessed of only lay knowledge about printers and their operation.

The other way in which the knowledge base had evidently been founded upon technical rather than lay reasoning related to how searches needed to be conducted and their outcomes understood. The knowledge base was open to being searched by using either keywords and phrases or via a side bar that specified a number of categories of problem, such as 'image quality', 'power', 'machine components', etc. The side bar could be used for category searches but tended to produce a disconcertingly large number of results. When using keywords or phrases, users were immediately confronted with the need to know the 'right' kind of terminology to be able to perform adequate searches. Furthermore, once a search had been initiated, the results brought back often lacked an *apparent relationship* to the original query. The results frequently made no mention of the keyword(s) used, or even anything seemingly related to the keyword(s). Indeed, they often had no visible relation to the problem to which a solution was being sought. For example, a search for 'screwed up paper' would return results like 'Paper tray 1, 2, 3, or 4 empty message'. Possessed of technical knowledge one might know that these kinds of results were premised on the possibility of a type of jam where some fragments of paper affect the sensor detecting the size of the sheets, resulting in a message for an empty tray. In the absence of such knowledge such results appeared nonsensical. Even where the results were more obviously related to the query there were almost always multiple options to choose between. However, the differences between the options were not, from a common-sense standpoint, readily understandable and again required a technical orientation to understand the differences.

The counterpart to the problem of technical reasoning embedded in the design of the knowledge base is the way in which users brought to the exercise their own common-sense understandings of the device. It was clear from the researchers' observations that users of the technology were bringing to the encounter an everyday understanding of device problems that were routinely articulated in *symptomatic* terms, such as 'the paper has smudges on it' or 'the machine is making a grinding noise'. It was these kinds of symptomatic descriptions that would get keyed into the search box. However, the knowledge base was organised in terms of a *technical taxonomy of faults* such as 'problems with the paper path'. The outcome of this was that searches framed around common-sense understandings of machine faults would most often fail to take a user to the right part of the knowledge base. The end result was that, although the knowledge base most often did contain information that would have enabled the users to solve their problems, the disjuncture between common-sense understandings and the technical understandings embedded in the knowledge base meant that the solve rate for users doing trouble-shooting on their own was alarmingly low, with many of them moving onto telephone-based support anyway.

There was thus a *misalignment* of ways of reasoning about and articulating problems; where users saw 'squiggles' engineers saw 'misaligned components'. Observations of the trouble-shooters made it perspicuous that they acted as mediators, 'translating' between the two forms of reasoning. In repeatedly using the knowledge base the trouble-shooters understood how it was organised, and in observing how they routinely handled problems they displayed that they knew, for example, that squiggles could be caused by a misalignment of the paper feeders, could query the knowledge base in appropriate technical terms and thus have the solution returned to them. Indeed, often as not, through repeated use, the trouble-shooters could offer up the answer without resorting to the knowledge base at all. Thus, in 'translating' between common-sense reasoning about a problem and the reasoning about problems done in the technical terms built into the knowledge base, the trouble-shooters *aligned and reconciled* the two forms of reasoning and arrived at solutions.

Bringing this alignment and reconciliation about was not a straightforward matter of translating A into B. The trouble-shooters were obliged to start the job of translation with the 'specifically vague' symptomatic descriptions provided by the customer (e.g., 'squiggles') and through discussion with the customer arrive at a 'specifically precise' description (e.g., 'misaligned paper feeders') consonant with the technical organisation of the knowledge base. This involved engaging users in elaboration of the specifically vague descriptions they had offered: "what's the paper coming out like", "what's the noise like", etc. One part of the work of translation thus involved working up the common-sense ways in which people were describing their problems into appropriate search terms for the database, which the trouble-shooters could then use to find potential resolutions. The other part of work here then involved translating the technical descriptions contained in the knowledge base of appropriate steps to take to resolve the problem into descriptions of actions users could understand to bring these about. These were shorn of their technical characteristics and articulated instead in a form better suited to ordinary common-sense ways of reasoning that tightly tailored description of the steps to take to the case in hand, as opposed to the generic propositions to be found in the knowledge base.

Both of these translational jobs turned in important, even critical respects, on the establishment of shared referents to ensure that customer and trouble-shooter were referring to the *same thing*. For example, "I've got a problem with the paper feed" – "You are talking about where you put the originals in aren't you?" Trouble-shooters would routinely perform checks to ensure that the customer knew what part of the machine they were referring to. A commonplace recourse here was to reformulate descriptions according to different features of a referent, such as its function, colour, shape, relative position, and so on. So an operative might ask the customer if they could see "a green lever that you have to push down, to the left hand side of the door". In observing the trouble-shooters at work it became clear that the work of establishing shared referents was intensely deictic in character. This was especially notable with regard to how operatives would work through the necessary sequences of action a customer might need to perform in order to arrive at a solution.

Here trouble-shooters were routinely seen to engage in two kinds of activity that were rich in deictic content yet utterly *lost to the customer*, who would only have available 'the talk track' so to speak. One of these was miming. As operatives described a sequence of actions to perform they would more often than not act out the manipulation of the parts as they were describing it. The other activity was literally going to a model of the same machine, which was a feature of the support centre in which they worked, and physically performing the actions they were describing. However, the lack of mutual access to the situation in play meant that the *embodied ways* in which instructions were articulated, including gestures, were unavailable to the customer and had to be re-described through talk. Furthermore, because a customer's orientation and actions were equally unavailable to the trouble-shooter, the trouble-shooter was obliged to rely on verbal feedback from the customer to understand how instructions might be being followed and what the outcomes of certain actions might be.

Consequently the trouble-shooters needed to recurrently check the state of the machine in order to be able to give further relevant and appropriate instructions. For example, they might ask if all the doors were closed. They might also ask customers to tell them what some part or other of the machine looks like because knowing what a machine in general looks like is not the same as knowing what this particular machine looks like in just this instance, and it is the features of this particular machine here and now which are pertinent for trouble-shooting. To uncover the relevant features 'here and now' operatives would often elaborate on their prior descriptions, for instance: "Can you tell me when you look in is the tray still lying flat or is it a bit off. Does it look as though it's skewed?"

The situation was compounded by a common organisational arrangement that directly affected interaction: in order to save costs many organisations locate print machines in a hallway or a room where they can be accessed by a number of users; phones, however, tend to be located in users' offices. This presents a problem when the trouble-shooter requests a user to engage in a particular activity and report back on the affects this has had on the operation of the machine. Unsurprisingly customers displayed a strong preference for using company telephones rather than their own, so calls from mobile phones in situ were relatively rare. This meant that the business of talk, as it were, was disconnected from the business of action, something users occasionally worked around by setting up a chain of people from the machine to the phone along which instructions and feedback was relayed. However, the absence of mutual access both to the state of the machine and what the customer was doing led on occasion to gross *mismatches of perspective*. Trouble-shooters would assume a certain default orientation to a machine, for example, though this was far from always the case. Thus a lever assumed to be at the left of the machine as one faced it might well be round the corner and to the right if the customer was already stood at the left hand side, the consequences of which could be fatal for problem resolution.

In summary, the studies revealed that customers reason about machine problems in vernacular and symptomatic terms, but that the knowledge base is built on engineers reasoning embedded in a taxonomy of technically defined faults. The two forms of reasoning (common-sense and technical) are then misaligned and this misalignment results in an apparent lack of relationship between a search query and the contents of the knowledge base. The two forms of reasoning are brought into alignment and reconciled by trouble-shooters through translation work, a two-way job of translating common-sense description into technical descriptions, and technical descriptions into common-sense accounts that can be 'followed' by ordinary users to effect repairs. Translation and repair turn upon establishing, and maintaining throughout interaction, shared referents to the machine, which is done verbally and in embodied ways. The latter are not available to the customer, however, just as the embodied actions of the customer are not available to trouble-shooters. Translation and repair is further impacted by the disconnect between the site of action (the machine) and site of communication (the phone in an office), which produces a mismatch of perspectives that can be fatal to repair.

These findings, which detail the methodical ways in which problems and repairs are articulated in interaction, including the methodical ways in which the interaction can and does break down, were drawn upon as a resource for redesigning the knowledge base to better enable the migration of problem-solving to customers and enhance mediated trouble-shooting when it is required. Redesigning the knowledge base turned upon overcoming the disjuncture between technical and common-sense reasoning. Here a number of design ideas came into play, many of which were premised upon the integration of natural language processing features into the tool that could offer a bridge between technical and common-sense vocabularies. These ideas included:

- Organising the knowledge base around a symptomatic taxonomy, with the structure reflecting symptoms and causes of problems, rather than a technical taxonomy based on faults.
- Providing the possibility of searching on either vernacular or technical terms or a mixture of both.
- Providing support for understanding the results of searches by giving technical terms lay descriptions and giving indications of what kinds of symptoms might accompany particular kinds of faults.
- Presenting search results in ways that would make clear how they were connected to the original search terms a customer had entered.

The second design solution was to provide 'on-the-machine' resources to facilitate both customer problem-solving and assistance from remote trouble-shooters. The core of the on-the-machine design was a two-way shared 3D representation of the machine and its current problem. This representation was to be presented on the machine itself, by using the medium sized screens that were increasingly being installed as standard, and on the trouble-shooter's terminal at the remote site. The representation was to be linked to the machine itself, such that actions on the machine could immediately be seen on the representation (e.g., if a user opened a door, that door would appear open on the representation). This was made possible through the many sensors already present on such machines. Additionally, both the customer and trouble-shooter would be able to indicate parts on the machine, and the trouble-shooter would be able to visually demonstrate the actions to be performed (e.g., lifting a handle and sliding a toner cartridge out of the machine). The customer was to be given access to technical support through audio-visual communication channels located on the machine itself, with the audio channel providing the means for conversing with the trouble-shooter. The visual channel, meanwhile, would be able to communicate current state, changes of state, overlays such as arrows, and separate animations. In this way, it was suggested, the machine itself would become the infrastructural mediator between users and technical support. Many new Xerox printers now carry these on-the-machine tools,[2] with a net result of improved customer support and a reduction in the multi-million dollar break-fix cost associated with providing that support. The achievement turns upon understanding members' methods for locally ordering, reasoning about and understanding interaction.[3]

8.3   Members' Methods and Ubiquitous Computing

We have gone back to basics in the previous two sections in order to emphasise that the methodological apparatus of the social sciences is *not required* to understand the social or to systematically build it into systems design and, in doing so, to *demonstrate* that there is a viable alternative: that design can be *instructed* in the social *by* society's members *in* methodological details of action's account-able conduct. This was recognised within design very early on in its engagement with the social – in writing *Sociologists Can Be Surprisingly Useful*, for example, Sommerville et al. (1992) described how in surfacing the methodological ways in which air traffic controllers ordered the flow of aircraft through the skies (Hughes et al. 1992) the ethnographers provided concrete insights for building the social into systems design:

> The ethnographic studies have already revealed a number of subtle system requirements which are unlikely to have been derived from a conventional requirements analysis process. For example, in studies of air-traffic control, we have discovered that apparently repetitive tasks such as rearranging paper strips representing aircraft being controlled, are a key part of the activity in that the manual manipulation serves to bring problems and details to the controllers attention. Furthermore, we have discovered much cooperation between controllers is implicit and relies on 'at-a-glance' understanding of other controllers' workspace. User interface tailoring which is usually suggested as a 'good thing' would be positively dangerous in this instance.

Elaborating the methodological ways in which members' order their activities, whether in doing air traffic control or doing any other activity, has subsequently turned out to be a rich resource impacting design in manifold ways, as we have previously described elsewhere in elaborating what is involved in doing ethnomethodological studies (Crabtree et al. 2012a). We note here that not only have ethnomethodological studies enabled designers to figure out what to build and to evaluate

---

[2] See www.youtube.com/watch?v=OO9fY5ovjBg [Accessed 06-03-2015]

[3] The studies on which this work was based have been reported in a number of scientific papers including Tolmie et al. (2004), Castellani et al. (2005), O'Niell et al. (2005a, b, 2011), and Crabtree et al. (2006).

systems with respect to the methodological ordering of action and interaction, they have also served to sensitise design to the 'real world, real time' nature of the social and allowed designers to explore their assumptions about it, ultimately challenging and changing received wisdom. It seems rather narrow to say then, as Dourish (2006) has said, that such studies are limited to 'facts' and developing 'implications for design' or 'requirements' for systems. Not that such matters should be lightly dismissed, for even in non-workplace settings designers still look to 'ethnographers' to inform them as to what they should or should not build, and to calibrate the fit of new technologies with the situated circumstances of their use.

We have not gone back to basics to champion the continuation of so-called 'workplace' or 'work practice' studies, however, as the study of members' methods has been narrowly defined by some. The idea that there is somehow a watershed moment – before ubiquitous computing and after ubiquitous computing – marked by an attention shift from the workplace to the wider world is misleading and wrong. The term 'ubiquitous computing' was coined in or around 1988, going public but not viral as it were in 1991 with the publication of Mark Weiser's landmark paper *The Computer for the Twenty-First Century*, but it was not until 1999 that what is now called 'the first international conference on ubicomp' took place. Clearly it took some time for widespread interest in ubicomp to gather pace. However, as far back as the early 1990s, just as 'ethnography' was coming to prominence as a means of understanding work in systems design, Christian Heath and Paul Luff (also noted for their own workplace studies, Heath and Luff 1991) were examining the local interactional ordering of *video-mediated communication* or VMC (Heath and Luff 1992). While this technology was developed for and studied within a workplace, Xerox's EuroPARC offices, the interactional order of video-mediated communication was not, in itself, tied to the workplace. VMC is today commonplace, found in workplaces, homes, even on the streets. Heath and Luff's studies elaborated the methodical ordering of this particular communicative arrangement wherever it occurs, and the methods they elaborated can still be seen 'at work' in video calls today.

The mid-1990s also saw the emergence of *collaborative virtual environments* or CVEs where interaction was not mediated by video but avatars. Here a broad range of studies elaborated the methodical ways in which interactants 'practically accomplished immersion' in virtual worlds (Bowers et al. 1996) and 'established mutual orientation' to interaction (Hindmarsh et al. 1998). These studies elaborated the unique interactional nature of CVEs, particularly that they 'fragment' interaction which in turn impacts interactants ability to design their actions for one another 'here and now' and thus places an overhead on the *necessary* interactional effort to make what is being done account-able (Hindmarsh et al. 2000).

Running alongside these early studies of non-workplace activities was an interest in the *home* as site for computing (O'Brien and Rodden 1997), and this has proved to be a profitable seam of interest that is still being mined today. From studies of the local interactional ordering of mundane artefacts of interest to design – including such things as set top boxes (O'Brien et al. 1999), mail (Harper et al. 2003), calendars (Crabtree et al. 2003), photos (Crabtree et al. 2004a), books (Rouncefield and Tolmie 2012), and the home network (Tolmie et al. 2007; Crabtree et al. 2012b, 2014) – to the leveraging of ubiquitous computing into the home (Tolmie et al. 2010), studies of smart homes (Randall 2003) and more recently the connected home (Harper 2012), long-standing interest in non-workplace activities is plain for anyone with the wherewithal to see. It can be seen too that studies of members' methods have accompanied other non-workplace interests in systems design: the development of computing for *cultural experiences* – e.g., museums (Hindmarsh et al. 2005) and games (Crabtree et al. 2004b) – or, alternatively, to support the development of *assistive technologies* for the differently-abled (Kember et al. 2002; Dewsbury et al. 2004). There are a great many other examples we could and probably should point the reader to where studies of members' methods have been done for the purposes of non-workplace design. However, even this cursory glance at some of the design-oriented work that has been done by ourselves and colleagues working in the ethnomethodological tradition should suffice to make it clear that the explication of member's methods as a resource for design is not and has *never been* just about the workplace. Indeed, that studies of a diverse range of non-workplace settings and activities have run in *parallel* to studies of the workplace from the outset of widespread engagement with 'ethnography' in systems design.

Concomitant with this observation, we suggest that any argument that makes the claim that 'new' approaches are required because design, under the auspices of ubiquitous computing, has moved out of the workplace is patently absurd. The absurdity of the matter is compounded when we consider that the very idea of ubiquitous computing was developed at Xerox PARC within the midst of the workplace and work practices studies that it is argued we need to move on from. Setting the confusion aside as to what the word 'work' means in ethnomethodological studies (see Chap. 7), Mark Weiser made no such argument or calls for 'new' approaches but developed the idea of ubiquitous computing "with Lucy [Suchman] sitting on my shoulder" (personal communication). Nonetheless, calls for 'new' types of ethnography have been made, and made by prominent members of the design community (Dourish and Bell 2011). In writing this book we have sought to make it visible to designers that these calls amount to replacing the methodological apparatus that society's members use to order action and interaction with the methodological apparatus that the social sciences use to talk about and describe action and interaction. Such calls seek to bring design to the heel of social science, to tame its engagement with the wild, naturally occurring, naturally account-able orderliness of social life, and put professionally accredited mediators and interpreters – social or human scientists - in its place. The contrast in these calls for the 'new' is not then a contrast with workplace and work practice studies, but a contrast between engaging with the social through the methods of social science *or* engaging with the social though the methods of society's members.

8.4   Conclusion: Eyeless in Gaza

It is a fact of systems design that the idea of the 'social' has turned out to be as important as the idea of the 'user'. Just how it is addressed by designers is not, to reiterate, a matter we wish to prescribe, though we have sought to elaborate just what is being bought into in making certain choices. If design finds scenic descriptions of action or interaction that gloss over the methods of its assembly relevant to a particular undertaking, or that some particular social theory or cultural interpretation speaks to design's interests in computing and society, or if design wants to know about the meanings that people attach to objects (or at least what social scientists say about such meanings), or if design wants to reflect upon how it is itself constitutive of the social in placing its designs into that world, we are not particularly vexed. Design has a history of dipping into and out of other disciplines and we, along with others, look with interest at the results. However, we are not alone in systems design in having ambitions for ubiquitous and interactive systems that go beyond current piecemeal, case-by-case, efforts to build-in the social, whether the 'building in' is done for the purposes of generating systems requirements, evaluating systems, sensitising exercises or general reflections on computing and how to approach it within the various social and cultural contexts in which it is today embedded. Our argument is not against those designers who engage selectively with the social, but is aimed at those who seek a more rigorous and thus *systematic* basis on which to build the social into systems design. This book is aimed, then, at those in design who want to move beyond the current piecemeal approach of dipping into (and out of) the social.

On the face of it many designers may be of the impression that a systematic method is already at hand and that ethnography will give them all they need to know about the social. The overwhelming tide of engagement with the social in systems design to date has, in its broadest sense, been 'ethnographically' based and not, for example, informed by statistically based approaches to social enquiry. In the past, characteristically, ethnography has been empirical and descriptive, that is, grounded in actual situations, producing descriptions of what has been observed, and the ways in which observable matters are organised and put together by the parties to them. However, in the last decade design has been told this conception of ethnography is outmoded, tied merely to the generation of requirements, tied just to the workplace, and tied just to work activities. Not only is design told that this approach is past its sell-by-date, it is also argued that it provides a narrow conception of ethnography. This is displayed in its demonstrable failure to appreciate that observing settings and what goes on within them is itself a methodologically constituted affair, one which impacts what is seen and one that, in placing emphasis on empirical matters, ignores the importance of theorising for understanding the social and its role in viewing the empirical world. It is therefore argued that new forms of ethnography are required as designers' interests move out of the workplace and the systems they build transcend societal and cultural boundaries. Attendant to this is a call for design to engage with social and cultural theory and contemporary methodological understandings of how ethnography is done to support the move.

In writing this book we have addressed an array of concerns that underpin and drive calls for the 'new' and have attempted to show that there is *nothing new* to them at all. They are founded in one way or another on the traditional ways in which social science addresses its subject matter by providing general theoretical accounts that interpret, define and explain society and social action. It is in light of this that we have said, and say again, that ethnography can be considered *harmful* to interdisciplinary efforts to build the social into the systems design mix (Crabtree et al. 2009). The reason for this, to re-emphasise, is that design is being invited to engage with the social through the methodological apparatus of social science rather than through the methods that society's members use to conduct, reason about and understand social life in the very course of *doing it*. The substitution of members' methods of doing social life for social scientists' methods of talking about it ensures the disappearance of the social as a lived interactional reality. All that remains are competitive versions of common-sense reasoning, rivalling members' versions and putting reified sociological abstractions in their place.

In short, systems design is being confronted with traditional social science and the old social science problem of how to account for the social order, whether it be the orderliness of an obstinately familiar world in which systems will be placed or the orderliness of brave new worlds being crafted in the work of design labs. In surfacing the 'problem of order' that confronts the old and new alike, we have attempted to show that Harold Garfinkel's ethnomethodology has created a fork in the road for social science and, through its engagement with social science, albeit unwittingly, for systems design as well. Calls for 'new' approaches to ethnography seek to place design on the well-trodden path of social science. It is a path though that leads nowhere. Garfinkel made it perspicuous that the social sciences simply cannot provide accounts of the social that are *different in kind* to the accounts that anyone else can provide, for social science accounts are, without remedy, predicated on common-sense methods of reasoning and understanding. In place of interpretation, definition and explanation, Garfinkel reconfigured the role of social science as one of *explication*, of surfacing, of revealing, of making visible the organised properties of common-sense reasoning and understanding. In doing this social science becomes a matter of studying how people use the organised properties of common-sense reasoning and understanding locally 'here and now' to order the concrete achievement of action and interaction in any actual case, and thereby produce the settings, scenes and events that make up social life (Garfinkel 1996); settings, scenes and events that computational devices, applications and services are (methodically) embedded within.

Just as social science has at hand members' methods, then so too does systems design. A body of work amassed over the last 30 years demonstrates that design efforts to change the world through the development of computational artefacts may be *constructively* 'informed' through the explication of members' methods; that systems can be *configured* around these methods to *build-in* the social and make computational artefacts *account-able* to action and interaction. We are aware, in saying this, that some in design have argued that ethnomethodologically-informed ethnography may limit or constrain the imagination of designers and inhibit the impetus towards change that characterises their endeavour. This is an old argument that suggests understanding how action and interaction is ordered 'here and now' effectively privileges the status quo at the expense of change. It is a fallacious argument, for whatever way you look at it design inevitably rubs up against an already organised world and must find its place within it. Designers may well invent new technologies that change the ease and frequency with which we can talk to one another, for example, but those technologies do not change the methodical ways in which we order our conversations. Far from constraining change, knowing how people order action and interaction enables design to intervene in ways that *gear into* the social – to construct expert help systems, video-mediated communication, collaborative virtual environments, and a wealth of other computational machines that *mesh* with the methodical ways in which action and interaction is done. Systems design has at hand the very resources that society's members use to order the doing of action and interaction, with one another and with computational machines. Those resources are taken for granted, seen but unnoticed, and ignored by mainstream social science. Nonetheless, in elaborating members' methods, as Garfinkel reminds us,

> … ethnomethodological studies have begun to reveal immortal ordinary society as a wondrous thing … professionals in the worldwide social science movement, with straightforward normal thoughtfulness are able to read it out of relevance, eyeless in Gaza. (Garfinkel and Wieder 1992)

It is our sincere hope that design does not follow the social sciences at large and end up in the same blind alley as it attempts to build the social into computational systems in a rigorous, systematic, *methodical* way.

References

Bowers, J., O'Brien, J., Pycock, J. (1996). Practically accomplishing immersion: Cooperation in and for virtual environments. In *Proceedings of the conference on computer supported cooperative work* (pp. 380–389). Boston: ACM.

Castellani, S., Grasso, A., O'Neill, J., Tolmie, P. (2005). Total cost of ownership: Issues around reducing cost of support in a manufacturing organisation case. In *Proceedings of the 7th IEEE international conference on e-commerce technology workshops* (pp. 122–130). Munich: IEEE.

Crabtree, A., Hemmings, T., Mariani, J. (2003). Informing the design of calendar systems for domestic use. In *Proceedings of the 8th European conference on computer supported cooperative work* (pp.119–138). Helsinki: Springer.

Crabtree, A., Rodden, T., Mariani, J. (2004a). Collaborating around collections: Informing the continued development of photoware. In *Proceedings of the conference on computer supported cooperative work* (pp. 396–405). Chicago: ACM.

Crabtree, A., Benford, S., Rodden, T., Greenhalgh, C., Flintham, M., Anastasi, R., Drozd, A., Adams, M., Row-Farr, J., Tandavanitj, N., & Steed, A. (2004b). Orchestrating a mixed reality game 'on the ground'. *Proceedings of the SIGCHI conference on human factors in computing systems* (pp. 391–398). ACM.

Crabtree, A., O'Neil, J., Tolmie, P., Castellani, S., Colombino, T., Grasso, A. (2006). The practical indispensability of articulation work to immediate and remote help-giving. In *Proceedings of ACM conference on computer supported cooperative work* (pp. 219–228). Banff: ACM.

Crabtree, A., Rodden, T., Tolmie, P., Button, G. (2009). Ethnography considered harmful. In *Proceedings of the SIGCHI conference on human factors in computing systems* (pp. 879–888). Boston: ACM.

Crabtree, A., Rouncefield, M., & Tolmie, P. (2012a). *Doing design ethnography*. London: Springer.

Crabtree, A., Mortier, R., Rodden, T., Tolmie, P. (2012b). Unremarkable computing: The home network as part of everyday life. In *Proceedings of the conference on designing interactive system* (pp. 554–563). Newcastle: ACM.

Crabtree, A., Rodden, T., Tolmie, P., Mortier, R., Lodge, T., Brundell, P., & Pantidi, N. (2014). House rules: The collaborative nature of policy in domestic networks. *Personal and Ubiquitous Computing, 19*(1), 203–215.

Dewsbury, G., Clarke, K., Randall, D., Rouncefield, M., & Sommerville, I. (2004). The anti-social model of disability. *Disability and Society, 19*(2), 145–158.

Dourish, P. (2006). Implications for design. In *Proceedings of the conference on human factors in computing systems* (pp. 541–550). Quebec: ACM.

Dourish, P., & Bell, G. (2011). *Divining a digital future: Mess and mythology in ubiquitous computing*. Cambridge, MA: MIT Press.

Dourish, P., & Button, G. (1998). On 'technomethodology' – foundational relationships between ethnomethodology and systems design. *Human Computer Interaction, 13*(4), 395–432.

Garfinkel, H. (1967). What is ethnomethodology? In *Studies in ethnomethodology* (pp. 1–34). Englewood Cliffs: Prentice-Hall.

Garfinkel, H. (1996). Ethmethodology's program. *Social Psychology Quarterly, 59*(1), 5–21.

Garfinkel, H., & Wieder, L. (1992). Two incommensurable, asymmetrically alternate technologies of social analysis. In G. Watson & S. M. Seiler (Eds.), *Text in context: Contributions to ethnomethodology* (pp. 175–206). London: Sage.

Harper, R. (Ed.). (2012). *The connected home: The future of domestic life*. London: Springer.

Harper, R., Evergeti, V., Hamill, L., & Shatwell, B. (2003). The social organisation of communication in the home of the twenty-first century. *Cognition Technology and Work, 5*(1), 15–22.

Heath, C., & Luff, P. (1991). Collaborative activity and technological design: Task coordination in London underground control rooms. In *Proceedings of the 2nd European conference on computer supported cooperative work* (pp. 65–80). Amsterdam: Kluwer.

Heath, C., & Luff, P. (1992). Disembodied conduct: Interactional asymmetries in video-mediated communication. In G. Button (Ed.), *Technology in working order: Studies of work, interaction, and technology* (pp. 35–54). London: Routledge.

Hindmarsh, J., Fraser, M., Heath, C., Benford, S., Greenhalgh, C. (1998). Fragmented interaction: Establishing mutual orientation in virtual environments. In *Proceedings of the conference on computer supported cooperative work* (pp. 217–226). Seattle: ACM.

Hindmarsh, J., Fraser, M., Heath, C., Benford, S., & Greenhalgh, C. (2000). Object-focused interaction in collaborative virtual environments. *ACM Transactions on Computer-Human Interaction, 7*(4), 477–509.

Hindmarsh, J., Heath, C., Vom Lehn, D., & Cleverly, J. (2005). Creating assemblies in public environments: Social interaction, interactive exhibits and CSCW. *Computer Supported Collaborative Work: The Journal of Collaborative Computing, 14*(1), 1–41.

Hughes, J., Randall, D., Shapiro, D. (1992). Faltering from ethnography to design. In *Proceedings of the conference on computer supported cooperative work* (pp. 115–122). Toronto: ACM.

Kember, S., Cheverst, K., Clarke, K., Dewsbury, G., Hemmings, T., Rodden, T., Rouncefield, M. (2002). Keep taking the medication: assistive technology for medication regimes in care settings. In *Proceedings of the Cambridge workshop on universal access and assistive technology* (pp. 285–294). Cambridge: Springer.

O'Brien, J., & Rodden, T. (1997). Interactive systems in domestic environments. In *Proceedings of the 2nd conference designing interactive systems* (pp. 247–259). Amsterdam: ACM.

O'Brien, J., Rodden, T., Rouncefield, M., & Hughes, J. (1999). At home with the technology: An ethnographic study of a set-top-box trial. *ACM Transactions on Computer-Human Interaction, 6*(3), 282–308.

O'Neill, J., Grasso, A., Castellani, S., Tolmie, P. (2005a). Using real-life troubleshooting interactions to inform self-assistance design. In *Proceedings of 10th IFIP TC13 international conference on human-computer interaction* (pp. 377–390). Rome: Springer.

O'Neill, J., Castellani, S., Grasso, A., Roulland, F., Tolmie, P. (2005b). Representations can be good enough. In *Proceedings of the 9th European conference on computer supported cooperative work* (pp. 267–286) Paris: Springer.

O'Neill, J., Tolmie, P., Grasso, A., Castellani, S., & Roulland, F. (2011). Ethnographically-informed technology for remote help-giving. In M. Szymanski & J. Whalen (Eds.), *Making work visible: Ethnographically grounded case studies of work practice* (pp. 53–73). Cambridge: Cambridge University Press.

Pollner, M. (1978). Constitutive and mundane versions of labeling theory. *Human Studies, 1*(3), 269–288.

Psathas, G. (1979). Organisational features of direction maps. In *Everyday language: Studies in ethnomethodology* (pp. 203–223). New York: Irvington Publishers.

Randall, D. (2003). Living inside the smart home: A case study. In R. Harper (Ed.), *Inside the smart home* (pp. 227–246). London: Springer.

Rouncefield, M., & Tolmie, P. (2012). Digital words: Reading and the 21st century home. In R. Harper (Ed.), *The connected home: The future of domestic life* (pp. 133–162). London: Springer.

Sacks, H., Shegloff, E., & Jefferson, G. (1974). A simplest systematics for the organisation of turn-taking for conversation. *Language, 50*(4), 696–735.

Sommerville, I., Rodden, T., Sawyer, P., Bentley, R. (1992). Sociologists can be surprisingly useful in interactive systems design. In *Proceedings of the 7th conference of the British computer society human computer interaction specialist group* (pp. 341–341). York: BCS.

Suchman, L. (1987). *Plans and situated actions: The problem of human-machine communication.* Cambridge: Cambridge University Press.

Tolmie, P., O'Neill, J., Castellani, S., Grasso, A. (2004). Users solving technical troubles with a remote expert. In *Proceedings of the 6th international conference on ubiquitous computing* (workshop 5. Giving help at a distance), 7–10 Sept. Nottingham: Springer. http://ubicomp.org/ubicomp2004/prg.php?show=workshop#w5

Tolmie, P., Crabtree, A., Rodden, T., Greenhalgh, C., Benford, S. (2007). Making the home network at home: Digital housekeeping. In *Proceedings of the 10th European conference on computer supported cooperative work* (pp. 331–350). Limerick: Springer.

Tolmie, P., Crabtree, A., Egglestone, S., Humble, J., Greenhalgh, C., & Rodden, T. (2010). Digital plumbing: The mundane work of deploying ubicomp in the home. *Personal and Ubiquitous Computing, 14*(3), 181–196.

Wall Street Journal. (2011). 2011 winners. In *Innovation awards*.www.wsj.com/articles/SB10001424052970203633104576623261551755704

Weiser, M. (1991). The computer for the 21st century. *Scientific American, 265*(3), 94–104.

Printed in the United States
By Bookmasters